JOEL BARLOW

Also by Peter P. Hill

Napoleon's Troublesome Americans: Franco-American Relations, 1804–1815

French Perceptions of the Early American Republic, 1783–1797

William Vans Murray: Federalist Diplomat The Shaping of Peace with France, 1797–1801

JOEL BARLOW

American Diplomat and Nation Builder

PETER P. HILL

Potomac Books
Washington, D.C.

Library of Congress Cataloging-in-Publication Data

Hill, Peter P., 1926–

Joel Barlow, American diplomat and nation builder / Peter P. Hill. — 1st ed.

p. cm.

Includes bibliographical references and index.

ISBN 978-1-59797-682-4 (hardcover edition)

ISBN 978-1-59797-772-2 (electronic edition)

1. Barlow, Joel, 1754–1812. 2. Poets, American—18th century—Biography. 3. Diplomats—United States—Biography. 4. Politicians—United States—Biography. I. Title.

PS705.H55 2012

327.730092—dc23

[B]

2011045397

Printed in the United States of America on acid-free paper that meets the American National Standards Institute Z39-48 standard.

Potomac Books
22841 Quicksilver Drive
Dulles, Virginia 20166

First Edition

10 9 8 7 6 5 4 3 2 1

Echoing Joel Barlow's expressed love for his wife Ruth, this book is dedicated to the late Barbara Hill, who was "the wife that my youth has chosen and that my advancing age has cherished," and to our son, George, who has always been "steady as a clock."

CONTENTS

1 Seeking Fame but without Fortune

Writing to a classmate shortly after he graduated from Yale, Joel Barlow joked, "Sometimes I do nothing, and sometimes I don't."[1] If meant to be self-deprecating, this remark famously belied the young man's already hard-driving determination to make a name for himself, to win public recognition, if not as the new nation's epic poet (soon to be his chosen vocation), then in whatever leadership role might win him a place among the thinkers and doers of his generation. And to another classmate, more in keeping with his usual high spirits: "We are not the first men in the world to have broke loose from college without fortune to puff us into public notice, [but] if ever virtue [and merit] are to be rewarded, it is in America."[2]

In this vein, Barlow's poetry would speak out exuberantly to those for whom the dawn of nationhood marked an intoxicating beginning of limitless possibilities. And yet, when his public career was over, his biographers seemed to have difficulty defining his place in American history—or literature—amid the plethora of his successes and failures. What, after all, could they say of this polymath who, at one time or another and sometimes simultaneously, wrote bad poetry, taught school, preached out of necessity, disgraced himself as a cheerleader for the French Revolution, and sold bogus Ohio lands to French émigrés? That he also practiced law (briefly) seems incidental. That he was a cofounder and editor of the *American Mercury* proved to be a passing fancy. Only during seventeen years of self-exile, mostly in Paris, would he come to serve his country in ways he found more satisfying than penning heroic couplets. By this time, his success as a commercial broker having finally freed him of financial worries, he would launch a bookended diplomatic career that began in 1796–97 when he completed some much-needed peace treaties with Algiers, Tunis, and Tripoli, and resumed fourteen years later when James Madison sent him back to France to try to cozen Napoleon into halting French depredations on American shipping. Although this last mission ended in failure and cost him his life, Joel Barlow had by then unquestionably won the notice of his countrymen and left his mark as a person of influence on the political and diplomatic scenes of his day.

Witty or pompous by turns, prophetic or just plain wrongheaded, Barlow seemed to sense from his earliest years that what he put on paper would be the engine of his advancement, though he also counted on the goodwill of his friends and admirers. Although some of his contemporaries saw him as an irrepressible pamphleteer and a self-conscious social climber, others appreciated his strong humanitarian impulses, born of the Enlightenment and cultivated throughout his life. He once told a former classmate, "I am determined to love mankind if they kill me."[3] In 1798, having just finished his successful if harrowing mission to Algiers, he rejoiced in still having an "undivided taste for tranquillity, study & doing good." By then in his mid-forties, he also admitted to having a taste for good food, had grown "fleshy," as he put it, and now weighed 170 pounds.[4]

Like many of his generation, the young Barlow felt a personal responsibility for the new nation's survival, a sensitivity far more acute than Americans feel today when, despite dangers from abroad, they know their country can hold its own. Like his contemporaries, he rallied at first to the unifying figure of George Washington but soon came to believe the nation would survive its birth only if it produced leaders working full time to hold it together, giving it the legacies, traditions, and groundings in permanence that would carry it safely into the bright future that he himself envisioned when he delivered his address "The Prospect of Peace" to the Yale graduating class of 1779.[5]

His country's future as a republic, Barlow also sensed, depended on leaders who could resist the temptations of stability offered by the European norm of monarchy. So believing, he swore a lifelong allegiance to Jeffersonian principles as he understood them, both in the United States and in France, coming to know and appreciate the challenges faced by the "founders" of republics. He cherished their steadfastness, whether in contesting the aristocratic pretensions of homegrown Federalists or in the benighted obtuseness of European royalists.

And because he never shrank from publishing his partisan loyalties, he paid a painful price in lost friendships and public obloquy when his republicanism fell briefly out of favor.

But to begin near the beginning, one might ask how this self-described farm boy born in Redding, Connecticut, was able to find a place among the nation's notables, how he exploited his youthful advantages, cultivated his talents, and made the social connections he sought so avidly? According to tradition, this fourth and last child of Samuel and Esther Barlow might have remained behind his father's plow had not a perceptive local pastor named Nathaniel Bartlett seen talent in the boy's penciled verses, undertaken to tutor him, and reportedly urged his parents to send him to college. Consequently, his father enrolled him at Dartmouth in the fall of 1773, where in lieu of paying his son's tuition, he cunningly arranged to pay the wages of a college housekeeper.[6] This arrangement expired, however, when Samuel died the following spring. Fortunately, his father's will stipulated that Joel be given a hundred pounds to complete his education. But not at Dartmouth, it turned out. One biographer speculates that he transferred to Yale in the fall of 1774 in order to be nearer to his widowed mother, a supposition borne out by a letter he wrote to her in July 1775 offering to ride back to Redding any time she needed him ("just send a horse").[7] Significantly he also asked her to send money for his tailor, a request that revealed the young man's awareness that in an age when clothing marked the visible divide between gentlemen and others, even in republican America a gentleman must look the part.

How Barlow came to fancy himself as America's epic poet traces, perhaps, to the juvenile versifying that attracted Parson Bartlett's attention. Or perhaps to the acclaim he won for his poetic description of a snowball fight between Yale freshmen and sophomores.[8] Whatever the source, soon after beginning his studies at Yale he convinced himself that the new nation deserved the grandeur of an epic poem. One biographer holds that he was already composing humorous verse in the epic style while still a sophomore and may have begun to outline his major and more serious work, *The Vision of Columbus*.[9] Barlow himself, however, first mentions his literary plans in March 1779. To a former tutor who had urged him to enter the ministry, he replied that he doubted he would be a good clergyman and would try to find other ways to better mankind. What attracted him, he wrote, was the sweep of history suggested by the "revolutionary" events following Columbus's voyage of discovery, a subject he believed worthy of epic treatment.[10]

Summer and fall of 1779 found him starting to outline *The Vision* while supporting himself as a teacher at Timothy Dwight's school in Northampton, Massachusetts. At the outset, he used a copy of William Robertson's *History of America*, which gave him a handy chronology of discoveries and events. Eight years and 258 pages later, his work would be published.[11] In early 1780, however, having spent his inheritance at Yale, he needed some sort of stopgap employment if he were to continue. An army chaplaincy proved to be the solution. He was already thinking about it when he got an encouraging letter from a former Yale graduate, Abraham Baldwin. Already a chaplain with the Third Massachusetts Brigade, "Prom" Baldwin assured him the duties were light: a weekly sermon, the occasional wedding, and plenty of time to work on his poem.[12]

The idea of getting paid for preaching apparently jolted Barlow out of his winter blues. Enlivened by the prospect, and after six weeks of theological prepping, he passed the required oral exam administered—somewhat warily—by New Haven's Association of Ministers.[13] (His unorthodox views on religion, fashionably deistic, were already showing.) While waiting for a chaplaincy to open, he devoted his energies to working up more verses for *The Vision* and ramping up his courtship of Abraham Baldwin's sister Ruth. He had known Ruth and her brother during his Yale days and had even boarded with her family after graduating—that is, until Baldwin, père, sent him packing in early 1779. Michael Baldwin, a prosperous blacksmith of Guilford, Connecticut, who had recently retired to New Haven, clearly frowned on Barlow's career prospects and doubtless hoped to nip what he saw as a budding romance. Barlow was not easily discouraged, however, nor was Ruth unresponsive. Their correspondence in 1780 was sprinkled with endearments and updates on each other's activities.

Barlow was not new to army life but found it far more congenial now than when he had served briefly as a Connecticut volunteer during Washington's defeat on Long Island in August 1776.[14] He left no record of an active part, if any, in this early debacle. Now in the fall of 1780, posted to various campsites in New Jersey, he told of keeping pleasant company with Prom and adding more lines to his epic. He was also surprised at how warmly Washington's officers received his sermons. Jokingly he told Ruth he was "in awe of such a thing as myself."And "yesterday I had another preaching scrape which kept me awake awhile, whether it had the same effect on others I am not sure."[15]

His superiors, however, far from sleeping through his flights of eloquence, thought especially highly of what he described to Ruth as "a flaming political sermon" titled "The Treason of Arnold and the Glory of America." This one earned him a dinner with Gen. Nathaniel Greene and led him to muse on how mortified "the Rev'd Fathers of the Association [would be] to see their heretic son gain such applause." Two weeks later Washington, too, invited him to dine. Awed by the honor, he confided to Ruth, "How do you think I felt when the greatest man upon the earth placed me at his right hand."[16]

Though praised for his sermons, Barlow dismissed the idea of pursuing a clerical career. His poetry came first, and when the time came to market *The Vision*, his contacts among Washington's officer corps began to pay off. Meanwhile, his chaplain's pay (twenty-two pounds a month) meant he could now afford to marry Ruth—even if he could not afford to house her. Mindful of her father's disapproval, the couple married secretly on January 26, 1781, in Kensington, Connecticut. At twenty-seven, the groom was a cheerful, healthy, heavyset young man who, as noted, would have to watch his weight in later years. Ruth, two years younger, was slim, flirtatious, and later plagued by intermittent if not always identifiable health problems. Described by one of Barlow's biographers as "gay, loving and amiable,"[17] Ruth Barlow continued to enjoy what had been a lively social life in New Haven. When Joel went back to camp, she kept him abreast of local gossip and managed to bear up cheerfully in his absence. Periodic separations soon became the hallmark of their marriage. While she visited with friends that summer, Joel repaired to various encampments, preached more sermons, and composed more lines of poetry. On July 19 he told her of having just ridden to Vermont on a secret mission. On his return to West Point, he had fallen ill—a rare occurrence—but was now fully recovered. Two weeks later, writing from the family farm in Redding, he noted unhappily that they had not been together for nine weeks. He must have sensed, however, that his wartime duties were drawing to a close. News of the victory at Yorktown effectively ended his chaplaincy and gave new urgency to completing his poem. In late October he promised Ruth he would come to New Haven and "carry her" to Hartford.

Typically their reunion was short-lived. Driven now and sensing that his vivacious bride would distract him, he rode back to Redding that fall, assuring her he would "attack the poem with all severity & finish it this winter."[18] In effect, Barlow spent the first four months of 1782 cadging off his older brother Aaron at the family farm, cranking out more verse and preaching the occasional sermon for pocket change. Except for a conjugal visit to Hartford in late January, he stayed in Redding, periodically giving Ruth line counts of his progress. Worn out by early March, he reflected that he was "as happy as a hermit can be." And some may wonder, he added, "that I drive myself so violently as to waste whole days & nights & months in the most laborious employment," but, as she should know, it was all "for the sake of shortening the time of absence from a sweetheart."[19]

The spring of 1782 also brought a reckoning of sorts with Michael Baldwin. Inevitably word of his daughter's marriage had leaked out. Barlow supposed the old man now knew of it and was angry at not having been consulted. Hoping to put things right, he wrote a letter to Ruth's father in which he apologized for their earlier secretiveness and gave assurances he now had the means to support her. A reproachful biographer describes this letter as an ingenious defense of an indefensible action.[20] Michael Baldwin's response, if any, remains unrecorded. Rather, it was Ruth's supportive brother Abraham, later a U.S. senator from Georgia and cofounder of that state's university, who maintained the Baldwin family tie in later years.

Barlow probably need not have reported to the army's regional headquarters at Peekskill, New York, that summer. The fighting was over and peace talks had begun in Paris. But besides needing to collect his pay, he planned to gather as many letters of introduction as possible from the officers he had befriended. These letters, he hoped, would help him secure funding from potential patrons in Philadelphia, where he planned to head next. Basically, he would be selling "subscriptions," intended to defray the costs of publication. When he saddled up in Peekskill and rode south in late October, he had fifteen such letters and was pleased to have the distinguished company of Secretary of War Benjamin Lincoln, "as amiable as he is great," he told Ruth.[21]

His marketing campaign in Philadelphia succeeded slowly at first but was ultimately rewarding: by mid-November he was sending money back to Ruth. His reception, he told her, was "flattering beyond our expectation," and the "populous [sic] seems starved for the kind of uplifting poetry that will exalt their new nation."[22] By the time he published *The Vision of Columbus* in early 1787, he had nailed down a total of 769 subscribers, among them George Washington and Louis XVI of France, from whom he received permission to dedicate the work. This royal imprimatur, though a coup at the time, prevented its being published in England. The first edition grossed $1,500.[23] How much he netted no biographer has yet uncovered.

The Vision of Columbus has met with what sheepish authors often refer to as mixed reviews. Over the years most have been negative. Before the modern-day critics weighed in, however, his first biographer wrote in 1886 that "for years no literary American was so well known, so much read, or the subject of so much eulogy, as Joel Barlow."[24] Present-day reviewers have been markedly less kind. They range from Robert Durden's allusion to the poem's "insufferable rhetoric,"[25] to Charles Woodress's reference to it as an "unending parade of heroic couplets." The latter assigns it the coffee-table quality of being "more admired than read."[26]

Some neither read nor admired it. George Washington gave his copy away.[27] Theodore Zunder is more specifically analytical. In his definitive study of Barlow's early years, he finds *The Vision* neither great nor good, too imitative of Pope and Milton, its ideas not well expressed, and many of its end-rhymes annoying."[28] Others have pointed out that Barlow's work appeared at a time when epic poetry had fallen out of popular favor. The *Edinburgh Review* made this point in 1810 when it remarked on Barlow's sequel to *The Vision,* recently published under the title *The Columbiad.* That Barlow persisted in the epic mode some have ascribed, in part, to the uncritical encouragement he received from his friends and tutors at Yale. He never voiced regrets, however, and later affirmed his original intent: to inspire his countrymen with a vision of the unfolding splendor that he believed had preceded and now attended their nation building.

Axiomatically poets seldom grow rich, and in a world sparsely populated by literary patrons, Barlow's modicum of fame promised little fortune, and he knew it. During the years 1784 to 1786, he groped for a profession that would keep him afloat financially while still honing his literary talents in his quest for public recognition. For more than a year, he seemed headed for a career as a publisher. In July 1784 he teamed up with an experienced printer named Elisha Babcock to launch the *American Mercury*, a Hartford weekly that survived Barlow's departure a year and a half later but meanwhile provided a useful vehicle for his occasional poetry. The partners' principal money makers were the books he and Babcock published. They included an almanac, Noah Webster's first textbook, and, somewhat controversially, a book of psalms that the Congregational churches of Connecticut hired him to edit. Creative as always, Barlow added some new psalms and revised others in ways that some readers felt had damaged the originals.[29] His edition nevertheless circulated widely in New England until the onset of the French Revolution, when his apparent lapse from orthodoxy led the reverend fathers to hire Timothy Dwight to put out another edition. Dwight's orthodoxy was never in doubt.[30] Barlow quit the *Mercury* in late 1785, parting on good terms with Babcock but convinced their partnership would not support them both.

Barlow next fixed his sights on a law career, possibly with a view to entering politics. Had he lived a century earlier, he might have reverted to the ministry as a path to public notice. Colonial clergymen had once wielded considerable influence in an agrarian society where few others had the time or inclination to publish their opinions. Besides airing theological issues, their writings often took on social, even political matters. By the late eighteenth century, however, the anticlerical rationalism of the Enlightenment—which Barlow shared—had sapped the primacy of the clergy, giving way to activists for whom perfecting man's law seemed a better way to serve the needs of mankind than preaching God's law. In sum, lawyers, especially lawyers as politicians, were fast setting the standard for leadership, becoming the most vocal and visible avatars of a new elite. Barlow also had before him the example of Ruth's brother Abraham, whose law career had already paved the way to a seat in Congress. The changing times and Prom's example may well explain why the erstwhile poet spent the winter and spring of 1785–86 preparing for the Connecticut bar exam. In April he presented the required treatise—a document Milton Cantor places well within the Jeffersonian canon—that the law, far from being immutable, should evolve to meet the changing needs of society. Or, as Barlow put it, "citizens of a new nation must make over legal fundamentals for their own use and adapt law to peculiarly American conditions."[31]

Already legal anachronisms like "entail" and "primogeniture" were disappearing from the statute books in the United States, and Barlow, having familiarized himself with the arguments against them, would refresh those arguments when he joined the British radical movement in London a few years later. His political ambitions, meanwhile, if they bore any connection to his study of law, culminated obscurely in his election to the New Haven Common Council in 1786.[32] He was practicing law at the time but, according to a handwritten note in the Barlow papers, "indifferently." The anonymous writer speculates that Barlow failed as a lawyer because "he was thought deficient in the happy impudence which is so essential to the success of an advocate."[33]

If the law failed to hold his attention, Barlow found a more congenial outlet for his literary energies when he joined the Hartford Wits in 1786. This group of like-minded law-and-order satirists published an extended serial poem titled *The Anarchiad.* Though loosely affiliated, the Wits were united in urging the need for a stronger central government to defend against the political unrest brought on by the sharp economic depression of the mid-1780s. Shays's Rebellion in Massachusetts was the principal manifestation of this unrest and appeared to some, at least, to threaten the Union. In retrospect the Wits seemed unkindly prone to poke fun at farmers who, unable to meet mortgage payments, were forcibly resisting foreclosures. Their motives were patriotic, however, if also somewhat patrician, and some have speculated that the case they made for a stronger central government may have rallied support for the handiwork of the Constitutional Convention, meeting a year later. This remains speculative. Certainly popular at the time, these poetic essays now gather dust, and perhaps the best that has been said of the Wits was that they were "the first serious group of writers America produced."[34]

Given his evolving Jeffersonian views on political issues, Barlow must have looked back in dismay at having fallen in with such future hardcore Federalists as David Humphreys, Timothy Dwight, and John Trumbull. More in keeping with his philosophy on civil unrest was the response he had made to Noah Webster in 1779. "I think," he wrote, "the civil dissensions you mention are a necessary evil in a republic . . . and will make candidates for public office more cautious and more faithful."[35] Whatever those dissensions in 1779, Barlow clearly chose the side of political stability in 1786. The siren call of the French Revolution had yet to beckon.

2 Selling Western Lands to French Émigrés

Poetry in the new nation may have been short of both supply and demand, but not western lands, where acreage for the taking seemed inexhaustible, and the demand needed only be nudged. In a sense, Barlow's transition from selling poetry to selling shares in western land companies was not as abrupt as it might seem. The spectacle of pioneers settling new lands, after all, evoked the same aura of romance he had trumpeted in *The Vision of Columbus*. Be that as it may, he would have been the first to admit in retrospect that his career as a land agent marked the sorriest chapter of his life. He never quite shook the taint of its ultimate disgrace.

Barlow's career in real estate began in 1787, shortly after the newly formed Ohio Company contracted to pay Congress $1 million for a million and a half acres of public lands in southeastern Ohio. Congress welcomed the prospect of being able to lower the national debt by that amount, and the company saw a profitable way to exploit the country's greatest natural resource. The principal deal makers in the transaction were the Rev. Manasseh Cutler, still the godfather of successful lobbyists, and William Duer, the not-too-scrupulous secretary of the Treasury Board created by the Continental Congress in 1779. Cutler closed the deal in July 1787 when he breezed into New York City and "worked" the members of the Confederation Congress as they spun out their final session. Quite likely he also offered shares in the company to members who needed persuasion. Duer contributed by lending Cutler $100,000 of government money to make the first down payment.[1] Despite the dubious activities of its founders, the Ohio Company ultimately met its contract and succeeded in establishing its first settlement at Marietta.

Not so the Scioto Company, the Ohio Company's semi-secret offshoot. While midwifing the Ohio Company, Duer and his friends also milked Congress for an "option" to buy an adjoining three and a half million acres bordering the Scioto River. Thousand-acre shares in this company were priced at a thousand dollars apiece. Owning the shares, however, conveyed only the option to buy, not title to the land itself. And while one biographer suggests that Barlow may not have understood this difference,[2] the latter's correspondence indicates that he expected the company to use its receipts from the sale of "options" to buy the land and thereby confirm the shareholders' titles. Complicating matters, Duer deceitfully provided Barlow with documents that attested to the company's actual ownership of the land.[3]

That Barlow attracted the company's notice in the first place seems to have followed more or less logically from his success in selling 113 of the Ohio Company's shares in less than four months, mostly in Connecticut.[4] But because shares in the Scioto Company moved more slowly, Duer and his associates hit on the idea of enticing European bankers to swap their nearly worthless holdings of U.S. government securities for American land shares. If Congress accepted those securities at par, the Scioto Company could then pay for the lands, actually take title, and profit from whatever was left over.[5] Unfortunately, European bankers were to show no more interest in buying options than potential investors in the United States, which explains why Barlow, when he reached Europe, made not a single sale for almost a year. Only when the French Revolution spewed forth a flood of fleeing émigrés would the Scioto Company begin to do serious if somewhat fraudulent business.

Barlow's recent success in selling lands for the Ohio Company may explain why the Scioto Company chose him to be their European representative. Or company officials may have hoped he could trade on his public recognition as a literary figure or counted on his outgoing personality to win the confidence of would-be buyers. Or, as Robert Durden suggests, "Perhaps Duer realized it would take abundant poetic license to sell lands for which he had no title."[6]

Barlow, for his part, accepted because he clearly relished the challenge and needed the money but also because he was beginning to nurture what would become a lifelong love of travel. He was seldom happier than when he was on the move. Ten years later, for example, while still enduring the hardships of his mission to the Barbary Coast, he suggested the State Department might send him next to make a treaty with Turkey. While admitting to a tourist's curiosity about the Ottoman Empire, he also insisted he knew of no one better suited to the mission. To Ruth, then in Paris, he hinted they could tour the sights of Italy on the way. Touristic appeal aside, however, the reality of doing almost any business in the eighteenth century required moving about. Without electronic conveniences and with a mail service that was truly snail-like, men on business either saddled a horse, ordered a carriage, or took a boat. They rarely sat in their offices. For Barlow, the prospect of doing business in Europe while having the opportunity to see the continent firsthand must have been irresistible. In high spirits, he left New Haven in the spring of 1788, predictably loaded with letters of introduction. He left Ruth behind to stay with her brother Dudley but promised to write frequently and assured her she would follow as soon as he had settled in.[7]

Barlow sailed from New York on May 29 on what was to be a fairly short passage of twenty-seven days. It must have seemed an eternity, however, when he discovered immediately and to his dismay that seafaring was not the most comfortable way to satisfy his wanderlust. From the moment his vessel cleared Sandy Hook, he was unremittingly and severely seasick. His long and graphic description of it later became the subject of an article published in the *Yale Journal of Biology and Medicine*.[8] Whatever else went overboard, however, his sense of humor was still intact when he landed at Le Havre. "The mouth of the Hudson," he wrote, "received my first sacrifice and the mouth of the Seine was honored with the last."[9] The severity of his suffering he blamed on the shipboard food, mostly superannuated hardtack. At one point, after fasting for nearly two weeks, he was able to keep down boiled rice until the ship's stores ran out. After that, he had to weigh his chances with a thick soup made daily of onions, garlic, and "musty bread."[10]

Still dizzy after five days ashore, he was scarcely able to write but, like most tourists landing abroad, felt compelled to mark down the salient European-American differences. Grimacing, he began with a description of French fleas, which, he recorded, were bigger and more ferocious than their American cousins. On this score he was reminded of Thomas Jefferson's well-known put-down of the comte de Buffon, the French naturalist, who "famously asserted that America's environment stunted the growth of its inhabitants [and] which Jefferson even more famously disposed of when dining with a mixed dinner of

Frenchmen and Americans, he asked the company to stand up and take each other's measure." But, he added, Buffon was right about the unstunted size of European fleas. Not satisfied with estimates and with an amateur scientist's penchant for weighing and measuring, he estimated that "the European flea is at least heavier by one third of a grain than that of America."[11]

Setting out for Paris, he wrote praise in his diary for the quality of French roads but noted irritably that customs officials stopped their carriage at nearly every town, always charged tolls, usually required bribes, and diligently ransacked their belongings for contraband.[12] His first impressions of France were predictably mixed. He enjoyed what he could see of the countryside and decided the people were not as miserable as he had been led to believe. Rural French cuisine, however, was not to his taste, and he found French cathedrals and public buildings generally dirty. "French cleanliness," he later observed, "will never become proverbial except in the language of irony."[13] Nor did he believe everything he was told en route. While he was touring the cathedral at Rouen, his guide announced that its bell weighed forty thousand pounds. With Yankee skepticism, Barlow took his own measurements "that I might calculate its weight at my leisure."[14]

Given the Scioto Company's plan to unload its land-purchase options on European bankers, the most likely dumping ground was the firm of Van Staphorst and Hubbard, which, having invested heavily in the American cause, held large quantities of U.S. government securities. Logically, then, Barlow's immediate target should have been the Van Staphorst office in Brussels. After only a few days in Paris, however, he took off for London in company with Daniel Parker, an expatriate businessman whom William Duer had asked to help him get started.[15] Parker would ultimately shepherd Barlow to Brussels, but in July he had pending business in London, and Barlow was happy to tag along.

Duer chose well in connecting the two men. Parker stood near the top of the American business community in Paris. Indeed, his estate on the Seine would soon become a meeting place for Americans bent on hatching joint ventures or seizing opportunities to forge profitable commercial ties with a succession of French regimes. The initial Barlow-Parker connection matured into a friendship that would last more than two decades and at one point very nearly produce a diplomatic solution to Madison's problems with Napoleon. But that came later. Meanwhile, rather than getting on with his mission for the Scioto

Company, Barlow spent more than two months in England, touching base with Parker between what can only be termed sightseeing forays in and around London. He did not reach Brussels until mid-September 1788.[16]

Barlow denied wasting time during this hiatus. He admitted to his diary the luxury of dining out six nights a week but defended these outings as "the best way of collecting information."[17] Experience having taught him the value of making personal contacts, this explanation was not implausible. Other diary entries, however, suggest he had fewer encounters with potential business associates than with members of Britain's scientific and political elite.

During this English interlude, he seldom missed an opportunity to make himself known to the famous. He was pleased, for example, to meet Sir Joseph Banks, president of the Royal Society. In this instance he found himself discussing with Britain's foremost scientist "the progress of the hessian fly in America" and, winking at stereotype, observed that Banks was "a large man, more able-bodied than most philosophers are."[18] He also called on Lord Shelburne, whom he identified more or less accurately as "the man who made peace with America," and noted admiringly that Shelburne's library contained fifty thousand volumes.[19] The highlight of these brushes with celebrity was his impromptu staring contest with King George III. It happened during chapel at Windsor Castle. "When his eye met mine, I saw he marked me for a stranger, & I endeavoured to outstare him but in vain. Well, thought I, if a cat may look upon a king, by the same ascending scale, a king may look upon me—& so stare away."[20]

Ruminating near Runnymede as his carriage drove back from Windsor, Barlow mused on the disconnect between Britain's legal legacy and her present-day political scene. On one hand, he expressed an American's profound gratitude for the heritage of habeas corpus and trial by jury but then considered glumly how corrupt the British political system had become. Filling seats in Parliament, he knew, too often consisted of wealthy men buying and selling election districts, known as rotten boroughs. "What shall we think of the political freedom of this people," he asked himself on hearing "that such a duke *sends sixteen members to Parliament* & that such a gentleman has *bought a borough*?"[21] Britons may have written the rules, he concluded, but Americans knew better how to play by them.

His British interlude also awakened what was to become Barlow's abiding interest in mechanical innovations. He talked to Thomas Paine about the latter's iron bridge, described a "new harpoon gun," and marveled at "a kind of rolling press called the mangle [used] for smoothing table linen." And after seeing James Rumsey's model steamboat, he predicted that once it was developed, "the commerce of the world will be carried on with one half the expense & double the expedition that it is now."[22] Considering how much of the American economy relied on merchant shipping, Barlow's fascination with steamboats was not unique and later took on a personal dimension when he and Ruth befriended Robert Fulton and made him their intermittent houseguest in Paris for more than seven years. But that, too, came later.

Barlow happily reported only a slight queasiness during a five-hour crossing to Calais on September 10. He and Parker set off for Brussels the next day. Curiously, he left no clue in his diary as to why he failed to do business with the Van Staphorsts. His entries seem to suggest that he and Parker had spent the week touring the city and its environs. He described climbing a two-hundred-foot Chinese pagoda from which he could see Antwerp in the distance. He also added to his store of knowledge about steam engines when he talked to workmen in charge of a pump boasting a cylinder five feet in diameter designed to fill a large basin in the park. Told it could throw thirty-six tons of water per minute and fill the basin in thirty-six hours, he calculated that it pumped 246,915 cubic feet.[23] This compulsion to measure every novelty he came across might be written off as an endearing idiosyncrasy. Earlier in London, for example, he had paced off the dimensions of Vauxhall Gardens and the living quarters in the Tower of London. He may simply have planned to use these factoids as future conversation pieces, although his fascination with the mechanics of new inventions doubtless had a more calculated purpose. Keeping abreast of the unprecedented surge in scientific advances also served a social purpose by putting him at ease in the company of the new elite. The wide-eyed farm boy was being left far behind.

Returning to Paris on September 25, Barlow stayed only long enough to record having dined with Jefferson and Lafayette at the American legation. Four rainy days later, the Van Staphorsts sent word asking him to return to Brussels. Again Parker accompanied him. They caught up with the bankers at Antwerp but left two days later—Parker to revisit London, Barlow back to Paris. Again his diary gave no explanation of the rebuff that had clearly transpired.[24]

Hereafter, unable to unload Scioto shares in banker-size bundles, he would have to try to sell them piecemeal to individuals. Until the summer of 1789, however, his prospects for finding such a market must have seemed bleak. He was still living, albeit comfortably, off Duer's expense account but had little hope of finding customers short of some change in the political climate. That change would come with the fall of Bastille in July, when aristocrats and others fleeing the fury of an increasingly bloody revolution would present him with more sales opportunities than he ever expected but quickly seized.

The previous fall he had been in Paris long enough to pick up on the breathless anticipation of those who hoped that France's legislative body, the Estates-General, soon to meet, would bring much-needed reforms to the French monarchy. "The Patriots of Paris," he wrote, "are very sanguine in their expectation that they will effect a peaceable & complete revolution in the government & establish a free constitution." Unlike most of his countrymen who, even today, picture American democracy as a universal model for strugglers against oppression, Barlow harbored serious doubts. He was wise enough in his own time not to expect an easy transfer of political institutions: "I presume there are not to be found five men in Europe, who understand the nature of liberty & the theory of government as well as they are understood by five hundred men in America."[25] Despite such misgivings, Barlow, like most Jeffersonians, ardently supported the early goals of French revolutionaries, wishing them success and occasionally putting up signposts to point them in directions he thought they should take. Curiously for a man who later threatened to write a history of the Revolution, he kept no diary in 1789. One of the few extant letters he wrote to Ruth that year, dated July 20, expressed a tumult of mixed feelings: "All the true things which you see published, however horrible, however cruel . . . have passed under my eye, and it is really no small gratification to me to have seen two complete revolutions in favor of liberty."[26] That the revolution in France was not "complete" would dawn on him soon enough. Five years later at the height of the Terror, he assured his friend and fellow Yale graduate Oliver Wolcott that he had given up all thought of writing a history of the Revolution. With unerring prescience, he foresaw the Revolution to be "of such an extraordinary nature, as scarcely to stand a chance of being treated impartially by its friends or enemies."[27]

Turning to business, Barlow wasted no time casting a wide net among would-be emigrants. In early August he enlisted a group of eight investors to form the Companie du Scioto. Jointly, they pledged to "buy, improve, and sell the company's three million acres."[28]

Barlow clearly hoped this larger investment group would attract enough buyers to enable the parent company to fulfill its contract with Congress and thereby validate the land titles. From the beginning, however, everything went wrong. Most critical perhaps, William Duer had no plans to receive settlers, a fact that Barlow was innocently unaware of when he sent off his last shipload of émigrés in January 1790, urging Duer to look after their welfare. In all, five small vessels carrying some six hundred would-be settlers straggled into Alexandria, Virginia, and New York City that spring.[29] Gradually the arrivals learned that although the Scioto Company had collapsed, the Ohio Company had subsumed its lands and had taken responsibility for settling them. Belatedly the company did provide for them, building four blockhouses and several huts ready for occupancy by June. Here at Gallipolis, perched on the banks of Chickamauga Creek, several dozen citified Frenchmen did their best to adapt to frontier life. Their plaintive letters home inevitably dampened hopes for further sales.[30]

Although Barlow in January claimed to have sent remittances to the parent company, they were not enough for Duer to convert options to ownership. Indeed, by 1793 Duer himself was in debtors' prison. The cash shortfall is most readily explained by the likelihood that at least two of Barlow's Paris associates were accomplished embezzlers. Probably a Frenchman named La Chaise de Soissons and certainly an English businessman ironically named William Playfair made off with much of the company's receipts.[31] And while Barlow himself may have been complacent in circulating a gaudy prospectus touting the idyllic attractions of the Scioto Valley, Playfair was most likely its author. In desperation Barlow reorganized the company in the spring of 1790, but by fall the Scioto speculation had collapsed in ruins amid bitter charges of fraud and threats of bodily harm to its agents.

Predictably, perhaps, Barlow's biographers have lined up to clear him of wrongdoing. Some find him too trusting of others or shockingly inattentive to detail, but none believes he had any part in the disappearance of company funds.[32] For evidence they rely largely on the exonerating report of Benjamin Walker, whom the parent Ohio Company sent to Paris to audit the company's books in late 1790. Walker cleared Barlow of any malfeasance but was unable to track down the money the French purchasers had paid. The most he could do was to place newspaper ads warning the public not to deal with Playfair. Walker expressed little sympathy for Barlow. He gave Gouverneur Morris, the U.S. minister to France, what the latter called "a lamentable Account of the Agency of Mr. Barlow in the Scioto Com'y."[33] And Theodore Belote, looking back, wonders why Barlow continued to deal with Playfair well into the spring of 1790, even after he suspected him of embezzlement. Why, he asks pointedly, did Barlow not take Playfair and Soissons to court?[34] Part of the answer lay in Playfair's having gone into hiding in late 1790.

Voicing both hope and despair, Barlow's letters to Ruth that spring reflected the uncertainties of his situation. On New Year's Day 1790, he described the past year as having been filled with "anxiety and distress." Money was coming in, he told her, but added significantly that he was not sure that it was reaching his "friends" in New York. Sales in Paris were still brisk, and "many respectable & wealthy families are making their purchases & are going this spring." But everything depended on how well the Scioto Company received the settlers.[35] When some weeks later news began to trickle back of how poorly they had been received, Barlow worked desperately to revitalize the company, adding new members and proposing to recruit buyers by allowing them to pay in installments, a plan Duer flatly rejected. Finally, washing his hands of the whole affair, he stayed in Paris only long enough for Colonel Walker to complete his audit and clear him of any criminal complicity.

By this time, Ruth had arrived in London where Joel was to join her, but not before he had blocked out a new career path. In July 1789 he and eleven other Americans sent a well-received letter to the French National Assembly, congratulating that body on its first steps toward dismantling the ancien régime. This letter met with "thunderclaps of applause," he reported happily, and it contained enough high-flown verbiage to suggest that he was one of its authors.[36] It also signaled a renewal of his literary output, most of it from England where shortly he took up company with like-minded British reformers later that year. Having failed to make his fortune in land sales, he would try his hand at writing political tracts.

Among its legacies, Scioto's spectacular failure did "great mischief" to the efforts of legitimate land companies trying to entice European buyers, a point noted peevishly by Gouverneur Morris, who himself dabbled in such enterprises.

As a royalist sympathizer, Morris had little use for revolutionary cheerleaders and as a businessman even less sympathy for Barlow's now widely known financial embarrassment. In a diary entry of August 31, 1790, he noted that Barlow had refused Duer's draft for $100,000. Again in November, he confided to a business associate in America that Barlow "sends back under Protest a Bill for 100,000# drawn for account of the Scioto Company," adding that this was the "same Company, against whose Deceptions the cry is general here, and whose Conduct will not . . . be agreeable on your side of the water."[37] Nor would Barlow's connection with Scioto soon be forgotten in Paris. More than two decades later, when serving as U.S. minister to France, he offered a complicated plan to indemnify the victims of French maritime depredations, only to have a suspicious underling remind the French foreign minister of Barlow's role in defrauding hundreds of Frenchmen during the Scioto affair. The American minister's indemnification proposal, he wrote, was not to be trusted; Barlow was an "impure source."[38]

3 Joining the French Revolution

Though sorely embarrassed as he put Paris behind him, Barlow nevertheless seems to have profited from the experience. He would choose more reliable business partners in the future and not be betrayed again. Meanwhile, although no record remains of how he and Ruth managed their personal finances in London, his political writings doubtless produced a modest income. At least his tracts were influential. Historians, for example, typically cite Thomas Paine's *Age of Reason* as the most potent rebuttal to Burke's defense of traditional institutions, but Barlow's *Advice to the Privileged Orders?*, published in February 1792, spoke out with equal force against Europe's feudal remnants. In it he advised European elites to embrace as inevitable the reforms initiated by the revolution in France, changes he believed would produce long-term benefits at all levels of society. Besides targeting the well-recognized evils of priestly abuse, indirect taxes, standing armies, entail, primogeniture and so forth, he also voiced a not-so-familiar condemnation of capital punishment.[1] By and large, what his *Advice* lacked in originality it made up in eloquence and well-reasoned argument. Thus, while Paine's work earned him a conviction for seditious libel, Barlow's less inflammatory critique, though frowned on, drew praise in Parliament from Charles James Fox, the one-time Whig opponent of Lord North in the run-up to the American Revolution. In October 1791 Barlow explained to Ruth's brother his personal reasons for writing it. Alluding to the Scioto project as "time ill spent," he told Abraham Baldwin he now intended "to chin up to the level of the politics of Europe, & not to suffer these great events to pass without my leaving an impression & leading to reflexions." His essay, as he called it, focused on "the necessity & propriety of a Revolution in the Governments of Europe."[2]

Advice also secured him entrée to London's quasi-seditious Society for Constitutional Information whose members held up the revolution in France as a model for parliamentary reform, a dangerous view at the time. In this and other radical circles, Barlow exchanged ideas with such luminaries as litigator and pamphleteer John Horne Tooke, the son of a grocer, whose published advocacy of parliamentary reform brought him to trial for high treason three years later. (He was acquitted.) Another of Barlow's "radical" associates, the scientist Joseph Priestly, is remembered as the codiscoverer of oxygen and, incidentally, the first person to carbonate water. As a former cleric, Priestly had been burned out of home and church in Birmingham for preaching Unitarian sermons. And another Unitarian, the ethicist Richard Price, had expressed enough sympathy for the French Revolution to be singled out for reproof in Burke's *Reflections on the Revolution in France.* Also on the fringes was Thomas Hardy, a London shoemaker, who was later acquitted of high treason for having been a war protester and an advocate of universal manhood suffrage.[3]

Altogether they made for heady if somewhat perilous company. Nor did Barlow play a minor role in their activities. He won the society's particular notice in October 1792 when he published *A Letter to the National Convention*, recommending thirteen amendments to the French constitution of 1791 and urging that body to top off its revolution by abolishing the monarchy and disestablishing the church.[4] The society promptly appointed Barlow and three others to draft its own *Letter to the National Convention*, and before the end of November Barlow and a colleague named John Frost set off for Paris to deliver the *Letter* in person.

They arrived at a time when the Girondin faction was riding high. Military victories at Valmy and Jemappes had offset earlier wartime reverses, and the paranoia that would spawn the Terror was still in the offing. Remembered for their all-encompassing expansionist fervor, the Girondins would, if they could, liberate and extend a fraternal embrace to all the world while adding a province or two to *la patrie* along the way. Thus, in November they voted to annex the Italian province of Savoy and sent off Edmond-Charles Genêt to try to persuade the Washington administration to launch liberating campaigns against Canada, Louisiana, and the Floridas. At another level, they expanded the pantheon of revolutionary heroes by awarding honorary French citizenship to those Americans, Britons, or anyone else they believed supportive of their cause. By early 1793 Barlow was among those so honored, along with a half dozen British radicals, who now joined such earlier honorees as Washington, Madison, and Hamilton.[5]

Always receptive to grand designs, Barlow let himself be swept up in the excitement. He exulted at the Convention's warm reception of the society's letter and when the Convention's president, Henri Grégoire, invited him to stand for election as a Girondin deputy from Savoy, he accepted the challenge and gamely set off for its capital city of Chambéry. Although Savoyards generally welcomed the prospect of annexation, the political divisions among its various factions militated against Barlow's candidacy, and he knew it. In a letter to Ruth in early December 1792, he downplayed his chances of election but said he relished the prospect of touring southern France and seeing the Alps, all at "the expense of the Republic."[6] Not to be thought a freeloader, however, he wrote and published an appeal to the people of neighboring Piedmont touting the advantages of following Savoy's example.[7] The Piedmontese needed persuasion, he told Ruth, because they hated both the French and the Savoyards.[8] After more than three months in the Alps, however, he had not persuaded Piedmont to join Savoy, nor had the latter elected him to the Convention. But his sojourn at least kept him out of harm's way. Had he been seated as a deputy, he might well have shared the fate of those Girondin leaders whom, after losing control of the Convention in June, the Jacobins proceeded to execute in September.

While Barlow's mission to Savoy bore no political fruit, it did produce a poem that his literary critics agree is his finest, his ode to *The Hasty Pudding.* Written after dining at an inn in Chambéry back in January, he recalled in sensuous, almost slurpy detail his robust enjoyment of real American cornmeal mush. This poem now graces nearly every literary anthology of the era. One of his biographers writes appreciatively that *The Hasty Pudding* "was worth a dozen *Visions of Columbus* or *Columbiads,*" pointing to the irony that its author never realized how well it would be received.[9] Another finds it even more ironic that "the man who most of all wanted to be remembered as the epic poet of America is best known today for his poem about corn-meal mush."[10] Proof that Barlow was sincerely attached to his favorite dish surfaced a decade later when he wrote Ruth from Paris that he had just "murdered" a mouse he found eating its way into a bag of Indian meal. To prevent further inroads, he planned to have mush for breakfast hereafter. He would instruct their cook to make a daily "polente, as the barbarous coxcombs of the Great nation are wont to call it who know as little about a hasty pudding as they do about a republic."[11]

While Barlow rusticated at Chambéry, the National Convention plunged into ever more feverish activity. In January it tried and executed Louis XVI, and then declared war on Britain, an event that immediately put American shipping at risk and pitted the cause of American neutrality against the inherent claims of the Franco-American alliance of 1778. In March, the month Barlow returned to Paris, the Convention bloodied itself still further when it created a revolutionary tribunal to hunt down and punish the nation's enemies, real or imagined, while at the same time fighting to put down a large-scale royalist uprising in the Vendée.

After Savoy, Barlow had no choice but to return to Paris. Ruth had written him in January that London was out of the question. "You are very obnoxious here," she warned. "You cannot return with safety. The Alien bill would prevent you if nothing more," adding that Edmund Burke had lumped him with those who had conspired with French revolutionaries "for the express purpose of overturning the constitution of this country." She also felt keenly about her own situation. If France and Britain went to war, she asked, "what will you do with me?" She would not feel safe in France and dreaded the prospect of returning home alone.[12] After these first alarms, however, she promised to weather their separation with more "philosophy" than he imagined and asked what she could do to look after his literary affairs in London. Whatever he was up to, she trusted his good judgment and told him to "follow entirely your own inclination, in so doing, know that you will always gratify me. I know your conduct will always be directed by humanity, integrity & a desire to promote the good of your fellow creatures." At the same time, she deplored the conduct of the National Convention whose execution of the king she thought was both "impolitic" and "unjust."[13]

Throughout March 1793 Barlow bombarded his wife with letters urging her to join him in Paris and promising they would soon sail home together.[14] By early April, however, he had found a reason to stay. A prominent American businessman, Benjamin Hichborn, had just made him a "proposal" that would require him to remain in Europe through the summer. This proposal clearly promised substantial financial reward, because Barlow, if his letters to Ruth are to be believed, had been fully prepared to return to the United States. On April 19 he wrote her that Hichborn, soon to be in London on business, would visit her; she should take his advice as to whether to stay or join him in Paris.[15] Ruth stayed in London until June.

Barlow had no sooner returned from Savoy than he figured briefly in an offbeat plan to liberate Spanish Louisiana. While the Girondin leadership hoped that Citizen Genêt could persuade Philadelphia to do this with his help, they also toyed with the idea of sending a French military force directly to New Orleans. Here the initiative centered on the Girondin minister of finance, Jacques Pierre Brissot de Warville, a recent traveler in the United States, whose account, *Nouveau voyage en Amérique,* Barlow had undertaken to translate and have published in England the year before.

When, in March 1793, the Committee of Public Safety entertained a proposal to send troops, Barlow's name came up as one who might help to organize the expedition. Nothing came of this project at the time, but nine months later Barlow and a fellow Yale graduate and businessman named Mark Leavenworth revived the idea when they submitted a "*plan pour prendre la Louisiane, sans couter rien à la nation.*" Specifically, they offered to lead an army of two thousand Frenchmen at their own expense.[16]

Why Barlow would invite a potentially threatening French presence at the mouth of the American West's major commercial outlet poses a question of judgment. The historian Robert Durden offers perhaps the best explanation, suggesting that "Barlow, like Paine, Brissot, and countless others of that generation, pictured himself as a 'self-conscious citizen of the Western world,' one who crossed quite easily over national boundaries because of the cosmopolitan world economy that characterized the late eighteenth century." To Durden, the Girondin phase of the French Revolution "dramatically epitomized that cosmopolitanism and internationalism." If these "isms" seem to cast doubt on Barlow's patriotism, he was not entirely indifferent to American national interests. He and Leavenworth explicitly stipulated that nothing arising from the proposed expedition should "hinder the free navigation of the Mississippi."[17] Seen in retrospect, free navigation of the Mississippi plus a right to deposit goods at New Orleans were the most that even the Washington administration could hope for at the time, and its emissary, Thomas Pinckney, would shortly extract these concessions from Madrid. Meanwhile, the Girondins, who might have acted on the Barlow-Leavenworth proposal, had long since been overthrown, and their Jacobin successors showed little interest in overseas venture.

Barlow's "cosmopolitanism" took a somewhat more combative turn when Oliver Wolcott wrote him glowingly about the success of the American experiment. Wolcott, then Washington's treasury secretary, found much to boast about. Despite lingering factionalism, he wrote, the country was more united, more prosperous than ever and remained a republican example to "enlighten men of all nations."[18] Barlow agreed that his country was a "useful example to the world" and surely had no need of a French-type revolution, but he believed there was still room for improvement. Governments in both countries could do more to improve the human condition if they fostered greater access to education, improved public morals, and encouraged "a degree of equality [that] tends to their dignity and happiness." Some of his old friends, he knew, "consider my head as turned by these ideas . . . but had you seen and felt what I have, I am confident you would have been of my opinion."[19] Moreover, the prospect of encountering friends who thought him hopelessly infected with French radicalism also helps to explain why he repeatedly deferred plans to go home.

Barlow had only sporadic brushes with the Terror after his return from Savoy. On one occasion he testified before a revolutionary tribunal on behalf of Francisco de Miranda, the would-be Latin American liberator who, though he had served as a French general, was thought to have been corrupted by his association with the Girondins. And in January 1794 Thomas Paine showed up at his door in police custody, asking Barlow to accompany him to his quarters to pick up some "papers," among them his manuscript for *The Age of Reason*. When Paine subsequently went to prison, Barlow circulated a petition for his release and obtained signatures from eighteen members of the American community but not that of the U.S. minister, Gouverneur Morris.

Paine languished in prison for nearly a year before James Monroe, Morris's successor, managed to spring him.[20] For the most part, however, Barlow kept a cautious low profile. In May 1793 he told Ruth, "I meddle in no politics," adding to reassure her, "Paris is quiet & I believe it will be."[21] The Jacobin Terror had yet to reach full bloodletting.

By late 1793 Barlow had outwardly abandoned both poetry and politics in favor of repairing his finances. To that end, he teamed up with a group of Americans whose business expertise France desperately needed to maintain her external commerce. For the French this meant employing knowledgeable American merchants and brokers to figure out how to move cargoes in and out French ports in the face of Britain's near control of the adjoining seas. Most prominent among them was James Swan, a Boston merchant and financier who in 1794 won the distinction of becoming chief purchasing agent for Robespierre's three-member Commission des Subsistances. Under the commission's aegis, Swan specialized in importing much-needed American foodstuffs and shipping back a variety of French luxury goods, which, though not much in demand, were plentifully obtainable from the confiscated estates of French aristocrats.[22] Barlow's first contact with Swan is unclear, but, significantly, as early as April 1793 he was telling Ruth to address her letters to Swan's residence in Paris.[23]

Among those who also flourished under the commission were Barlow's longtime friend, Daniel Parker, his fellow would-be Louisiana liberator Mark Leavenworth, and of course Benjamin Hichborn, who first broached the "proposal" Barlow had related to Ruth in April. Like much wartime commerce, Hichborn's skirted the traditional ban against trading with the enemy. In what was apparently their first venture together, Barlow, Parker, and Leavenworth arranged for Hichborn to go to England where in late 1793 he hired a British vessel, laded it with flour and rice, papered it for a Spanish destination, then sneaked its cargo into Bordeaux.[24] Given the demand for foodstuffs, such stratagems proved highly profitable. Why Barlow's business associates enlisted him in this and other ventures possibly reflected their hope to exploit his latent political connections. Although by late 1793 he had eschewed all political activity and taken up residence in the quiet Paris suburb of Mendon, he still had standing as a French citizen, and his letters of introduction from Jefferson doubtless made him welcome at useful levels of French officialdom. Or perhaps the group simply accepted him on Hichborn's nod of approval. As Barlow told Ruth, he and Hichborn had hit it off at a personal level. They were friends as well as partners, a plausible explanation in light of Barlow's gift for making friends.[25]

In early 1794, acting under the commission but on his own account, Barlow successfully brought a Swedish cargo into Le Havre.[26] His success in this

Scandinavian venture may explain why he moved closer to the source. In April 1794 he and Ruth left Paris for Hamburg where he opened a brokerage office within easy walking distance of their living quarters in Altona. Given his earlier affiliation with the Girondins, his decision to leave France was likely cautionary as well. In light of the Jacobins' relentless pursuit of their fallen foes, he was obviously safer beyond their reach.

Whatever the reason or combination of reasons, it was a rewarding move. Barlow prospered in Hamburg as never before, ultimately making enough money as a cargo broker to free him and Ruth from financial worries for the remainder of their lives. Records of this interlude are sparse, but his instructions to a Capt. Benjamin Parks reveal the perils of transporting cargoes in wartime. Writing in November 1794, he told Parks that if the British waylaid his vessel, he should seek help from John Lyle at the London firm of Byrd, Savage, and Byrd. If the French brought him in, he was to call on John Higginson on the rue de la Réunion.[27] A sketchy secondary account pictures him repeating much the same pattern as his first venture with Hichborn, in these instances chartering "neutral" American vessels, lading them with cargoes either in Hamburg or in Britain, furnishing them with papers showing Spanish destinations, but routing them into Bordeaux.[28] From there the ubiquitous James Swan handled their disposition. Scattered references in the commission's files suggest that Barlow's vessels often carried cargoes of potash and pearl ash, variously used in the manufacture of soap, glass, and ceramics.[29]

If, in turning a profit, Barlow felt any qualms about "feeding" the Terror, whose excesses he clearly abhorred, he could, and probably did, rationalize that as long as French republicans were battling the forces of European monarchism, he could support them. And when those same Frenchmen proved incapable of sustaining a republic—any more than they could make a hasty pudding—he bore the disappointment with philosophical resignation.

4 Waiting for a Diplomatic Opening to Algeria

Northern Europe's bitterly cold winter of 1794–95 froze Hamburg harbor solid from November to March, effectively ending Barlow's brokerage business. Nonetheless, they were free of financial worries, and he and Ruth idled away their days learning German and enjoying each other's company. For the Barlows, their winter in Altona was a pleasant if isolated interlude. By spring, both were eager to get back to Paris—always a center of attraction—and now quiescent enough to hold no dangers for a former Girondin hanger-on. With the end of the Terror, France had acquired a drab and barely functional regime known as the Directory, a five-member ruling committee whose agreed-upon raison d'être was to prevent a resurgence of either monarchists or Jacobins at home while using Napoleon Bonaparte to keep foreign enemies at bay. In this quieter French capital, he and Ruth looked forward to renewing old acquaintances, and for Barlow it would mark the beginning of a widely spread-out career in public service.

By the spring of 1795, the U.S. government had already spent more than a decade trying to ransom American seamen taken captive by Algerian corsairs. Barlow, now footloose and financially secure, must have seemed an attractive choice to carry that effort forward. Wittingly or not, he made his presence known, if not also his availability, when he called at the American legation to pay his respects to James Monroe, the new U.S. minister. Subsequent encounters with an old friend, David Humphreys, clinched it.[1] Also a Yale graduate, Humphreys had risen to the rank of colonel as an aide to General Washington and had crossed paths with Barlow in 1780 when he had introduced him to Gen. Nathaniel Greene who, in turn, had encouraged Barlow to seek a chaplaincy. The two men also had in common their ties with the Hartford Wits. Humphreys, now U.S. minister to Portugal and charged with Algerian affairs, was in France that spring hoping to win French diplomatic support for an Algerian settlement. Barlow arrived on the scene just as Humphreys had given up on Paris and realized the need for the services of a special emissary. One biographer suggests that Barlow agreed to go to Algiers because he was just plain bored.[2] Barlow himself later admitted that his motives were touristic as well as humanitarian.

He later offered Humphreys two reasons: "One was to try to extricate our citizens from slavery, and the other was a curiosity (perhaps a very idle one) of seeing a people and government who make so singular a figure in the great picture of human activity."[3] Unfortunately, the most prominent aspect of that activity consisted of North African regencies nominally under Turkish rule capturing the vessels of shipmasters whose governments either refused or were unable to afford the cost of "peace" treaties. Algiers easily outstripped Tunis and Tripoli in such depredations, although the rulers of all three depended for much of their revenue on captured shipping. As the price for immunity, they extorted payment in the form of costly treaties plus annual tribute plus consular "gifts" and held seamen for ransom when such safeguards lapsed. Barlow later put his finger on the revolving-door nature of this process and its imperatives. Because Ali Hassan, the dey of Algiers, needed to reward those who kept him in office, his corsairs were constantly at sea, plundering the shipping of one nation after another. The fixed point of Algerian policy, he wrote, "is that the regency must be at war [and] whenever one power makes a treaty, others are put at risk.[4] And as he later learned, successful diplomatic maneuvering often depended on which nation's shipping was next on the hit list. As to why the civilized world allowed this borderline piracy, the time-honored explanation holds that the great powers tolerated, even encouraged it because it gave them a competitive edge over those lesser Mediterranean powers that, unable to pay the costs, were driven from the seas.

For Americans, winning independence obviously meant losing the protection they had enjoyed as British subjects. Still, American vessels remained relatively safe in the Atlantic as long as Spain or Portugal kept the Barbary corsairs bottled up behind the Straits of Gibraltar. When the straits were twice left unguarded, however, the U.S. government faced the problem of securing the release of its captured seamen. A relatively small number fell victim when Spain made a truce with Algiers in 1785; a much larger group was captured when Portugal did likewise in 1793. The Spanish truce did minimal damage, costing Americans only two vessels seized off the coast of Portugal in July 1785. Significantly, two of the twenty-one seamen taken prisoner at this time figured prominently in later negotiations. One was James Leander Cathcart, a young Irish American crewman aboard the *Maria,* whose language skills and insinuating personality ultimately won him an influential post as the dey's "chief Christian secretary."[5] Barlow would come to regard Cathcart for what he was—a self-important intriguer whose counsel was sometimes useful. The other was Richard O'Brien, captain of the *Dauphin* out of Philadelphia, soon to be a de facto spokesman for the prisoners and a knowledgeable insider whom Barlow would come to trust implicitly.

Shortly after the first captures, the Portuguese took over blocking the straits for the next eight years, their prime motive to keep the corsairs from pillaging their important commerce with Brazil. When the Portuguese unexpectedly removed their guard in 1793—curiously, the result of an unauthorized truce arranged by the British consul in Algiers—the capture of a much larger group of Americans forced the U.S. government to engage in more sustained diplomacy.

With no shipping losses between the first and second episodes, the fifteen survivors of the original twenty-one were more or less, but not entirely, forgotten. Word of their capture soon reached Paris where Jefferson had just "succeeded" Benjamin Franklin (no one could replace him, he insisted), and London where John Adams was being asked snidely whether he represented one nation or thirteen. Adams played a peripheral role in what followed. After several meetings with a self-styled Tripolitan ambassador in London, he concluded that whatever ransom Congress might offer Algiers would not be enough.[6] He was right in that respect. Jefferson's first response was to seek assistance from the Maturins, a French religious order that had recently succeeded in ransoming three hundred French seamen at a reasonable $200 a head. Unfortunately, the Revolution overtook the Maturins before Jefferson could mobilize their willingness to help.[7]

The Confederation Congress, meanwhile, anticipated post-independence dangers when in early 1785—even before news of the first captures—it accepted the offer of a Connecticut sea captain named John Lamb to undertake a treaty mission to Algiers. Impressed by Lamb's claim to familiarity with North Africa and his willingness to serve without pay, Congress authorized him to draw funds through John Adams from a "treaty credit" of $80,000 it had established with the Dutch bankers.[8] In retrospect Congress might better have run a background check on Lamb. Jefferson, of course, was glad to see him when he arrived in Paris in September and sent him off to touch base with William Carmichael, the longtime U.S. chargé d'affaires in Madrid. Unfortunately, Carmichael's part in this first official mission was to mislead Jefferson into believing that $80,000 would suffice not only to ransom the captives, but also to cover the cost of treaties with all three North African powers.[9]

Lamb's mission quickly went from bad to worse. He landed in Algiers in late March 1786, only to have the British and French consuls refuse to introduce him to Ali Hassan because he had not brought the customary gifts required of such ceremonies. (Barlow would not make that mistake.) When the dey finally agreed to see Lamb, it was as a ransomer, not a treaty maker. The mission climaxed on April 7, 1786, when Lamb tentatively agreed to the dey's ransom demand of $50,000, to be delivered within four months.[10] This was the last that was heard of him. Jefferson later claimed that Lamb had never notified either him or Adams of his contract with the dey. Nor, Jefferson added, had Lamb ever settled his accounts or explained what happened to the $12,000 in walking-around money he took with him.[11]

When Lamb's failure dawned on the captives, Captain O'Brien asked bitterly how Congress could have sent an emissary so ill prepared, moreover a man he also described as coarse, vulgar, tactless, and much too friendly with the British consul. But the door was still open, he believed. Ali Hassan had no settled dislike of Americans, and their coastline was too far away to be routinely ravaged.[12] Cathcart, however, from his listening post in the dey's palace, doubted the likelihood of a treaty in the near future. He pointed out that the dey, then negotiating with Spain, was not likely to treat with Americans whose shipping he might want to plunder if Madrid met his terms. Like O'Brien, Cathcart also lamented Lamb's negotiation, primarily because it raised false hopes among the captives, while leading the dey and his Turkish grandees to conclude that the American government was trifling with them.[13]

In July 1791 Jefferson, now secretary of state, wrote Humphreys that the administration's current policy was "to take no notice of our captives." Any further effort to ransom them, he explained, would play to the dey's exaggerated view of how much he thought the U.S. government would pay. And as long as the Spanish consul in Algiers, Count d'Espilly, continued to provide the captives with subsistence, he thought it enough for Humphreys to make sure that the count was reimbursed. As for rescuing them, Jefferson added somewhat offhandedly, "It remains for us to see what other means are practicable for their recovery"[14] Humphreys was in Lisbon at the time, busily gathering intelligence broadly related to early stages of persuading Madrid to grant free navigation of the Mississippi River. Curiously, Jefferson neglected to tell him that he had already laid out to Congress what "other means" it might follow. Because using naval force in the Mediterranean was not an immediate option, he seemed to lean toward buying a treaty, although he recalled being told in Paris that it might cost up to a million dollars.[15] There the matter rested for more than a year. Then, in February 1792, shortly before Humphreys was appointed U.S. minister to Portugal, Congress authorized the president to spend up to $145,000 for treaty purposes and ransom.[16]

In a bid to add luster to the mission, Washington subsequently named the naval hero John Paul Jones to be the new federal government's first official emissary. Jones, unfortunately, died before he could carry out the mission, but his instructions recounted all the frustrations that had beset earlier ransom efforts. Here Jefferson listed his own abortive attempt to enlist the Maturins, as well as Lamb's fiasco and the efforts of several Mediterranean-based U.S. consuls acting on their own initiative. However well-intentioned these overtures, the dey obviously took them for eagerness and refused to budge from the $50,000 figure Lamb had purportedly agreed to. If the current appearance of "neglect" had the desired effect, however, Jefferson hoped the dey would agree to a more reasonable settlement. The ransom figure he had in mind was $10,000, but Jones could go as high as $27,000. The secretary also enclosed a copy of the recently negotiated U.S. treaty with Morocco for Jones to use as a model. As for the cost of a treaty, as distinct from ransom, time would tell whether O'Brien's estimate of roughly $300,000 would suffice. Besides making a treaty, Jones could agree to pay annual tribute but not in naval stores, "which we know they will employ to do wrong."[17] Jefferson later dropped this scruple when it became clear that without such items there would be no treaty.[18] North African corsairs were typically short of cannons, powder, and shot, and their shipyards needed reliable sources of spars, ship timbers, tar, cordage, and the like, especially when declarations of war against the powers of northern Europe cut off their traditional supplies from that quarter.

Humphreys had been at his Lisbon post for a full year before Jefferson authorized him to "undertake the mission to Algiers." By this time the secretary had news of Jones's death, followed by word that Thomas Barclay had also died. The latter was Jefferson's fallback designee, having successfully negotiated the Moroccan treaty. Why Humphreys, so near the scene, was not tapped earlier remains uncertain, although one might speculate that Jefferson's growing alienation from Washington made him reluctant to appoint an individual whose closeness to (and covert correspondence with) the president was well known. In any event, on March 21, 1793, the secretary of state, now on the brink of retirement, told Humphreys to go to Algiers. He envisioned a quick settlement. Enclosing a copy of Jones's instructions, he merely told Humphreys to return to Lisbon as soon as he had finished negotiating. Whatever a treaty might cost, he could offer to pay the first half in naval stores, the remainder in specie.[19]

Headed for Algiers six months later, Humphreys reached Gibraltar only to learn that a secretly negotiated truce with Portugal had again allowed Algerian corsairs to slip into the Atlantic. Although he promptly dispatched warnings to American consuls and sea captains, ten more vessels were seized that fall, raising the number of American captives to more than one hundred. Curiously, the Portuguese truce surprised not only American shipmasters, but Lisbon itself. Unbeknownst to the latter, the British consul in Algiers, a man named George Logie, acting on orders from London, had arranged it with the connivance of a minor Portuguese official. Britain's purported motive was to facilitate naval operations in the Mediterranean.

Acting swiftly, Edward Church, the consul whom Humphreys had left in charge of the legation, obtained an apologetic disclaimer from the Portuguese foreign office and the promise that Portuguese warships would convoy American merchantmen until the truce could be officially disavowed and a Portuguese squadron once more placed at the straits.[20] Humphreys later told O'Brien not to worry: the truce did not herald a formal Portuguese peace treaty. The dey's exorbitant asking price of $3 million was absurd because it failed to take into account how little merchant shipping Portugal had in the Mediterranean.

Moreover, he added, any treaty that opened the straits would put at risk vessels carrying Portugal's much-needed imports of American grain.[21]

Humphreys, now bound for Algiers but fearing capture at sea, traveled overland from Lisbon to Alicante, a port on Spain's eastern coast routinely used for communicating with Algiers.[22] From here he probed Ali Hassan's willingness to receive him and was sorely miffed when the latter brusquely refused to grant him a passport. Writing to Washington on November 23, Humphreys quoted the dey as saying that he "would not treat with us, even if we were to lavish Millions."[23] An explanation of the dey's rebuff came largely from Pierre Eric Skjoldebrand, younger brother of the Swedish consul in Algiers and a man whose unremitting support of American interests later led Barlow to offer to reward him out of his own pocket. The dey's hostility, Skjoldebrand explained, arose in part from Lamb's broken promises but also because his corsairs' recent captures had led him to believe he had little to gain from making peace with the United States as long as more American vessels might be had for the taking. Also, as the dey reminded Skjoldebrand, treaties with Spain and Portugal were still pending. "If I make peace with everyone," he asked the Swede, "what will my corsairs do?" Gamely Skjoldebrand dismissed the likelihood of a Portuguese treaty, telling the dey he had asked too much. Then, hoping to capitalize on the regent's dislike of the British, he remarked on how nobly the Americans had fought them for their independence. Moreover, unlike the British, Americans had never made war on Algiers.[24] Although this attempt to play the "British card" proved unavailing at the time, Barlow would use it with greater success two years later.

Looking to the immediate future, Skjoldebrand advised Humphreys to be patient. Ali Hassan might look more favorably on a treaty once the tottering prospect of peace with Portugal fell off the table, as he was sure it would. Until then he urged Humphreys to designate a foreign consul, someone already in Algiers, to monitor the situation. The regent, he noted, was wildly unpredictable and could change his mind "on matters of great significance" in the space of a few minutes. Skjoldebrand did not ask to be that agent, but Captain O'Brien thought he would be ideal, describing the young Swede as a "gentleman of first-rate abilities and a strong friend of the United States," and urged Humphreys to empower him to act on behalf of American interests until the dey decided to negotiate.[25]

Significantly Skjoldebrand also advised that any American agent sent to Algiers be prepared to cultivate the goodwill of Micaiah Coen Bacri, a Jewish banker whose house wielded great influence at court. Bacri, he added, was already working to persuade the dey "in your favor." This advice did not go unheeded. Although Humphreys chose not to act on it, Barlow arrived well briefed on the banker's potential usefulness and immediately struck up what proved to be a rewarding friendship.

Barlow later confirmed what O'Brien and others disliked about Humphreys: he seemed congenitally incapable of taking an initiative. His hesitancy when faced with critical decisions would soon leave Barlow, who expected better, gasping with impatience. Here, after all, was a decorated war hero who had skillfully gathered intelligence during the Paris peace conference and a man whose military bearing was so striking that Abigail Adams had once commented on it.[26] As minister to Portugal, however, he showed himself to be more comfortable taking orders than giving them. While still at Alicante, to be sure, he did arrange for Robert Montgomery, the U.S. consul there, to supply the captives with clothes and money. But he insisted—to both O'Brien and Skjoldebrand —that he had no authority to "delegate my powers to any other person." Skjoldebrand's brief junket to Sweden at this point gave him more reason to do nothing.[27] Uncertain where to turn, Humphreys left Alicante for Madrid in late December, ostensibly to consult with William Carmichael and William Short, who were busy laying the groundwork for Thomas Pinckney's treaty with Spain. The two Williams merely urged him to be careful.[28] Humphreys needed no urging. By mid-April 1794 he was ready to wash his hands of the Algiers mission entirely. He wrote Edmund Randolph, Jefferson's successor in the State Department, that he was determined "to have no further agency in this business." He would continue, of course, to watch over the Algerian situation pending further instructions from Philadelphia, and he would act if the dey made an overture that conformed to his existing instructions.[29]

Prospects for negotiation seemed to brighten that spring. A letter from Skjoldebrand, then en route to Sweden, pictured Ali Hassan favoring a settlement with the United States in light of Portugal's firm refusal to meet his terms. Skjoldebrand quoted the regent as saying angrily: "If those damned Portuguese . . . won't pay me what I have asked, I shall summon the American Ambassador, because it pleases me more to be at peace with those I like and at war with those I don't like." Skjoldebrand warned Humphreys, however, that absent an invitation, it would be risky to come to Algiers. The latter needed no persuading. O'Brien, too, thought the rupture with Portugal had improved the American position. He quoted a furious dey as saying that he would never again free another Portuguese prisoner. Half an hour later, betraying the fickleness for which he was renowned, the dey impulsively signed a treaty with the Dutch.[30]

By this time, Humphreys hoped to saddle someone else with the Algerian mission and had it in mind to go home to explain why. On May 13 he broached Randolph with the suggestion that he pay a short visit to Philadelphia "to make such oral & expeditious communications" as could not be conveyed effectively in writing. Five days later he wrote that he wished "to have nothing further to do" with Algiers and urged the "necessity of having some [other] suitable person appointed as Agent or Consul General for Barbary."[31] Having put this alternative in motion, the colonel spent much of the year 1794 fending off somber letters from O'Brien, who periodically gave him body counts of plague victims and insisted that Ali Hassan was still open to making a peace treaty. Hoping to prepare the way, he echoed Skjoldebrand's earlier advice that an American observer be put in place to signal the moment the dey might agree to talk. It could happen at any time, O'Brien wrote, picturing the regent as so unpredictable that "our peace and treaty might be settled in one hour."[32] Humphreys responded blandly: he would continue to correspond with O'Brien and Skjoldebrand but only in his "private character," repeating his lack of authority to "delegate the Powers with which I was formerly invested and from the functions of which I now consider myself exonerated."[33]

Humphreys's reluctance to go to Algiers in person may have stemmed from more than his professed lacked of instructions. Ali Hassan's initial rebuff had clearly rocked his dignity with its shocking disrespect for his country. He may also have shied at the prospect of being personally humiliated, even threatened with bodily harm. As he noted to O'Brien, the dey often seemed ready to threaten physical punishment to those who crossed him.[34] But the financial aspects of treaty making also perplexed him. What Humphreys seemed to fear most throughout his diplomatic career was that he might be accused of mishandling public funds, even small sums. In fact, he conditioned his acceptance of the Lisbon post on the administration's appointing Nathaniel Cutting, an

American shipmaster, to do the bookkeeping. He must have blanched when O'Brien estimated ransom at $250,000 and a treaty at another $300,000.[35]

In August, Humphreys made a final attempt to elicit reasonable peace terms. He asked Skjoldebrand—not officially, but "only as a Friend of Humanity"—to find out if the dey "*will or will not name the very terms* on which he would make peace with the United States." If such terms were forthcoming, however, they should be sent via Montgomery either to the president or to whomever had been charged with Algerian affairs. He did not mean himself.[36] That same day, he wrote Randolph asking why he'd had no response to his request to be replaced in the mission. The answer soon arrived. Writing a month earlier, the secretary of state insisted that because Humphreys had detailed knowledge of the situation, he should stay the course. "It is impossible to discharge you from this service," Randolph wrote but added that if Humphreys thought it "unsafe or impractical" to go in person, he was to contact and work with an unnamed agent, whom Gouverneur Morris had asked to accompany the new French consul to Algiers. Humphreys agreed that French support could be the key to success but had received no word from the agent.[37] The hope for official French backing died hard in Philadelphia.

Humphreys offered multiple reasons for deserting his post, most having to do with money. Although Randolph had authorized him to draw as much as $800,000 on the Van Staphorsts, he claimed that the French invasion of the Netherlands had frustrated his best efforts in that direction.[38] Money remained a factor even after Skjoldebrand conveyed the dey's announcement in October that Humphreys "can come when he pleases" and would be well received. The colonel still insisted that he needed more "definitive instructions."[39] What he really needed was someone who knew how to access the available funds and bring them within reach. Unfortunately, Cutting, who probably had this expertise, had left for Ireland. Also, having heard from Skjoldebrand that neither ransom nor treaty would come cheap, he was certain the dey would ask too much—-perhaps more than a million dollars—and, by implication, he was not sure whether or how to meet those demands. To these reasons he added Skjoldebrand's warning that foreign intriguers were at work to scuttle a U.S. treaty. If this were the case, he supposed—however unlikely the supposition—that his absence would divert the attention of "those most hostile to our plans."[40] Just before he left his post, he shielded himself from the secretary of state's wrath by hinting that he had some ideas about giving "a greater prospect of success to the negotiations" but wanted to communicate them directly to the president.[41]

Humphreys's timidity contrasts sharply with the boldness Joel Barlow would show under similar circumstances. For one, Barlow *did* know the mechanics of money transfers and would hound Humphreys and others to act on them. Also, he did not suffer Humphreys's qualms about dickering over dollar amounts, nor would he shrink from making financial commitments the administration might disavow. He would arrive determined to pay whatever it cost to ransom his countrymen and fulfill a treaty that would safeguard American shipping. Not least, whereas Humphreys may have feared humiliation at the hands of the dey, Barlow would take the regent's threats in stride while playing the game of court intrigue with consummate skill.

5 Setting Out to Complete Donaldson's Treaty

Even before Humphreys sailed for home in late November, the administration was scrambling to find someone who would actually go to Algiers. By early 1795 it had run through four candidates: first a Virginian named Gabriels, a shadowy figure at best; then a Danish sea captain named Heysell who got as far as Algiers only to have the dey reject his credentials.[1] It even assigned the consulship to Pierre Skjoldebrand, who later declined lest it conflict with his brother's official position. The administration finally settled on Joseph Donaldson, Jr., an obscure and aging Treasury official who, despite meager qualifications, gout, and a bad temper, actually signed the treaty that Barlow would be sent to implement six months later. Donaldson's name would be on the treaty, but no captive would be freed, no vessel made safe from capture, until Barlow had arranged to pay for both treaty and ransom.

Humphreys found Randolph disgruntled when he arrived home in January 1795, but he more or less justified his return by producing a list of military and naval stores he believed would jump-start the negotiations. Congress promptly appropriated funds.[2] Whatever unrecorded conversations he had with Washington quite likely reinforced the administration's predisposition to look to the French government for diplomatic support. Not surprisingly, then, Humphreys on his return was instructed to go to Paris,[3] and Donaldson was told to befriend the French consul in Algiers, a man named Vallière. At this stage, using the French connection seemed promising. From his consular post in Alicante, Montgomery enclosed a letter from Vallière, written at the dey's request, inviting a negotiation. With it came O'Brien's report that the French consul had asked Paris for permission to support such a negotiation.[4]

Heading back to Europe that spring with Donaldson in tow, Humphreys bore instructions that appeared to cover every contingency. He had consular commissions for both Skjoldebrand and Donaldson and could use his judgment as to whether to employ both men or Donaldson alone. And if the latter took sick or died, he could appoint a replacement.[5] From the outset, Humphreys showed little confidence in the consul-designate's abilities. Writing to Washington just before he sailed, he sketched out the minor role he envisioned for him. He planned to have Donaldson merely contact the dey but not negotiate until he (Humphreys) had ginned up French support in Paris.[6]

During their passage to Gibraltar, however, and as he came to know Donaldson better, he began to wonder if the old man could carry it off at all. His low expectations registered when he told Donaldson to present himself in Algiers as a private person, be guided by Vallière, and if he could not put a negotiation in train, as seemed likely, he was to gather what intelligence he could and return to Lisbon as soon as possible.[7] Five days later, however, he put Donaldson's departure on hold, ordering him from Gibraltar to Alicante but telling him to wait there for an unspecified "change in circumstances." Confused, Donaldson wrote for an explanation, but Humphreys had already sailed for Le Havre.[8] Unfortunately, storms in the Bay of Biscay prolonged his voyage by nearly a month. When he arrived in Paris in June 1795, he found that the French had just learned the terms of the Treaty of London of 1794 (also known as Jay's treaty, for chief negotiator John Jay) and were furious at what they regarded as Americans' treacherous knuckling under to Britain's somewhat more limited view of a neutral power's maritime rights than had been agreed to in the Treaty of Amity and Commerce between the United States and France of 1778. Parenthetically, one might speculate that the French officials who actually read Jay's treaty were less outraged by its terms than by the sheer audacity of Americans having anything to do with their hereditary enemy. As their anger grew, any hope for enlisting French diplomatic support in North Africa quickly faded, although Humphreys continued to count on that support because he doubted Donaldson could succeed without it. His misgivings on this score go far to explain why he approached Barlow when he reached Paris. Ironically the colonel had misgauged the old man. Much to everyone's surprise, Donaldson did succeed in making a treaty. News of it reached Paris just as Barlow was preparing to leave for Algiers and momentarily cast doubt on the wisdom of his going.

Donaldson, it turned out, though ordered to stay in Alicante, saw no reason not to prepare the way for his mission. His probing letters to Skjoldebrand and O'Brien, received in mid-August, set off a flurry of activity in Algiers to persuade the dey to receive Donaldson as a fully empowered negotiator. To this end, O'Brien and Skjoldebrand counseled Cathcart to skirt the fact of Donaldson's "private" character and assure the dey that he would come with full powers. The dey, still miffed at Humphreys's side trip to Paris, nonetheless yielded to Cathcart's blandishments and agreed to receive Donaldson if Cathcart would "take responsibility" for him. As the dey's chief Christian secretary, Cathcart wrote the letter accepting Donaldson's credentials, the dey signed it, and Skjoldebrand sent it off to Alicante forthwith. Vallière, who had been left out of the loop, scolded O'Brien for not telling him of these preliminaries.[9] In light of the French consul's later efforts to scuttle the negotiation, however, keeping him in the dark suggests a certain prescience on O'Brien's part.

Although James Cathcart often exaggerated his influence on the regent, his closeness to Ali Hassan inevitably figured in the diplomatic maneuvers that followed. Now ten years into his captivity, the twenty-seven-year-old Irish American already owned three taverns and would have enough money, when the time came, to buy the vessel that would take him to freedom. Though he started his captivity as a palace gardener, he later recounted having suffered extended periods of hard labor in the dockyard, shifting rocks and unloading cargoes. For most prisoners, it might be noted, the workday ended at 3:00 p.m., giving them freedom to earn money plying whatever crafts and skills they had. At night they were confined to prison barracks called bagnios, and when foreign vessels were in port, they were chained up. Escape was not an option, but unless the plague killed them or they died from an excess of corporal punishment, most managed to survive. Some, like Cathcart, even prospered. Before the old dey died in 1791, Cathcart had opportunely made himself useful to Ali Hassan, clerking for him when the latter had charge of the port. When Hassan became regent, Cathcart borrowed enough money from him—and from Skjoldebrand ($500 from each)—to buy the office of chief Christian clerk.[10] Thereafter, the bond between regent and clerk remained close but fragile—Cathcart obsequious for reasons of self-preservation, Hassan alternately showing disdain due an infidel and threatening him with the bastinado.[11] The regent did, however, rely on him in dealing with other infidels, which meant that Cathcart would play a strong supporting role in Donaldson's success.

Amazingly, that success came in record time. Donaldson signed his treaty within forty-two hours of his arrival on September 3, 1795. Cathcart later recorded how he, O'Brien, and the banker Micaiah Bacri had met Donaldson at dockside and walked him to his quarters. Cathcart, who had arranged housing for him, graphically described the angry old man, his gouty right leg swathed in flannel, his face streaming with sweat, stumping painfully up the marble steps, caught up in a "paroxysm of rage" as street children crowding around him laughed at his agonizing progress. When he reached his quarters, Donaldson threw himself on a couch cursing volubly. When Bacri asked for a translation, Cathcart replied that the "ambassador" was saying his prayers. "His devotion is very fervent," the banker observed.[12]

In the end, the treaty committed the United States to pay $585,000 plus annual tribute—not a bad package when weighed against the dey's initial expectation of more than $2.2 million. Although Cathcart's principal activity consisted of carrying messages back and forth, he contributed in a major way when he persuaded the dey that Vallière was a flat-out liar in spreading the rumor that the American envoy had financial carte blanche. The negotiating scene opened when the dey threw a tantrum at Donaldson's initial offer of $543,000. He told Cathcart the French consul had assured him that the American "can give what he pleases for peace."[13] Then, having blunted Vallière's untruth, Cathcart joined O'Brian and Skjoldebrand in what appeared at first to be a vain effort to persuade Donaldson that the dey might still agree to sign a treaty if another forty or fifty thousand dollars were added to the initial offer. Donaldson refused and seemed vindicated when the regent counteroffered with the still unacceptable asking price of $982,000. Cathcart expressed alarm at the prospect of returning to the palace without offering at least a fractional increase. The dey would probably expel the emissary and give the messenger "five or six hundred bastinados." Cathcart flinched at Donaldson's casual observation that he would at least have the "consolation" of knowing he had "served the interests of his country."[14]

Cathcart was almost right on both counts. The dey did order Donaldson to leave and at least threatened his Christian secretary with a beating. While Donaldson was packing to leave, however, a breakthrough occurred when Philip Sloan approached him with a letter he had received from Humphreys. Former captain of the *Rachel*, Sloan together with O'Brien had long served as spokesmen for the captive community. Humphreys had written him that if Donaldson "should exceed his orders by fifty or sixty thousand dollars, it would be of no moment." Apprised of this latitude, Donaldson yielded, and the negotiations went forward quickly.[15]

At 7:00 a.m. on Saturday, September 5, while Donaldson continued to go through the motions of packing, Cathcart, Sloan, and Bacri conveyed his "final" offer of $584,000. The dey grumbled at the meagerness of the increase, repeated the canard about Donaldson's having carte blanche, but finally agreed to sign if only "to pique the British who are your inveterate enemies."[16] The aftermath was disconcerting. Three hours later, when Donaldson came to sign the treaty, he found the dey had mellowed to the point of offering to release the American captives from hard labor and from their nightly lockup in the bagnios, warning, however, that he would punish them if they got drunk and insulted his Turkish soldiery. To Cathcart's dismay, Donaldson refused the offer of leniency and allowed that he "did not care if they all turned Moors."[17]

Though his response seemed callously indifferent, Donaldson did believe the funds were already in Lisbon and would soon arrive. He may also have feared that if the captives had more freedom, their drunken sprees would complicate the endgame. Or, as one author suggests, the tightfisted envoy foresaw that if the captives were released from the bagnios, the U.S. government would have to pick up the tab for their room and board.[18] For their part, the prisoners were predictably outraged. Four months later, when the ransom money was still in London, an angry crowd of American seamen, revealing how much freedom of movement they already had, sacked and for several hours occupied Donaldson's house in the suburbs. It took armed guards to rout them.[19]

Looking back, Cathcart took most of the credit for Donaldson's treaty, observing dryly that "peace was made by a lame old man who understood no language but his own, without funds or credit and surrounded by enemies." Moreover, the treaty "was made and written out for him without his either discussing or seeing it until I presented it to him for his signature."[20]

Cathcart's hurt feelings aside, Donaldson did rely on his knowledge of court intrigues and profited from his willingness to risk the dey's displeasure even as he influenced him to make concessions. Not to be discounted in the outcome, however, was the prodding Donaldson received from O'Brien, Sloan, Skjoldebrand,

and Bacri. In the end, the grumpy, penny-pinching old man became the unlikely instrument of a successful group effort.

After the signing Donaldson wisely chose to stay in Algiers, lest his departure remind the dey of John Lamb's vanishing act. He also chose O'Brien (whom the dey released for the purpose) to carry the good news to Lisbon and, like the others, hoped for the speedy return of enough money to pay for both treaty and ransom. O'Brien, in turn, convinced a resentful Cathcart, who himself hoped to be the messenger, that someone should stay behind to keep a watchful eye on the gaffe-prone Donaldson.[21] As O'Brien set off for Lisbon, no one could foresee how long it would take to fulfill the treaty and free the captives. Soon it would be Joel Barlow's turn to try.

Humphreys's quest for French support succeeded in Paris only insofar as Monroe, at his urging, managed to extract vague assurances that Vallière would assist in the Algiers negotiations. Monroe later complained how undignified he felt asking a favor from a government increasingly outraged by the terms of Jay's treaty.[22] Coupled with this hostility came news that Donaldson had signed a treaty without French assistance, which meant that Paris no longer felt any obligation, if it ever had, to support American policy in the Mediterranean. But while Monroe faced the everyday reality of growing French ill will, soon to take the form of maritime reprisals, Humphreys remained curiously optimistic. Writing from Lisbon on September 7 before he knew of Donaldson's treaty, he gave Barlow "full powers" to negotiate, with or without Donaldson, insisting only that he cooperate with French officials at every step. The administration, he wrote, had "unbounded confidence in the French Republic to yield effectual assistance."[23]

By late September Humphreys was again in France but about to leave from Le Havre when Barlow wrote him of Donaldson's success and urged him to hurry back to Lisbon because the Algiers treaty was "provisional." Only the arrival of the promised funding would make it whole. And because Baring Brothers in London held $800,000 earmarked for American treaty purposes, he urged Humphreys to move the "credit" availability from London to Lisbon as quickly as possible.[24] As he soon discovered, however, telling Humphreys what he should do and waiting for him to respond defied all expectations of cause and effect. Nor was Barlow alone in questioning Humphreys's inaction. Timothy Pickering, Randolph's successor in the State Department, when he learned of Humphreys's trips to Paris, observed acidly that if he had stayed in Lisbon he could have "drawn the necessary monies from London in October and November" at a time, he added, when the Barings had written that "Portugal gold and Spanish dollars could easily have been procured."[25]

Although Barlow fully expected to arrive in Algiers armed with enough money to complete the treaty and free the captives, he knew that more would be required. Unlike Donaldson, he sensed that dealing with Turkish officials would entail a great deal of gift giving. With Monroe's blessing, he contracted lavishly with Paris jewelers and couturiers and then, predictably, fretted over their delays. What he called his "difficulties" in assembling the finished products delayed his own departure.[26] Altogether the gifts cost the U.S. government more than $30,000, leading Cathcart to grumble later that Barlow had spent too much; he should have asked Bacri to buy these items.[27] Moreover, such gifts as women's dresses were totally inappropriate. Barlow later admitted as much and suggested that four of the dresses (worth roughly $8,000) he might take to Istanbul, should the State Department decide to send him there.[28]

Also mindful of protocol, he asked Humphreys to assign him the title of "temporary consul," pointing out that if Donaldson had left Algiers, whoever represented American interests should have official standing until the naming of a permanent consul, a position he made very clear he did not want for himself. Indeed, he envisioned staying in Algiers only long enough to free the captives and fulfill the financial terms of the treaty, a few weeks at most, he hoped.[29] Had he known he would not see Paris again for almost two years, he might have left that city—and his affectionate wife—in a less buoyant mood.

Traveling by carriage to Lyon, then by boat down the Rhone—he noted but did not dance on the bridge at Avignon—he arrived in Marseille the first week in January 1796. His social instincts intact, he immediately mixed business with pleasure by attending the theater with U.S. Consul Stephen Cathalan and his wife, and later talking to the consul about undertaking joint mercantile ventures. "Cathalan and I," he wrote Ruth, "we shall do business together, and we are good friends."[30] If Ruth decided to come to Marseille to meet him on his return, the Cathalans would look after her. Again he explained why it had been best for her to stay behind. A consul arriving in Algiers with a wife would be expected to rent a house, buy a carriage, and settle in. If Ruth had come, his posting would have given the dey a false impression of permanence.[31] He didn't want Ruth to get that impression either.

Before he left Marseille, Barlow befriended a group of Algerians just out of quarantine who were headed toward Amsterdam on an unspecified diplomatic mission. They assured him the dey was a "most gentle, most amiable" ruler who awaited his arrival with impatience. Barlow suspected they were simply trying to hurry him on his way but warmed to their company over a dinner, where he muddled through linguistically in "bad Italian and Spanish."[32] Although he seemed heartened by the Algerians' show of goodwill, he had no illusions about the difficulties ahead. Earlier, he had written Ruth, "I have never taken a voyage with so much inquietude."[33] Or, he might have added in retrospect, with so many delays. The latter began when the vessel he boarded in Marseille on January 22 met with such heavy storms that he was glad to be set ashore three days later at the Spanish port of Figueres. Traveling overland now by mule-drawn cabriolet, he arrived at Alicante, his takeoff point, by way of Barcelona on February 5, 1796.[34] There, uncertainties continued to dog him for almost a month.

His first impulse was to go to Algiers at once, if only to explain to the dey, if he could, why the treaty payment would be delayed. A letter from Donaldson warned of Ali Hassan's growing impatience, and although Montgomery had gone to Lisbon ostensibly to secure the necessary funds, Barlow half expected more delays from that quarter. Humphreys, he grumbled, should have had the money in hand two months ago. Then, abandoning plans for an early departure, he told Ruth it would be pointless to go without the money. Instead, he would await Montgomery's return.[35] Waiting, however, did not mean sitting idle. Always a compulsive sightseer, he managed to treat himself to a day trip to Cartagena where he toured its arsenal and navy yard, taking a friend with him. He was seldom without friends. Back in Alicante on February 22, he learned of further delay. The vessel Humphreys had sent to London to pick up the money had not returned. "All this difficulty could have been prevented," he huffed to Ruth," if they had followed the advice I gave in September, of transferring the credit from London to a more accessible place."[36]

Despite Barlow's complaints, Humphreys in early February 1796 was doing his best to save the treaty. Reaching out to the man he knew had influence, he appealed to Cathcart to explain to the dey how many obstacles had arisen. Wartime conditions, he began, had defeated his hopes to secure specie from the Dutch bankers. His search for funding, he explained, had taken him to the United States and later to Paris, travels repeatedly held up by "contrary winds and long passages," nearly two months en route to America and more than a month in transit from Paris back to Lisbon. He was sure the dey would acknowledge his "zeal" when he learned of these shipboard sufferings. More time was lost, he continued, when Captain O'Brien took more than a month to bring news of the treaty to Lisbon. By then specie was known to be available from the Barings, but heavy weather had prevented O'Brien from sailing to London until the end of December.[37] If he hoped to end this letter on an upbeat note, Humprheys's last-minute postscript forecast still more delay. Late word from O'Brien, he regretted to say, had informed him that neither gold nor silver was available in London; the captain would try next in Hamburg. Chagrined, he added: "We had every assurance and reason to believe the money was in readiness for us in England."[38] The fate of the treaty had now reached at a critical stage.

Cathcart, meanwhile, needed no prompting. Long before Humphreys's letter reached him, he took it on himself to explain to the dey why time-distance factors had delayed the delivery of specie, and if Donaldson had not balked at sweetening this explanation with a "small present," he believed his persuasion might have succeeded. As it was, the dey rejected everything Cathcart told him and announced that unless the money arrived within a month, he would send Donaldson packing and return to the shipyard those American captives who had been released from hard labor. Cathcart told Humphreys that this deadline might be pushed back, but only if a portion of the promised specie were to arrive in the near future. Meanwhile, he seemed to share the dey's irritation that the colonel had made no effort to contact the regency since the signing four months earlier.[39] Humphreys himself must have realized the oversight, for on February 10 he wrote the dey of Barlow's appointment as a "temporary agent" and asked that he be welcomed. Bestowing the title of agent, he told Barlow, would allow him to avoid the gift-giving required of newly installed consuls, but, whatever his title, Barlow had full powers to treat, with or without Donaldson.[40]

What galvanized Barlow to action were letters from Algiers in late February announcing the dey's one-month deadline. He might not have credited

Cathcart's intelligence on this score, but Donaldson's had confirmed it. The treaty had only a month to live. He promptly wrote Monroe that he would sail to Algiers at once. "This month will certainly elapse before I can arrive. But I am determined to go on, as it can do no harm, since the affair has become so desperate. And it is possible I may save the treaty." Like Cathcart and Donaldson, he also worried lest a failed treaty lead the dey to make peace with Portugal and once more expose American shipping to capture in the Atlantic.[41] As he prepared to board ship for Algiers, he assured Ruth he did not expect to linger. Either the treaty would fail or the money would come "if O'Brien hasn't drowned."[42]

6 Saving the Treaty, Freeing the Captives

Rowed ashore soaking wet, Barlow landed in the port of Algiers on March 5, having survived five days of stormy seas and the worst seasickness he could recall. His arrival, unlike Donaldson's, caused little stir. Notified, the dey merely asked whether the envoy had brought the treaty money or at least some gifts. Clearly Ali Hassan was in no mood to receive an empty-handed emissary. Barlow, for his part, was relieved to find the treaty "not yet lost" and wrote Ruth he was more hopeful of success than when he had left Alicante.[1] Being at the scene of action seemed to infuse him with a self-confidence that, in any case, he seldom had in short supply. His first move was to ask Micaiah Bacri to use his well-known influence at court to secure him an audience. Bacri obligingly approached the dey several times during Barlow's first week but without success. Perhaps made surly by Ramadan fasting, the regent expressed no interest in meeting the new envoy and, indeed, said he would see no more Americans until the treaty money arrived.[2]

Reconciled to waiting, Barlow filled his time writing a nineteen-page dispatch to the secretary of state that omitted nothing of possible interest. He described the regency's history, geography, demographics, and political structure, its current relations with other powers, the role of the Turkish soldiery, and evidence of the dey's reputedly "ungovernable temper." Though a quick study, Barlow could scarcely have amassed so much data without borrowing from Cathcart's journal. Nor did Cathcart forgive him for having cribbed without attribution.[3]

Toward the end of March, strained relations between Cathcart and Donaldson seemed certain to complicate what remained of the mission. A mutual dislike had long simmered, with Donaldson chafing at Cathcart's know-it-all arrogance and often poking fun at his fear of the dey's periodic outbursts. In return, Cathcart bridled at the envoy's failure to take the dey's threats seriously. Back in January, for example, when the dey had threatened beheadings if the money failed to arrive, Donaldson had joked that he and Cathcart had such short necks, the executioner would have difficulty carrying out the sentence. Somewhat out of character, Skjoldebrand had joined in, saying he would try to have their punishment commuted to a live roasting. Cathcart, all too familiar with the dey's murderous wrath, was not amused. A more serious clash occurred in early March when Cathcart, at the dey's request, penned a secret letter to Humphreys. When Donaldson learned of it, he blasted Cathcart for not telling him about it. On this occasion, however, Barlow was there to defend him, pointing out that the chief Christian secretary, having promised the dey not to disclose the letter, "could not have acted otherwise with any degree of propriety or self-respect."[4]

Cathcart especially deplored Donaldson's resistance to bribing officials, failing even to tip their servants, when the goodwill of the both could often determine an outcome. He was only somewhat less critical of Barlow whom he saw as a latecomer who should have sought his advice in dealing with the dey and was mortified when Barlow made clear from the outset that he preferred to rely on Bacri for official contacts. Neither man fully trusted the other. An aggrieved Cathcart later came to believe that the public had credited Barlow with a larger role than his on the diplomatic scene. Peevishly in his memoirs, he wrote: "All the services which I had rendered before he was ever thought of as an agent have been erroneously attributed to him."[5] The charge of erroneous attribution was partly true: Cathcart was right to remind his readers that he was, in fact, a central figure during the Donaldson phase of treaty making and that his pre-Barlow success in making a truce with Tunis deserved greater recognition. His other claims to fame, however, seem to arise more from a bruised ego than from a strict regard for the truth. What piqued him was Barlow's suddenly replacing him at center stage, relegating him to the role of messenger instead of accepting him as the major player. He did, however, find a welcome contrast between Barlow's willingness to spend whatever was necessary to keep the treaty alive and Donaldson's seeming reluctance to spend enough to save the treaty—or free the captives.[6]

On March 15, his ninth day in Algiers, Barlow wrote Ruth that the dey had repeatedly threatened to expel them but now seemed relatively quiescent. He was reluctant to "awaken" him. To fill his time, he regaled Ruth with some of the more barbaric aspects of Islam, its low regard for women and Jews, and the harsh punishments meted out by Islamic law. Christian lawbreakers, he wrote, were hanged, Jews were burned alive, and "a Turk has the honor of being beheaded or strangled." Mosques were impressively large and airy but off limits to visiting infidels. Any nonbeliever who entered a mosque must either convert or be executed. He assured her that if he inadvertently wandered into one, he would "become a Mahometan on the spot, for I have not enough religion of any sort to make myself a martyr."[7]

Tensions began to crackle in early April when the dey set new deadlines, warning the two envoys that they had eight days to produce the treaty money or he would expel them and that if the money did not arrive within thirty days, his cruisers would resume capturing American vessels. Alarmed but mostly frustrated, Barlow wrote Humphreys that he had done all he could "to ward off the fatal stroke," but there was not much he could do "considering the ignorance in which we have been left relative to the state of the funds & to your intentions as to fulfilling the conditions of the treaty." Donaldson, he observed, had signed the treaty believing the funds were at hand. Had he foreseen this problem, his treaty might have stipulated a year's delay before delivery. Had he been in Humphreys's place, he chided, "I should not have hesitated to order the payment as soon as possible" or at least warned Donaldson if he had anticipated delay. He painted a somber picture of what would happen if the treaty failed now. Our captives will be "spit upon by Jews & Strangers, as well as Turks & Moors who will say that America has no money, credit, or good faith, and that she never intends to redeem her people." Then, amending his reference to Jews and strangers as detractors, he added, "I ought to make three exceptions. The Skjoldebrand brothers are our frank and disinterested friends [and] Baccry the Jew is likewise a warm friend. He appears to be a man of uncommon merit for one of a race so degraded & debased as are the Jews of Algiers." Clearly fed up, Barlow allowed he would stay in Algiers no longer than necessary and Humphreys could forget about his voyaging on to make treaties with Tunis and Tripoli. He had too much of his own business to attend to. Perhaps, he suggested, the colonel could persuade Donaldson to go to Tunis. The latter's health was good, and in Barlow's view he "merit[ed] confidence as a man of talents & integrity," the kind of confidence Humphreys had not shown him when he appointed them jointly. Humphreys would have to reassure the old man on that score.[8]

The diplomatic skies brightened abruptly during the first week in April. Writing to Ruth on the 2nd, he was sure his mission had failed, but three days later, he exulted that the dey, after uttering "the most insupportable threats, injuries, and insults, has agreed to give us three more months to produce our money."[9] What he left unsaid was that he himself had managed to extend the deadline by offering the dey the additional gift of a frigate, ostensibly as a present to his daughter. In the foreground, Barlow had first put it to Micaiah Bacri that the offer of a twenty-gun frigate might win a six-month reprieve. Bacri countered that a twenty-four-gun frigate would have greater appeal and agreed to run the idea by the regent. On April 4, after paying several visits to the palace, the banker found an opportunity to make the offer. Overall, his timing was good. The dey, now at war with Denmark and basking in a surfeit of captured Danish vessels, apparently decided he could afford to wait, although he told Bacri the gift must be a thirty-two-gun ship. Then, warming to the prospect, he invited Donaldson and Barlow to an audience the following morning where Barlow made such a favorable first impression that the dey gave him a fine horse several days later. As the deal stood, in return for the frigate, now upped to thirty-six guns, the regent agreed to wait three months for the treaty money "but not a day longer."[10] Even Cathcart was impressed. And for Barlow, this meeting marked the beginning of, if not a beautiful friendship, more cordial relations with Ali Hassan. He certainly left a better impression than had Donaldson. After the audience, Cathcart quoted the dey as saying that Barlow had "the appearance of a Cavaliero but the old fellow . . . might be a great man, but he never saw one that look'd less like it than he did."[11]

For Humphreys's benefit, Barlow did the math. He estimated the cost of the frigate at $45,000, plus an outlay of $18,000 for Bacri's services in bribing various officials. The $53,000 total might be reduced, however, by deducting the cost of freight charges if the frigate brought the naval stores promised by the treaty.[12] He and Donaldson admitted they risked being disavowed but felt the value of the Mediterranean trade justified the additional expense. "We expect to incur blame," he wrote, "but we are perfectly confident in having acted right."[13] And to Secretary Pickering, with the same misgiving: "I shall be extremely unhappy but not at all surprised if the president should think we went too far." Giving the dey a thirty-six-gun frigate was his idea, he admitted, not Donaldson's, although the latter agreed to it. "I shall therefore be the cause of this additional expence to the United States."[14] And to Monroe, still in Paris: "I am sure of incurring a heavy portion of blame, but this [was better than] not being able to deserve the blame." Tongue in cheek perhaps, he expressed satisfaction at having given Humphreys "another chance to save the treaty."[15]

His impatience with Humphreys spilled over in a letter to Ruth. The colonel, he told her, "seems to have too much beef in his head to be a good manager of such affairs." He especially deplored Humphreys's withholding information from those who needed it. No one in Algiers had heard from him since he wrote on February 7: "His eternal mystery & silence (I will not say inattention & folly) will probably lose us the treaty yet." He observed wryly that "a good banker's clerk" in Lisbon would have finished the business by now and spared the U.S. government the additional cost of the frigate.[16]

Barlow's next step was to lay hands on enough specie to fulfill the treaty. As he reminded Humphreys, the Barings could order it disbursed from London, Lisbon, or Madrid. Better still, a shipment from Leghorn to Algiers would minimize the danger of interception. Hoping Humphreys would act on this advice, he notified him that Donaldson had sailed for Leghorn two days after their audience with the dey and expected to hear from him.[17] Donaldson would have a long wait. Meanwhile, on another front, Barlow tried to dissuade the dey from dunning him for the customary "consular gift," on grounds that his appointment was temporary. When the dey insisted, Barlow relented, accepted the title of consul, and made the gift. An additional gift might be avoided, he told Pickering, if his "permanent" successor presented himself as Barlow's vice consul. This ruse might work, especially if Barlow left the impression that he intended to return. Ali Hassan apparently saw through this attempt to avoid future gift giving and threw a fit. Barlow was pleased to report, however, that with his own gifts in prospect, the regent forgot his anger and sent him "a very friendly message," saying that he believed Americans were "a good people" who had many enemies, "but he would be their friend, and he was now ready to receive the consular presents." Barlow apologized to Pickering for yielding to the dey's insistence on recognizing his consular status but felt he had had no choice.[18] To bolster the appearance of impermanence, he later told Ruth, he had rented a house in the country.[19]

With the treaty money presumably on its way, Barlow found occasion to mull over the pros and cons of paying tribute. Submitting to this kind of extortion, he wrote Monroe, is "doubtless unworthy of us. . . . But as long as the powers of Europe will persist in this policy . . . it is our duty, instead of being its victims, to partake of its advantages." The commercial profits, he calculated, far outweighed the costs of paying tribute. Alternatively, the high cost of buying commercial insurance would surely make American cargoes noncompetitive. Overall, the system appeared to be effective and relatively painless. Absent the tributary system, he repeated the conventional wisdom that the Italian states would take over the Mediterranean trade completely.[20] As it was, the great powers were wealthy enough to regard the payoffs as trifling, while lesser mercantile nations such as Denmark, Sweden, and the Netherlands could rely on their well-heeled chambers of commerce to foot the bill. Over time Barlow even came to view the tributary system as not altogether unjustified from the Turkish standpoint. He found a parallel between the possessiveness Americans felt about their own territorial waters and the way the Turkish regencies "view themselves honestly as proprietors of these seas." There was a certain logic, he felt, in their exploiting their most proximate resource.[21]

Always eager to combine travel with business, Barlow began to look beyond Algiers to landing a diplomatic mission to Italy. Because many of the Italian states were unable to pay tribute for the use of the Mediterranean, they might welcome the import-export services of American vessels. If Monroe thought it appropriate, he would be happy to go and try to negotiate commercial treaties with them. "It would give me the opportunity of seeing those countries," a motive Monroe might think "frivolous," but "no person . . . could do the business better than I, or would do it so cheap?"[22] Naturally he invited Ruth to share his pipe dream: "Perhaps we will go, tho' I don't expect it, but I should love to make that tour with my charming wife."[23] Not without guile, he doubtless hoped the prospect of sightseeing would reconcile Ruth to his ever-lengthening absence. Volunteering for other missions in the Mediterranean appeared often enough in his official correspondence to confirm his undiminished wanderlust, as well as his commitment to expanding American commerce.[24]

By late April, Barlow was multitasking with a vengeance. Once more, he urged Humphreys to waste no time in securing the treaty money; the dey would brook no further delay. He wrote the same to Montgomery in Alicante, expecting the latter to convey his sense of urgency to Lisbon. And to his friend Wolcott in the Treasury Department, he listed in detail the naval stores the dey expected to receive.[25] Donaldson, too, got one of his outgoing messages. If the latter could possibly send him a draft for $200,000, this amount—coupled with the recent and well-received consular gifts—might be enough to ransom the captives even if the treaty itself failed, or before it was *known* to have failed. He assured the old penny-pincher that paying $3,000 per captive would be "clearly within our limits."[26]

Not content to wait for one of the Baring Brothers' bank drafts to shake loose a source of specie, Barlow turned to puzzling out the best way to negotiate a treaty with Tunis. For several weeks he pinned his hopes on the goodwill of a newly arrived French consul named Aloïs Herculais. Not surprisingly, he and Herculais hit it off from the outset and remained on good terms even after Paris warned its consul to stop being helpful. At that juncture, mystified by his government's sudden coolness, Herculais was startled when Barlow briefed him on how severely Jay's treaty had chilled Franco-American relations. He urged Barlow to write Monroe to see if the latter could use his influence to restore Herculais's earlier orders to give the Americans every assistance. Even after he had been warned, the Frenchman offered "unofficially" to put Barlow in touch with the French consul in Tripoli, the third remaining treaty target on the North African coast. Although Barlow believed Tripoli posed "no great danger" to American shipping, he appreciated Herculais's continuing goodwill.[27] Meanwhile, it was Herculais, who, presumably in good faith, persuaded him to approach the bey of Tunis through the agency of a French merchant there named Joseph Étienne Famin. Unfortunately, despite Herculais's assessment of Famin's supposed influence with the bey, it was slow to bear fruit. Famin's diplomatic fits and starts would keep Barlow in North Africa for more than another year.

James Cathcart, critical as always, later observed sourly that Famin was "a very improper person . . . to negociate a treaty for us." In this instance, Cathcart considered himself an interested party, having negotiated an eight-month truce with a visiting Tunisian diplomat the previous November.[28] Now, by late May 1796, with time running out, Barlow invited Famin to act on behalf of the United States, either to make a treaty (he enclosed a draft copy) or get Cathcart's truce extended. To that end, he plied Famin with arguments and observations he hoped would be persuasive. Mindful of the bad blood between the two regencies, he believed the bey would appreciate making a treaty without the dey's intercession and would welcome the $20,000 he was prepared to offer. Otherwise, Famin was to warn the bey that if his corsairs attacked American shipping, the United States would retaliate in force. It had eight heavy frigates it could send against him. Assure him, Barlow continued, that Americans wanted only to conduct their commerce in peace, but if they were forced to make war, he should remind the bey that they had defeated a "more powerful and more invulnerable" enemy in their struggle for independence. On the positive side, Famin could offer the prospect of a profitable commerce with America, one that might soon make Tunis richer than Algiers. He could also promise the bey gifts of "jewelry, watches and hunting guns" once the treaty was signed. And to tempt Famin into accepting his agency, Barlow offered him a consular commission. His government, he explained, preferred its consuls to be American citizens but regarded French republicans as "brothers."[29]

Also in late May, Barlow's impatience with Humphreys once more boiled over. Lisbon had been silent for three months, he told Monroe, even as Donaldson reported that he could lay his hands on plenty of specie in Leghorn as soon as Humphreys sent him an order to draw on one of Barings' agents in London, Lisbon, or Madrid. He was sorry to be associated with so many "combinations of folly," he wrote, "but I shall be more sorry to see a hundred of our citizens & several hundred after them terminate their miserable existence in this place."[30] How miserably their existence might terminate struck home when plague broke out that month. Barlow at first hoped to "get leave" for some of the captives and "move them out into the country near me where I shall take a house & garden for them, to save as many of them as I can." His hope to "rusticate" a large number of captives, however, met with the dey's objection that they "were not yet paid for" and that such unprecedented leniency would not sit well with his Turkish soldiery.[31] By early July, with the plague still raging, Barlow told Ruth that "a pressing duty of humanity requires me to expose myself . . . in endeavouring to save as many of our unhappy citizens as possible." He believed his "exertions" may already have saved some. If he died in Algiers, he asked her not to "upbraid my memory by even *thinking* that I did too much."

"If you were here," he wrote, "you would do more than I shall do; for your kind, intrepid spirit has more courage than mine, and always had." If the worst happened, his new will (which he enclosed) would give her immediate access to their Paris funds. He estimated their worth at about $120,000, which, if later invested in U.S. bonds and real estate, should produce an annual income between $5,000 and $7,000. He made her his sole beneficiary not only because he owed her his "financial competency," but also for the joy she had given him in their life together. These solemn expressions of affection mixed with practical advice ended on an upbeat note. "I certainly hope to escape from this place and return to your beloved arms," he wrote. "No man has stronger inducements to live than I have. . . . I have a moderate but sufficient income, perfect health . . . and the wife that my youth has chosen and that my advancing age has cherished."[32]

In late June, Barlow reported bad news on several fronts. Four Americans had succumbed to the plague, he had heard nothing from Donaldson in Leghorn, and the dey, having just made peace with Denmark, was casting about to pillage some other nation's commerce.[33]

Humphreys, he believed, had finally sent Donaldson a "credit for the money," but, as he wrote Monroe, "I have every reason to believe it will arrive too late. . . . If so, I tremble for the consequences." Not content to wait on events, however, Barlow hinted at having begun clandestine talks with Micaiah Bacri, the only person in Algiers who could produce specie on demand. His "little maneuver," he told Monroe, might "save the treaty for another six months, if necessary, without a farthing of money or additional promises." He cautioned Monroe not to tell anyone because he might be wrong.[34] Barlow did not specify the details of his fallback plan, but his close dealings with Bacri would soon pay off handsomely.

When Barlow finally heard from Leghorn, the news was both good and bad. Humphreys had reportedly authorized Donaldson to gather up as much as $400,000 in specie. Shipping it to Algiers, however, presented problems. French troops had recently seized the city, and the British had put it under blockade. Even after Lord Nelson agreed to let a ship bearing only specie pass through his blockade, Donaldson held up shipment, unwilling to pay adverse exchange rates and high brokerage fees. Accentuating the positive, however, Barlow barely hesitated. With ransom money known to be within hailing distance, he moved quickly to assure the dey it would soon arrive.[35] Then, to nudge things along, he turned to the house of Bacri. To prepare the way, he "drew" on Donaldson for $253,000 (enough to ransom the captives) but told him to lodge bills for this amount in the Bacris' branch office in Leghorn, thereby establishing a credit that either Barlow or Bacri might draw on to procure the specie.[36] When Bacri balked at the risk of shipping specie from Leghorn to Algiers and questioned whether Donaldson had the requisite authority, Barlow agreed to pay him a "guarantee" against Donaldson's bills being protested.[37]

With this backup assured, Bacri came through with the loan. On July 6 Barlow paid the ransom and freed the captives. Writing to Humphreys the same day, he exulted that "for a snuff box of the value of a hundred dollars I have engaged a Jew house to advance without interest 200,000 [dollars] and to be answerable to the regency for 300,000 more." He had acted swiftly, he explained, because plague was ravaging the city and had already had taken the lives of six Americans. Indeed, he had just returned from the port where he had been overseeing the survivors' "purification" before they embarked.[38]

The "snuff box" explanation grossly understated what had transpired behind the scenes. Barlow had procured the loan largely because he had recently obliged the house of Bacri by ridding the political landscape of James Cathcart. The Bacris had long regarded the chief Christian secretary as their primary rival for the dey's favor and played along gratefully as Barlow persuaded the dey to believe it was his own idea that Cathcart should go to the United States to expedite the first shipment of naval stores. Cathcart had sailed for Philadelphia a month earlier.[39]

Still, Barlow might not have succeeded but for an unforeseen stroke of luck—an "accident," he called it. When he had first asked for the loan, the house of Bacri pleaded a temporary shortage of specie. For reasons that defy simple explanation, however, the French government owed the banking house a half million dollars. Thus, when Aloïs Herculais turned up and lavished enough gifts on the dey to get a loan of $200,000 in specie, he promptly paid it over to the Bacris. Barlow later described this chain of events to the secretary of state: "Sometime in June a new French consul arrived, and by some brilliant presents revived the influence of the republic with the Dey so as to borrow from the public treasury about 200,000 dollars which he paid into this Jew House. I immediately insisted that the Bacris should prove the sincerity of their friendship by lending me the sum . . . for which I would give them my bills on

Donaldson at Leghorn."[40] In short, Barlow, in one of the highlights of his diplomatic career, had ransomed the captives with the dey's own money. Understandably, he took some pride in how well he had manipulated Micaiah Bacri. Two months later, he recalled to Humphreys: "Had it not been for the confidence I had inspired in the Jews, which I must say was rather personal than national, our prisoners would still have been here, and many more of them dead with the plague."[41]

Having single-handedly liberated 101 of his countrymen, Barlow set about to assure their safe and speedy return. He instructed Samuel Calder, captain of the brig *Fortune* and himself a former captive, to carry them first to Leghorn and then, if possible, on to Philadelphia. Because he had only chartered the *Fortune* from the Bacris, he relied on Donaldson either to buy or lease the vessel from its part-owner, Solomon Bacri, the family's representative in Leghorn. Failing that, he told Donaldson to make other arrangements. He had given each man a month's pay, he wrote, but they would need warm clothing for the passage home.[42] The captives ultimately arrived safely in Marseille, but untangling the troubles that subsequently overtook the *Fortune* would require Barlow's attention long after he had left Algiers.[43]

Having bade the captives farewell, he could not refrain from needling Donaldson, boasting that "notwithstanding I have had no letter from you since the 3rd of May, and the time for our payment is expired, I have been able not only to keep the peace, but to liberate our people." That said, and now that the ransom was paid, he went on to address what he hoped would be Donaldson's role in producing the much larger amount of money needed to pay for the treaty. He knew from Humphreys that Donaldson had "a credit lodged in Leghorn for $400,000 & in Lisbon for 200,000 more for which you can draw."[44] Prodding Donaldson for part of the treaty money, however, proved to be a dead end. Even his efforts to reimburse the Bacris for the ransom loan were stymied. The British still blockaded Leghorn where, in any event, specie was not readily available, and even if it had been, the Bacris remained unwilling to ship it by sea. When the treaty money finally arrived, much of it would come from Lisbon—and Richard O'Brien would bring it.

Meanwhile, the dey's patience once more wore thin. On hearing of the delay occasioned by the blockade, he accused Barlow of lying about everything. "Is it possible, says he, that your money has been dancing all over Europe for a year & has happened to light at last in Leghorn just at the moment the British were to blockade the fort? No, you either have no money in Europe or you never intend to pay it." His tirade then adopted an abused tone: "You speak of patience, says he, I have more patience than God. I have resisted all your enemies who have tried to overturn your peace. . . . I think you honest. But I begin to think you are the most faithless nation of all the infidels."[45] Barlow could only hope for O'Brien's timely arrival.

7 Waiting Out Treaties with Tunis and Tripoli

Waiting for O'Brien as August lengthened, Barlow despaired of a quick and easy settlement with Tunis. Two months earlier on June 14, Tunisian corsairs had captured the American schooner *Eliza,* ironically one day before Famin's recently arranged truce came into effect but presumably protected by the truce Cathcart had negotiated the previous fall. The bey of Tunis, however, denied any knowledge of Cathcart's truce and claimed the captured vessel as fair prize. Barlow was furious. Remind the bey, he told Famin, that it was well known that one of his subordinates *had* signed that truce. Moreover, the dey of Algiers, who was the bey's nominal superior, also knew of the Cathcart truce and had promised Barlow he would enforce it. The U.S. government, he reminded Famin, was offering Tunis $20,000 for a treaty—more than the regent of Algiers thought necessary—and it expected both a treaty and the return of the *Eliza* without further expense.[1]

Threatening Tunis with Algerian coercion depended, of course, on the dey's willingness to oblige. Ali Hassan, however, was not in a cooperative mood, pleased to have received the ransom money but doubtful that the United States would ever pay for the treaty. From his standpoint, the difference affected him personally, because ransom payments traditionally went to the treasury, whereas two-thirds of any treaty payments would go directly to him and his family. Barlow described him as "mortified to see the treasury paid while nothing comes into his own pocket."[2] In sum, the moment to solicit the dey's assistance against Tunis was singularly inopportune. To Monroe he confided: "I should not be surprised if my mentioning the subject should throw him into a passion, and produce a declaration of war."[3]

The regent's well-known volatility, however, occasionally furnished Barlow with comic relief. In early August he recorded what he called the dey's forty-five-minute "war" on Great Britain. It started when the British, having promised the regent the gift of a twenty-gun ship, showed up with "an old rotten vessel of 6 guns." Barlow chuckled at what followed: "The Dey declared war. The battlements were manned, guns loaded & matches lit. The war lasted for three quarters of an hour to the utter distruction [sic] of several inchs [sic] of tow and brimstone; when, to prevent the extinction of the human race, the Dey relented, invited the commandant on shore and settled the matter; whether with or without presents I don't know." The dey's warlike temper, he explained, had cooled when three British frigates, acting as escorts, had followed the "rotten old vessel" into Algiers harbor.[4]

Waiting for the treaty money made Barlow edgy. He had covered his own bills with the Bacris, he assured Monroe, "but how to get the other three or four hundred thousand dollars here I cannot yet contrive." A failed treaty would seriously endanger those Americans who were already risking ships and cargoes in pursuit of markets. "The Mediterranean is full of American ships," he told Monroe. "They would sail into the mouth of hell, if the Devil was to turn Catholic, so as to make it a good market for codfish."[5] And in the same vein to Humphreys some weeks earlier: "You cannot keep the Americans out of the Mediterranean. You might as well try to shut out the Atlantic current. Wherever there is wind and water they will sail."[6] Half-admiring, he nonetheless had no wish to be called on to liberate more captured ships and seamen. He begged James Simpson, U.S. consul at Gibraltar, to do his utmost to prevent American vessels from passing the straits until treaties had been completed with all three Barbary powers.[7] Peevishly he suggested to Montgomery that he "send out a galley & sink every American vessel that attempts to pass Gibraltar, untill peace is made with Barbary."[8] Were it not for "other considerations," he muttered to Ruth, their capture would be richly deserved.[9]

Good news seldom came unadulterated. On September 24, six weeks after Humphreys had written that O'Brien had sailed from Lisbon with $200,000 in specie, Barlow wrote back that despite prevailing westerlies, the vessel had not arrived. He feared "some disaster had happened to him."[10] Coming away from a meeting at the palace, he reported the dey "seemed determined to treat all I could say with contempt & to disbelieve everything." Fortunately, he had left the regent "in a tolerable good humour," but if O'Brien failed to show up, "he will say he was never sent."[11] He tried to assure the dey that if O'Brien did not bring enough specie to fulfill the treaty, he had arranged for the Bacris to "make up the deficiency." The dey scoffed: "Do you think I believe all this?" To which Barlow replied: "Effendi, I know you believe it. That severity in your face is just the mask of an excellent heart, as you esteem the Americans, in spite of all their enemies." Upon saying this, the dey gave Barlow his hand and said, "We will be friends a little longer."[12] Hoping to prove that O'Brien had laded specie, Barlow wrote Humphreys to send bills of lading or "certificates of money being shipped." Such papers would at least convince the Bacris "and possibly thro' them the Dey. They can easily make him believe that black is white, but to convince him that white is white is a task more difficult." Reflecting on the dey's character, he mused, "I could get along well enough with his wickedness, if it were not for his ignorance." He thinks "all Christian nations are devoid of good faith . . . and that they are sure to decieve [sic] him when they can."[13]

O'Brien had in fact run into difficulties. A corsair commanded by a British "renegade" had captured his vessel and brought it into Tripoli. Nearly two weeks passed before it fully dawned on the bey that the money on board belonged to the dey of Algiers. Released, O'Brien made landfall at Algiers on October 1, where Barlow was pleased to report: "He has lost but very little of the money. The Dey's passport saved the Brig at last." In retrospect, he had nothing but praise for O'Brien. Without his combination of "pliability & firmness," he told Pickering, "no man could have done what he did."[14] The dey, thoroughly outraged at the delay, demanded that the bey send him the head of the British renegade or he would dispatch his corsairs to fetch it. To Barlow he raged: "I placed that ungrateful Boy on the throne of Tripoli & I know how to place another there."[15]

Now that hard cash had arrived safely, the dey overwhelmed Barlow with expressions of goodwill, even offering to lend him enough money to complete the treaties with Tripoli and Tunis. At a remarkable audience he told Barlow, "I have long admired your constancy & courage. I now find you are true to me as well as to your country. I always felt something at the bottom of my heart which told me *that man cannot lie.* God has rewarded you for all your sufferings. We will be friends forever . . . let me now prove to you my sincerity."[16]

At this point, Barlow believed he was about to conclude treaties with all three Barbary powers. He barely waited for O'Brien to offload the specie before sending him off to complete treaties already pending with Tunis and Tripoli. He later told the secretary of state that rather than wait for the capture of more American vessels, he was "determined to make treaties where I could & take the responsibility on myself."[17] Moreover, he believed he could lay his hands on enough funds to pay for all three. By his reckoning, the available sources totaled more than $600,000—O'Brien's $232,000 plus Donaldson's "bills" for $400,000. For $525,000 he could cover both ransom and treaty with Algiers, buy a treaty with Tunis for $50,000, and buy a treaty with Tripoli for $40,000.[18] Adverse exchange rates and brokers' fees would boost the final tab, but whatever the additional cost, he firmly believed the value of the Mediterranean trade justified the expense and hoped the administration would agree. Among the extra costs, he figured the U.S. government would ultimately owe the house of Bacri close to $150,000 for its services but reminded Donaldson that Micaiah Bacri's acting as broker and dispenser of bribes "has absolutely saved us in a number of instances." In all, he wrote, "our peace with Barbary will cost us a great deal of money, and a considerable portion of it goes to the Jews. But without the Jews it would have cost us a great deal more and pray what is the difference between Moses and Mahomet."[19] In the end, the house of Bacri provided most of the hard cash up front for all three treaties, leaving Barlow with the wearisome task of reimbursement. Ten months later, as he was preparing to leave Algiers, he was still dunning Humphreys to clear accounts with the bankers.[20]

Sensing a gathering momentum, Barlow worked into the night of October 8, feverishly writing letters. Some were instructions, others warnings; he even wrote thank-you notes to the British and Spanish consuls who had looked after O'Brien during his forced layover in Tripoli.[21] He also drafted instructions for O'Brien, who, on his return to Tripoli, was to drop off a new American consul, a merchant named Joseph Ingraham, deliver the $40,000 that had been promised the bey, and bring back a treaty. If he needed assistance, he should rely on the French consul there, a man whom Barlow had asked Herculais to alert to O'Brien's arrival.[22] And because that consul had been insulted earlier by an American sea captain, Barlow sent him a note of apology.[23]

Two of that day's letters went to Tunis. One told Famin to join O'Brien when he arrived and work with him to facilitate the payment of $50,000 for a

Tunisian treaty. Barlow hoped for a simple transaction, the outlines of which had already been agreed to. Unfortunately, coming to terms with the bey proved to be far more complicated and frustrating than he imagined. His other letter that day notified Captain Graves of the *Eliza* that $30,000 of the Tunisian treaty money had gone to ransom his vessel, its nine crewmen, and its cargo of brandy. The schooner, he reminded Graves, was now U.S. government property, adding that O'Brien would instruct him to come to Algiers and pick up "my dispatches for Philadelphia."[24]

Like everything else that came out of Tunis that fall, Graves gave Barlow a series of headaches. Put simply, he hijacked his own vessel, loaded a Jewish-owned cargo before he left Tunis, and sailed to Palermo where, having stolen the cargo, he flogged the young Jewish supercargo who had accompanied it and set him ashore. When the latter turned up in Algiers to complain, Barlow quickly sought out the dey before the Jewish merchants could get to him. He played down the value of the stolen cargo and assured the regent that if Graves were guilty, the American government would punish him. By this time, Barlow and Ali Hassan were on such good terms that the dey promised to give the Jewish agent a thousand bastinados if he exaggerated his losses.[25] The following April, on hearing that Graves planned to land his stolen cargo at Gibraltar, Barlow exhorted James Simpson, the U.S. consul there, to retrieve it if he could and send it to Algiers. Otherwise, because the U.S. government owned the vessel, it would have to pay for its stolen cargo "at probably ten times the value."[26]

Having set events in motion, Barlow waited impatiently to hear the results. Not until mid-January 1797 did he brace Humphreys with the good news that O'Brien had succeeded in Tripoli. The latter would deliver the treaty to Lisbon, he wrote, adding "I believe you will be convinced that we have done as well as it was possible under the circumstances."[27]

Parenthetically, this treaty with Tripoli is best known today for firing a shot across the bow of the Christian Right, specifically its Article 11, which begins "As the Government of the United States is not in any sense founded on the Christian religion" and ends with the mild predicate "no pretext arising from religious opinions shall ever produce an interruption of the harmony existing between the two countries."[28] Whatever angst or satisfaction today's partisans may draw from Article 11, its contemporary usefulness lay in reassuring Muslims that they had nothing to fear from a country that had never been party to a Crusade.

In announcing O'Brien's success in Tripoli, Barlow also alluded briefly to his continuing failure in Tunis. The bey had held out for more money, but, on the bright side, the latter's "obstinacy & bad faith" had so rankled Ali Hassan as to declare war on Tunis. A breakthrough seemed imminent. Barlow assured Humphreys "that the present war which the Dey of Algiers has undertaken against Tunis is wholly on account of our treaty—He will succeed, and our peace with Tunis as well as with Tripoli will be established on the most solid foundation." This assurance, though it proved premature, spoke volumes about Barlow's skill in exploiting the dey's goodwill.[29]

Events in Tunis soon underscored the futility of relying on Joseph Famin's supposed influence or, for that matter, on the probity of the bey who, when approached on treaty matters, expressed doubt that O'Brien and Famin were authorized to negotiate. Undaunted, O'Brien turned for support to the Algerian ambassador there. When the bey still refused to deal, the latter went home, and O'Brien made one last attempt. Calling on the bey, he asked him point-blank if he intended to make a treaty for the agreed-upon $50,000. The bey replied vaguely that O'Brien had no authority to conclude a treaty "without a reference to algiers [sic]."[30] That "reference" soon arrived. At Barlow's request, the dey sent letters to both beys, demanding they conclude their respective negotiations without further delay. Not content with sending off letters, he told Barlow: "My friend, I will do all this & more; for you have not asked enough. Your nation is brave and good. [But] you are not prepared with the money to send to those places. . . . I will give it to you from own treasury. And your nation will send me those two sums whenever it is convenient."[31] So it was that O'Brien was authorized to pay for the Tripolitan treaty with $40,000 of the dey's money. Once again, Barlow's charm had worked its magic.[32] Only Tunis remained to be dealt with.

The dey's winter war in 1796–97 brought no immediate results, nor did persons close to the scene offer details. O'Brien later alluded to Algerian forces having "actually invaded Tunisian territories," and Barlow in early February referred to "open warfare" between the two,[33] but not until April was there news of a signed treaty, and not until June did the bey agree to amend an article that Barlow found unacceptable. James Cathcart later wondered why, in light of Famin's incompetence, Barlow had not gone to Tunis in person. Barlow himself admitted that Famin was "not very zealous in our cause," but he likely decided that to undertake a personal mission would show a lack of confidence in the dey's more warlike and presumably more effective approach. Rather, he resigned himself to sending couriers to Tunis, hoping to hear back good news. Waiting clearly took a toll on his optimism. In early February he wrote Ruth despairingly that he had not heard from Tunis or Humphreys or Philadelphia. He promised never to leave her again and hoped she would forgive him "for the foolish indiscretion that made me undertake this interminable mission."[34]

His diplomacy stalled, Barlow's entrepreneurial impulses began to stir as the commercial scene brightened. By January 1797 he had purchased two vessels, which, thanks to the dey's passports, could sail with impunity wherever he chose to send them. In the case of the *Friendship*, a 150-ton brig, he told her captain, Chapin Sampson, a former captive, "to run the seas over as long as he pleases" and forward any proceeds to his Boston banker, William Little. To motivate Sampson, he promised him a one-third ownership, to be consummated when he reached Boston and paid Little the sum of $1,000.[35] By this time he had also bought the *Rachel,* a 250-ton prize vessel, and was casting about for a cargo. Half apologetically, he explained to Montgomery that he had hoped to avoid doing personal business during his mission but had been "brought in against my inclination to buy a prize vessel." Subsequently the Bacris had let him invest in half a cargo of wheat they planned to ship from the Algerian port of Bône. Philip Sloan, commanding the *Rachel,* would bring the wheat to Alicante where the Montgomery brothers were asked to dispose of it and, if possible, furnish Sloan with another cargo. He promised to reimburse the brothers for any dockside expenses and was pleased when the voyage proved profitable.[36]

Because the dey's passports would soon be a hot commodity, Barlow urged that American shipmasters furnish Algiers with various samples of the American flag. "At present," he wrote Pickering, "you will see all sorts of colours in our stripes,—they sometimes run parallel & sometimes perpendicular, to the staff. They are sometimes without stars, sometimes with stars & eagle & sometimes with the Irish Harp." Any vessel flying a flag at variance with those on deposit in Algiers, he warned, "will always be exposed . . . to pillage & possibly to condemnation." In the same vein, he urged legislation to punish American shipmasters who entered the Mediterranean whenever the United States was at war with a Barbary power. Writing at a time when treaties with

Tunis and Tripoli were still pending, he estimated close to a hundred American vessels were then in the Mediterranean, adding grimly, "American masters & merchants are more stupidly adventurous in this respect than those of other nations." If legislation failed, they should at least be convoyed.[37] Even diplomatic terminology posed a danger. He warned Famin, for example, not to refer to his countrymen as "Anglo-Americans" lest they be mistaken for Britons.[38]

While Barlow was working to make American commerce safe from North African predators, an uptick in French hostility posed a new danger. In March 1796 Paris had repudiated the principle of "free ships make free goods" in retaliation for its omission from Jay's treaty. As noted earlier, this principle, when stipulated by treaty, constrained the parties, when one was at war and the other was not, from seizing the neutral party's vessels even though they carried enemy-owned cargoes. The Directory's abandonment of "free ships" meant that French corsairs were now on the prowl for American carriers laded with goods of enemy origin. For Barlow this new threat struck close to home when a privateer fitted out by the newly arrived French consul, Jean Bon Saint André, promptly captured and brought in two neutral vessels—one Danish, the other Swedish, ostensibly for carrying goods belonging to an enemy of France. Fearing an American would be next, Barlow worked closely with the two consuls to remind the dey that all their treaties with Algiers upheld the principle of "free ships"—that a neutral flag "covers the cargo." Ultimately, the Swedish consul prevailed on the dey to "shut his port against all such [captured] vessels." Barlow was pleased, but, mindful of possible political fallout, he feared the French consul might "point the resentment of his government against the United States for the part I took in this business."[39]

He need not have concerned himself on this score. The Directory had already shown its teeth. In a fit of ideological pique, it had refused to receive Charles Cotesworth Pinckney, Monroe's successor as U.S. minister, because it found him "too aristocratic," thereby setting the stage for the XYZ Affair and the Quasi-War that followed. As for Saint André, Barlow described him to Pinckney as "the most fiery satellite of Robespierre," a man who relished predicting that Jay's treaty would bring war between France and the United States.[40] When in fact the crisis did reach the point of an undeclared naval war, Barlow would be back in Paris trying to stamp out the flames. Meanwhile, the unfinished negotiation with Tunis continued to delay his departure.

By early February 1797, the dey's coercive "war" against Tunis had succeeded in evoking the bey's apology and the promise of an early treaty. If further delays ensued, the dey told Barlow he would resume hostilities as soon the snow melted in the mountain passes. Barlow doubted he would.[41] By late March, however, a letter from Tunis gave him the impression that Famin was on the brink of sending him a signed treaty. A month later he felt confident enough to tell Cathalan that he would hand-deliver it in Marseille on his way back to Paris.[42]

In early June, however, Famin sent him shocking news of last-minute difficulties. The problem lay in the bey's insistence on adding a passage to Article 14 so damaging to U.S. customs revenue that Barlow, when he learned of it, told Famin, "neither you nor I nor the government has a right to accede to it." The bey's new wording, he noted, would allow Tunisian nationals to bring cargoes duty-free into the United States from any point of origin. Barlow was aghast. He read it to mean that "a single Tunisian in London can cover with his name any cargo that comes from England; another could so the same thing in France." Barlow calculated the resulting tariff loss in the millions.[43] Speculating that Congress might agree to a lesser loss, he told Famin to seek a modification that would allow Tunisians to ship duty-free cargoes but only in "merchandise of their own country." Even so, he should warn the bey that changing the tariff laws would delay the six shipments of munitions the treaty had promised.[44] Ultimately, the bey withdrew the offending clause, but not until after Barlow had left Algiers. Terminally frustrated by his inability to tie up the loose ends, Barlow boarded the *Rachel* on July 28 and sailed for Marseille, entrusting to Micaiah Bacri the financial details of completing the Tunis negotiation. He wrote: "If Mr. Famin should write that he has not concluded the treaty, do not fail to take such measures as I know will be within your power to conclude it immediately & on the best of terms."[45]

Arriving after twelve days at sea with only minor discomfort, he wrote Ruth that he now hoped to forget everything that had happened since he left her. She would find him a little fatter, he warned, but promised to shave off the thick black moustache he had grown. Giving himself "the look of a tiger," he explained, had been useful on certain critical occasions. Though tempted to show it off, he was sure she would prefer to receive him clean-shaven.[46]

Forty days of quarantine effectively immobilized Barlow but gave him ample opportunity to catch up on his correspondence. Famin needed another

$10,000, he wrote Bacri, but don't give it to him until he delivers a signed and sealed treaty and places it in the hands of George Clark, the agent he had left in charge of the U.S. consulate. He also bade a warm goodbye to the banker. "Be a good man," he wrote, "Be Macayo Bacry. My best affections to your good family. I shall not forget your goodness to me & you must not forget your old friend."[47] He also reminded Humphreys that the U.S. government still owed Bacri $50,000 and that any default "would injure us exceedingly in Algiers." His own travel expenses and back pay he would detail later, but he estimated them at about $5,000. He would not press for payment if the government balked, reminding Humphreys that money had never figured in his decision to undertake the mission.[48]

Mindful of how badly Franco-American relations had deteriorated in his absence, Barlow foresaw he might have difficulty returning to Paris when his quarantine expired. It was not easy for an American to get a passport to the French capital in late 1797. Hoping for official assistance, he asked Fulwar Skipwith, the American consul in Paris, to make the case for his return by pointing out to the appropriate authorities that he had lived in Paris since 1788, owned two houses there, and had been made a French citizen in 1793.[49] As a fallback, on learning that persons with active business affairs in France were more likely to be admitted, he asked his friend Robert Lyle to send him a predated letter attesting that he had a cargo waiting for him in Le Havre. He wrote: "If I can have a passport to go to Le Havre, you know I must take Paris on the way & that will answer my purpose."[50] In the end, it was Skipwith who came through. On August 24 Barlow wrote Ruth that officials in Marseille had orders to give him a passport to Paris. Because no other American had been so favored, he urged her to thank Skipwith, adding with a bow to understatement, "it seems we are a little at odds with our allies."[51]

During his quarantine in the spacious Marseille lazaretto (duly described and measured), Barlow had his first brush with the problem of rescuing American seamen stranded in France when French corsairs captured their vessels. Responding to Cathalan's query, he parsed the problem with considerable prescience. As U.S. minister to France more than a decade later, he would deal with the plight of "distressed seamen" at close range and at a time when the French were capturing American vessels in far greater numbers. As early as 1797, however, he put his finger on the central difficulty. French officials, he wrote, invariably pinned British nationality on every English-speaking seaman who came within their hearing. Proof of citizenship, he told Cathalan, was the key to their release. "It is so difficult to distinguish Americans from English that the French government will not allow any man to be American who cannot prove it." Cathalan, too, should seek such proof. Meanwhile, whatever Congress might rule, consuls by tradition were bound to help their fellow citizens, but they must make sure to identify them as such. "You ask me what I would do in your place, I would succour real American seamen in distress, untill I had advice from either the Sec'y of State or Mr. Skipwith."[52]

Although his advice was sound, the potential for mischief lay not only in the Anglophobic mind-sets of French officialdom, but also in the difficulty of sorting out the nationality of captives taken at sea. Some were British deserters who had taken berths on American merchantmen; others were Americans who had escaped British impressment. As time went on, some were repatriated, others interned. The problem would fester until Napoleon left for Saint Heléna.

8 Critiquing U.S. Policy toward France

The France that Barlow returned to in the fall of 1797 was riding a crest of military victories almost certain to put further strains on American neutrality. Having routed Spain and Prussia two years earlier, France now basked in Napoleon's victories over the Austrians in Italy, while in Paris a reconstituted and more belligerent Directory needed only a successful cross-channel invasion to complete French hegemony. With her corsairs making profitable inroads on Americans' trade with Britain and still resentful of Jay's treaty, France seemed unlikely to accept any terms American diplomats might offer in the name of neutral rights.

The French government's refusal to accept Charles Cotesworth Pinckney cast an ominous shadow over Franco-American relations, but as long as diplomacy held out hope, even the War Hawks of the Federalist Party could agree with John Adams to try again. The president, for his part, sincerely wanted peace, though not at any price, whereas the militants of his party calculated that if France were to reject another diplomatic mission, as seemed likely, Adams would be unable to resist the public outcry for war. In that event, militant Federalists relished the prospect of making an alliance with Britain that would serve as a bulwark against the spread of "French radicalism" at home and abroad. With intraparty tensions momentarily stilled, the Senate approved the appointment of John Marshall, a staunch Federalist, and acquiesced reluctantly in Adams's last-minute nomination of his friend Elbridge Gerry, a political independent. These two ill-matched envoys were to join a recommissioned Pinckney and proceed to Paris in a last-ditch effort to halt the slide toward war.

As noted in chapter 7, Pinckney, then at The Hague, had fled Paris in December when the Directory not only refused to receive him but also signaled it might arrest him. Whether his return to the French capital in company with Marshall and Gerry would make any difference remained to be seen. Symbolically perhaps, in light of Gerry's later "defection" from his colleagues, Marshall and Pinckney left The Hague for Paris on September 18 without waiting for his arrival. All three were in the French capital, however, soon after Barlow returned from Marseille. Here, happily reunited with Ruth and vowing never again to leave her, he watched anxiously from the sidelines as the notorious XYZ affair unfolded.

The American mission appeared to start promisingly. Gerry at least expressed optimism when, at their first meeting with Charles Maurice de Talleyrand, he described the foreign minister as having a "familiar & easy style."[1] Within days, however, the envoys were treated to an almost comical combination of Talleyrandian greed and deniability. It began when they were approached first by one, and then several, intermediaries later identified merely as Messieurs W, X, Y, and Z. These agents intimated that the United States might resolve its difficulties with France if the envoys agreed to pay a quarter-million-dollar bribe, arrange for an intergovernmental loan, and disavow passages hostile to France that Adams had uttered in a message to Congress the previous May. They were not able to specify the offending passages or the exact amount of the loan, but paying the bribe, they insisted, must precede any substantive negotiations.

The envoys' written reports of these early meetings, soon to be known as the XYZ Papers, reached Philadelphia in March 1798, where the president, realizing their inflammatory potential, was inclined to keep them secret. Congressional Republicans, however, suspecting that France had held out an olive branch, insisted on seeing them. One look was enough. Outraged at what it viewed as an attempt at national humiliation, Congress proceeded to abrogate all past treaties with France, suspended commerce, created a navy department, and, perhaps most significantly, authorized the seizure of armed French vessels. Thus began so-called Quasi-, or Naval, War with France. Thereafter only John Adams stood between the hawks of his party and an official declaration.

Until Talleyrand learned of the furor in Congress, he was content to play a waiting game with the envoys. During weeks of fruitless meetings, some face to face, others through his agents, he held Marshall and Pinckney at bay, stalling them with proposals they found unacceptable, while courting Gerry, whose dread of war made him more approachable. Once the news of congressional reprisals reached France, he drew Gerry even closer, warning him that if he left Paris, as his colleagues were threatening, his departure would surely mean war. Gerry, gullible perhaps but genuinely alarmed, opted to stay. Marshall and Pinckney left. Whether Tallyrand was truly shocked by the intensity of the American reaction—bribery and corruption were, after all, the familiar tools of European diplomacy—he shied at being held responsible for adding to France's declared enemies. He knew, of course, that Americans posed no direct military threat but feared they might well lay waste to the French Indies, even seize Louisiana before France had a chance to recover it from Spain. A declared war was not in France's interest nor in Talleyrand's.

Later, when the full measure of American hostility became known, he managed to disavow any knowledge of Messieurs X, Y, and Z (Monsieur W played such a small role that he is generally omitted from contemporary mention), and when Marshall and Pinckney left Paris in disgust in April, he became what one historian calls an "apostle of peace."[2] His problem thereafter was how to backtrack without losing face. Fortunately for the cause of peace, John Adams came to his rescue by offering a way out. On June 27 a presidential message to Congress backhandedly left the door ajar to further negotiations. Vowing he would "never send another minister to France without assurances that he would be received, respected, and honored as the representative of a great, free, powerful, and independent nation," Adams gave Talleyrand an opening.[3] By early 1799 the president had received the French foreign minister's word-for-word assurances on these points. By this time, letters from France, Barlow's among them, confirmed that France was indeed ready for a settlement. The following year, another three-man commission would negotiate the so-called Franco-American Convention of 1800, which wrote at least a temporary end to French hostility.

Few public figures emerged smiling from the Quasi-War era. Adams's courage in sending a third mission to Paris split the Federalist Party so badly that it never elected another president. Peace advocates like Elbridge Gerry, George Logan, Joel Barlow, and even William Vans Murray, the U.S. minister who conveyed Talleyrand's assurances from his post at The Hague, were reviled by the "High Federalists" as dupes or appeasers.[4]

Barlow, meanwhile, struck up a friendship with Gerry that enabled him to follow the envoys' early frustration. As weeks lengthened into months, he came to harbor strong feelings about the reasons for the impasse. In early March 1798, hoping to be heard where his views might count, he sent a long letter, intended for discreet circulation, to his brother-in-law Abraham Baldwin, now a U.S. senator from Georgia. In a searing critique of American foreign policy, he came perilously close to giving France a free pass, a flaw that Federalists attacked ferociously when the letter was later stolen and published in the partisan press. At the time, however, Barlow felt it important for his countrymen to know how resentfully France viewed Jay's treaty and how fully justified it felt in taking maritime reprisals. Specifically, he reminded them how little regard the Washington and Adams administrations had shown for French republican sensibilities from the outset, especially in their choice of envoys. French republicans, he pointed out, attached great importance to the political ideology of those with whom they chose to do business. In the first instance, they were sorely offended when Washington replaced Jefferson, who was well liked, with Gouverneur Morris, a man they came to regard as little more than a British agent. Then followed Monroe, whom they welcomed as a kindred spirit, only to see him recalled in disgrace for having failed to defend Jay's treaty with sufficient vigor. How London must have rejoiced, Barlow wrote, to see Monroe "recalled in the most abrupt & censorious manner, for the apparent crime of preventing a war." Still, the French had shown restraint, he observed, because they believed that Washington, now "in the dotage of his natural life, and near the close of his political career," would be replaced by someone who would bring Americans to their senses. Instead, his successor, John Adams, "a reputed royalist & enemy of France," had had the gall to recommission Charles Cotesworth Pinckney, "a man who had just been refused & could not be offered again without insult." Nor was the president wise to join him in the mission with John Marshall, a partisan whose "virulent defence" of Jay's treaty had reportedly inspired his fellow Virginians to burn him in effigy. As for Elbridge Gerry, Barlow ranked him dismissively as "a little make-weight man, appointed with the intention that he should have no influence," although he ventured the unlikely scenario that if Gerry had not been "shackled with the other two," the Directory would have negotiated with him. Barlow's overheated partisanship got the better of him at several points, especially in characterizing Adams's messages to Congress as intemperate and insulting to France.[5]

Although Adams would later join in the cries of outrage that followed the publication of the XYZ Papers, his earlier messages to Congress—the only ones available to Barlow at the time—show a president deeply disturbed by France's seizure of American shipping and her refusal to receive Pinckney but were in no sense inflammatory.[6] Still, in Barlow's view, the president had insulted France by alluding to its unreliability, and Congress, instead of echoing the president's sentiments, should have "sent him to the Mad-house." What may have colored Barlow's perception was not so much the content of Adams's messages as reading the contemporary speeches of Francophobic members of Congress, whose heated diatribes routinely found their way into the *Gazette of the United States*. Unfortunately, Barlow noted, French officials just as routinely read the *Gazette* and were convinced that it spoke for the administration.

The solutions Barlow proposed revealed how much he had yet to learn of the deep partisan divide at home. Fecklessly he suggested that Adams might find the Directory more willing to deal if he replaced Marshall and Pinckney with Madison or Monroe. The notion of a Federalist-controlled Senate endorsing the appointment of such towering opposition figures showed how tenuous his grip of political realities was. Nor was Adams likely to heed his supposition that all issues could be resolved if a new envoy brought messages of goodwill.

By the end of July 1798, Barlow knew from reading over Gerry's shoulder what terms the Directory was prepared to offer. Hoping to underscore their importance, as well as their reasonableness, he repeated them to his old friend Oliver Wolcott. France, he told the treasury secretary, was ready to treat with any envoy who might be sent, irrespective of that individual's ideological stripe. Bribes and loans were no longer on the table, nor were apologies for offensive speeches. A new negotiation, he predicted, would end the seizures of American vessels and free those the French government had interned after learning of Congress's hostile measures.

Convinced the Directory had gone as far as it could to achieve a peaceful outcome, he cautioned that "a refusal on your part to meet on this ground, would be considered as a declaration of war."[7] Again, only dimly aware of the political tensions in Philadelphia, Barlow failed to realize that such warnings were not likely to sit well with an administration that considered itself blameless in its dealings with France and had endured more than five years of French envoys meddling in American politics and endangering the country's neutrality.

In early October, with diplomacy still stalled, Barlow took aim at a loftier target when he sent an appeal to George Washington, urging the former president to use his influence to calm the increasingly turbulent political waters. As matters now stood, each side had worked itself up to believe that war was inevitable. He assured Washington, however, that the Directory was now "sincerely desirous of restoring harmony." As he had told Wolcott, the French government was prepared to deal with any emissary the United States might send and no longer demanded loans or apologies. Moreover, he had it from reliable sources that the Directory intended to restrict future privateering "to the legal objects of capture," a phrase unfortunately vague enough to leave lingering uncertainties. Still, Barlow wrote, he had been led to believe that France would not only restrain her corsairs, but would also agree to adjudicate Americans' maritime claims and accept the principle of "free ships, free goods." But, he cautioned, the administration must act quickly. Although prospects for peace were bright "at present," time was running out. And again, he overplayed the alternative. One can imagine the irritation Washington (and later Adams) felt at being told that to refuse the Directory's overture would bring "immediate war . . . a war of the most terrible and vindictive kind, producing incalculable calamities."[8]

Adams, to whom Washington forwarded the letter, later reflected that at the time he would sooner have expected to see a French army in heaven than in America. In early 1799, however, the president reacted furiously to Barlow's assumption that he would be deterred from accepting Talleyrand's overture by the threat of a French descent on the American mainland. Touchy because he had already decided to accept that overture in the face of heavy political fire, he blasted Barlow for writing a letter that "destroyed his own character." He advised Washington not to answer it. Barlow's having transmitted this "infamous threat . . . ought to be answered by a Mohawk," Adams rumbled. In his retirement, however, he thought better of this harsh judgment. Writing to the *Boston Patriot* some years later, he recalled weighing whether Barlow's letter was written with "a very good or a very bad design" and had now concluded that "it was written with a very good one."[9]

Even after John Adams confounded the War Hawks of his party and sent another mission to France, the bitter animosity between Federalists and Republicans continued to burn fiercely and would leave Barlow badly singed. In early March 1799, a year after sending his letter to Baldwin, he was aghast to see it published in the *Columbian Centinel,* Hartford's unforgiving Federalist organ. While admitting its authorship, he prefaced his rebuttal by charging, predictably, that he had been misquoted or misunderstood, stating flatly that "every part of it is mutilated and distorted more or less." But mostly less, it turned out.[10] The major points of his critique, having survived minor editing, were enough to infuriate Federalist critics. Barlow's instinctive response, however, was to give no ground, retract nothing, and repeat his belief that the United States should settle with France. His letter to Baldwin, he explained, had no other purpose than to focus on the shortcomings of American policy, because he believed his countrymen needed to know how Frenchmen perceived them. Had he known the letter would be published, he would not have left the impression, by omission, that he approved of France's misconduct. Quite the contrary, he had often "remonstrated" against France's "monstrous system of piracy and plunder."[11] Indeed, against such conduct he would always defend Americans' rights on the high seas. He only wished the U.S. government had done the same when the British had first offended by seizing American vessels in 1793. In that year, he wrote chidingly, the administration had lost a great opportunity to use its economic power. However vulnerable American seaborne commerce, he observed, its value to Europe gave Americans a "precious weapon, and the only infallible one." Instead of sending Jay to London, the administration should have sequestered the debts Americans owed to British creditors. "You had an invincible bulwark in the debts you were constantly owing." Unlike other forms of redress, sequestration, he insisted, offered an "honorable" way to compensate for "public wrongs" and would have been highly effective.[12] Clamors from hurt British creditors would have ended the depredations forthwith. To strengthen his argument, he rejected alternatives as being too costly. A retaliatory embargo, for example, would have left ships and cargoes rotting, their crews idle, while building a navy, as Congress seemed about to undertake, would drastically raise the national debt.[13]

Barlow's argument for sequestration, though well rounded, missed out in one particular. It failed to take into account how direly American commerce would suffer if those Britons who had financed it in the past now refused to do so.

Predictably, the partisan ruckus over Jay's treaty lent itself to exaggerated judgments on both sides. Federalist defenders touted it, though unconvincingly, as an alternative to war, while Republicans pretended to find no merit in any of its twenty-eight articles. Most distressing to Barlow, the treaty yielded to British maritime policy in ways destructive not only to neutral rights but also to the material interests of both France and the United States. He did not have to explain in detail. The treaty spoke for itself. Its failure to affirm the principle of "free ships, free goods" meant the British might seize as fair prize any "enemy goods" found aboard a neutral vessel. It was small consolation to France that the British, after looting American vessels of French cargoes, agreed to set them free. Worse in some respects, the treaty set the stage for expanding the list of contraband, usually defined as arms and implements of war, and invariably subject to confiscation. Jay's having agreed that Britain might at some point classify "provisions" as contraband clearly put at risk France's vital suppliers of American grain. Again, Paris could draw no comfort from London's avowed willingness to pay for such cargoes.[14]

Barlow's advocacy of neutral rights went beyond lamenting their absence from Jay's treaty. In December 1799 he addressed a memorandum to the Directory urging that France espouse those rights, as it had in the past, and even expand them. His advice seemed timely. French and American diplomats, he believed, would soon be negotiating, and he hoped they might be inspired to make a treaty that would sweep away the most egregious practices of maritime warfare. Both parties, he believed, had a stake in affirming the rights of neutral carriers—especially France, because she depended heavily on others to carry her seaborne commerce. For reasons of self-interest, then, she should embrace the principle of "free ships," using her prestige to give wider authority to the dictum that a neutral flag protects all cargoes in time of war. Nor would he exclude contraband from that protection. Radical for his time, Barlow favored scrapping the whole notion of contraband on grounds that belligerents had no right to change the rules. Cargoes lawfully traded in peacetime should not be subject to seizure in wartime.[15]

Indeed, the only acceptable impediments to neutral shipping he envisioned were the blockades belligerents levied on the ports of an enemy. And to be legal, those blockades must adhere to the time-honored canon of being effective—tight enough that "a vessel cannot enter without imminent danger of being stopped." Taking an even more liberal stance, he would give blockade runners a first-time free pass, proposing that no ship be seized unless it "shall have been stopped, and sent away, and shall return a second time."[16] In setting forth these proposals, Barlow may have hoped that the Directory, as the inheritor of the Revolution, still retained enough zeal for world-changing measures to take them on.

In urging France to give up privateering as well, however, Barlow went one step too far and must have caused its members to question his grasp of wartime realities. With France's regular navy bottled up by British warships, privateers were her only sea-going recourse, affording her at least the means of worrying occasional stragglers from British convoys. Whether Barlow seriously expected the French regime to call back its corsairs, he was mindful of the toll they had taken of American vessels. He gave it his eloquent best, condemning privateering as a practice unworthy of a great nation, a "loose piratical warfare," attracting the "most vitious individuals," many of whom would be caught and end up in British prisons, thereby depriving France of the crewmen her navy might put to better use.[17] There is no record of a response. Ironically Barlow himself had a brush with privateering. In settling a bad debt in the spring of 1800, he inadvertently acquired shares in a very successful French privateer, the *Uni*. Realizing the potential for embarrassment, he offered the U.S. consul at Nantes a commission to sell the shares and please keep his name out of the transaction. Privateering, he insisted "is a detestable form of robbery, in which I have never placed a farthing, & never will; especially in such as may be employed against the commerce of my own country."[18]

Although events in the year 1799 moved fitfully toward another meeting between French and American diplomats, what exactly they would negotiate remained an open question. Neither party seemed ready to talk specifics. Predictably this lack of substance emboldened Adams's critics to picture France's willingness to receive a new emissary as a mere formality. No concessions had been hinted at. Still, when Adams in early February received Talleyrand's assurances that an emissary would be received, he embraced the formality and hoped for the best. With this, the boldest and most costly decision of a long career, he promptly named William Vans Murray to go to Paris to test the sincerity of the French overtures. Senate Federalists, thunderstruck at the prospect of peace, did what they could to put up roadblocks. Hinting that Talleyrand had hoodwinked Murray into transmitting the assurances, they insisted on adding two staunch Federalists to the mission and then abetted delaying their departure for almost a year. The two additions were Chief Justice Oliver Ellsworth and

William R. Davie, the aristocratic governor of North Carolina. They did not arrive in France until the end of January 1800.[19]

In Paris Barlow did his best to hurry the peace process along. In February 1799, unaware of Adams's decision that month, he and Fulwar Skipwith cosigned a letter urging the Directory to send its own emissary to Philadelphia. Congress, they noted, would recess on March 4, and if the president were forced to call the Senate into special session, approval of a new envoy would be delayed until early fall. In particular, they hoped the Directory would furnish its interim envoy with decrees renouncing the worst abuses of privateering. They had already told their correspondents in America that France was willing to impose such restraints. A French envoy arriving with confirmation would resolve any lingering doubts. Privateering, they argued, had never served France's best interests. Without its interruptions, the free flow of trade in recent years would have made France three million livres richer. Had American vessels been safe from capture and confiscation, they would have flocked to France, their cargoes "nourishing" the agricultural and manufacturing bases of her economy. Nor had it made sense for French corsairs to target American vessels carrying British goods, inasmuch as such carriers deprived the British of freight charges and drew seamen away from Britain's merchant fleet. In sum, France had little to lose from recalling her privateers and much to gain from winning back the goodwill of a sister republic. As for naming an appropriate envoy, Barlow and Skipwith merely suggested that it be someone well known to Americans for his writings, "a citizen, if possible, who may have some acquaintance with our excellent philosopher & patriot, Jefferson." Or at least someone who would not be "disagreeable to the opposite party."[20] Therein, of course, lay the rub. How the Directory could identify a French republican who would not be instantly anathema to hardcore Federalists may explain why the Barlow-Skipwith letter went unanswered.

Although this correspondence suggests that Barlow may have had personal contacts with one or more members of the Directory, such was not the case. In June 1799 he explained to Stephen Cathalan, who had lost his consular post in Marseille, why he was unable to get him a government job in Paris: "I have not had the least acquaintance with any minister, or any director, or any of those secretaries or clerks. Ever since the year 1793 when I came near to perishing with the fathers of the Republic, I have avoided any connection with the men in power," remaining attached only to the ideal of "the Republic in general."[21] Soon, Napoleon Bonaparte would dispose of that as well.

Like others of the American community, however, Barlow felt uneasy about the instability of France's internal politics. By the end of June 1799, military defeats and rumors of corruption in high places had led the French legislative councils to oust all but one of the incumbent members of the Directory. This legislative coup, named "Prairial," for the French revolutionary calendar month in which it occurred, left pundits wondering what would come next. Predictably perhaps, the rudderless mood of the times spawned rumors of an impending Bourbon restoration, an expectation so widespread that when it crossed the Atlantic, Federalist War Hawks pressed Adams to delay the mission until a regime change could be certified. The president saw some merit in the case for delay but ultimately reasoned that if the commissioners arrived to find Louis XVIII on his throne, they could extend their congratulations and then write Philadelphia for new credentials. At his bidding, Ellsworth and Davie sailed from Newport, Rhode Island, on November 3, 1799.[22] Six days later, in what proved to be a fortuitous turn of events, Napoleon effectively seized the reins of power in Paris. Emerging as self-proclaimed first consul, he and two other conspirators quickly put an end to the Directory and set about to consolidate their coup by working toward a general peace settlement. Within two years, the treaties of Lunéville, Amiens, and Mortefontaine would end hostilities with Austria, Britain, and the United States, respectively. But until this new direction bore fruit, watchful Americans in Paris could only speculate as to whether the Ellsworth Commission would share in the peace process.

None doubted, however, that political uncertainties had worsened the economic hard times besetting American businessmen. Barlow, too, felt the pinch. Shortly after returning from Algiers, he had sold both his vessels, planning to invest the proceeds in outgoing cargoes. He soon discovered, however, that commercial opportunities were few and risky. To Robert Lyle, a one-time business associate, he wrote in July 1799 that the "present state of Paris with respect to business . . . is much worse than the worst times you have ever seen." Two months later, again to Lyle, he reported that James Swan, once the high-flying "provisioner" of the Terror, was dunning him for money. Swan would have to wait, he added, because he himself was short of funds. Government contracts, he explained, were no longer the life's blood of commerce, largely because the

Directory was too corrupt and untrustworthy to do business with. "I am forgetting as fast as possible all my acquaintances among men in power. I never speak to them on business, and never will if I can avoid it."[23]

If business was bad, the news from home was also unsettling. A letter from his older brother Aaron in the fall of 1799 warned him that if he remained in France, the government might seize his property. Publication of his letter to Baldwin, Aaron explained, had left him open to reprisal. He had heard it rumored that unless the "difficulties" with France were soon settled, "Congress will pass a law to confiscate property belonging to any person that resides in any part of the French nation." To prevent this, Aaron offered to assume power of attorney so that he could sell off Barlow's property in Hartford and Greenfield, Connecticut, and take possession of his speculative land holdings in Vermont and Ohio. He reported having already rescued Joel's moth-eaten furniture, books, and other belongings from the Hartford house, then observed ruefully that if his brother had come straight home after his mission to Algiers, he would have been welcomed "with greatful Honor, but since them letters was published thair is much [talk] about your being an enemy of your native country and renouncing all religion." And if he did come back, Aaron suggested that he and Ruth might be happier in Pennsylvania or Virginia or Georgia. Anywhere but Federalist New England was the message.[24]

Aaron asked for help as well as offering it. His foundry in Fairfield, he observed, was in dire need of investment capital, and because none of his sons was interested in the family ironworks, he was struggling to keep it solvent. Having heard that Joel had "made a fortune in Europe," he asked for a loan of a thousand pounds, promising to pay it back in two years at 5 percent interest.[25] Barlow never had to meet this request. Aaron died less than a year later, though perhaps not before he received word of Barlow's friendly attempt to persuade Oliver Ellsworth to take Aaron's nineteen-year-old son Stephen to Paris in a secretarial capacity, a good-faith effort that spoke both to Barlow's strong attachment to family and to the conventional wisdom of the day. Like other upwardly mobile figures, Barlow thought highly of exposing young Americans to the European scene, whether to complete their education or to prepare them for leadership roles in the new republic. In this instance, as he explained to Aaron, Ellsworth had refused the favor, presumably because he hated Barlow's "republican principles."[26] Twelve years later, however, as he readied for his own mission to Paris, Barlow was pleased to include Aaron's youngest son, Thomas, in his entourage.

If Ellsworth hated his "principles," Barlow fully reciprocated. Like many Jeffersonian Republicans, he suspected Federalists of conspiring to establish a hereditary aristocracy. Accordingly he lumped Ellsworth with those who would, if they could, "rivet the chains of monarchy" on their fellow Americans.[27] However exaggerated this view, it typified the partisan accusations of the day and, in this instance, underscored how little Barlow knew about Ellsworth or about the status of the negotiations. He no longer had an Elbridge Gerry to keep him informed. In late August 1800, for example, he mistakenly told Ruth the negotiation would run at least another two months because the commissioners were waiting for new instructions.[28] In fact, little more than a month later, on October 2, they and Napoleon signed what came to be known as the Franco-American Convention of 1800. Also referred to as the Treaty of Mortfontaine, this document effectively ended the Quasi-War, which, in any case, had begun to lose its raison d'être when the first consul set out to make peace with Britain. A year later, the short-lived Peace of Amiens removed maritime issues from Americans' immediate quarrels with both powers. And under the rubric of all's well that ends well, the Senate struck Article 2 from the convention, thereby effecting a trade-off that both parties found they could live with. This deletion wrote off France's liability with respect to past depredations, but it also foreclosed any future French efforts to revive the entanglements of earlier treaties. The protocol of understanding that William Vans Murray signed in June 1801 abandoned both maritime claims and old treaties.

Although Barlow made no mention of the Ellsworth Commission's handiwork, he must have welcomed its reaffirmation of the principle of "free ships, free goods," a short-lived about-face that reflected the first consul's larger designs in 1800. As part of his pressure on London to make peace, Napoleon tried, though not very successfully, to mobilize the neutral nations of northern Europe to unite against Britain's long-time interference with their commerce. The so-called Armed Neutrality of 1800 never amounted to much, except to put France forward, briefly, as a champion of maritime neutral rights.

The summer of 1800 found the Barlows enjoying their self-imposed exile, pleasantly occupied in a variety of activities and with no thought of returning home until the partisan storms had abated. Now financially well fixed thanks to the rising value of French government securities, Barlow negotiated at length and finally bought the property at 50 rue de Vaugirard, a building so large he furnished only four of its rooms. Ruth, for her part, spent August in Le Havre in the company of Robert Fulton whose latest steamboat project was then afoot.[29]

Between steam-driven experiments, "Toot," as they called him, lived with them in Paris. Over the years their letters to Fulton spoke to a relationship so affectionate that one of Fulton's biographers makes an arguable case they enjoyed a ménage à trois.[30] Whether Fulton actively participated in their marriage, we have his later declaration that his love for Ruth was "platonic."[31] Whatever the household arrangements, the Barlows supported Fulton's inventive genius both personally and financially. Barlow sent him money that summer, lobbied the French naval ministry for more funding, and told Ruth, "I would do any thing in the world that I think would do him good."[32]

However idyllic these turn-of-the-century years, Barlow could not escape reminders of how low his reputation had fallen among those who assumed his brush with the French Revolution had left him hopelessly radicalized, godless, and probably treasonous. His letter to Baldwin, in particular, had evoked a hostility that both puzzled and repelled him. How, he wondered, could his critics have surrendered their republican principles, merely because "a few of our fellow citizens, wish to be kings and nobles & ride upon our necks?"[33] In October he wrote his friend Alexander Wolcott of a conversation he had had with Zephaniah Swift, a Connecticut lawyer and former Yale classmate who had served as secretary to the Ellsworth Commission. Swift had told him that he and Wolcott were probably "the only friends" he had left in Connecticut. Reflecting on this conversation, Barlow told Wolcott he would like to return home, but this "will probably never be, for the people of your state, tho' they may soon come to their senses, will not easily forgive those who told them they had lost them."[34] Even those with whom he corresponded, he feared, might suffer taint by association. He would have sent a set of French classics to enrich the library of the new University of Georgia, he told its president, Josiah Meigs, except that "every thing coming from me would be Sedition or Treason—so my project must be adjourned." Nor was Meigs to mention him to "any of my old friends lest they should take it as an affront. I am told they have all turned my enemies. God bless them! I wish them all as happy as I am."[35] Even James

Watson, his broker in New York, saw fit to denounce him for his political heresies. Barlow had written earlier to remind Watson that he had asked him to sell off his Ohio Company lands and deposit the funds in Ruth's name. In response to Watson's "angry letter," Barlow enclosed two explanatory pamphlets, which, although "they contain nothing but old fashioned republican principles, such as you and I were nourished in, . . . I cannot suppose they are any longer to your taste, & therefore I do not ask you to read them."[36]

One bruised friendship Barlow found particularly painful. His distress appeared in a letter he wrote in reply to William Lee, who had charged Barlow with slandering him. Barlow replied that he had done nothing of the sort. He was especially hurt because he and Ruth had earlier befriended Lee when he was living in Paris and liked him. Now, writing from Boston where his family had commercial interests, Lee demanded to know why Barlow had badmouthed him. Mystified and suspecting the influence of political undercurrents, Barlow asked sorrowfully, "Is then the air of that country so contagious, her calumny against me become so fashionable, so seducing, as that you cannot refuse to join the cry?" He denied ever having said anything derogatory about Lee and certainly had never accused him of "infidelity or want of talents in business. No, my friend, I never accused you in thought, word or deed, of any thing farther than *neglecting to write me.*"[37] Whatever the specifics of this misunderstanding, they were soon glossed over. By the time Lee took over the U.S. consular post in Bordeaux in 1801, he and Barlow were fully reconciled.

Among Barlow's other burdens was the charge of atheism, a reproach typically leveled at those French revolutionaries who, hoping to put behind them the oppressive aspects of traditional Christianity, had embraced the concept of a single "Supreme Being." Barlow's religious views, like those of many of his enlightened generation, were familiarly deistic in that they reflected a belief system that accepted the existence of a creative force (manifested in nature), adhered to the moral teachings of Jesus and rejected the institutional and theological accretions of organized religion. For traditional Christians, however, deistic simplifications were close enough to atheism as to make no difference. Once labeled an atheist, Barlow found the epithet stuck. Eight years later, for example, his old friend and fellow wordsmith Noah Webster explained why he could not review Barlow's recently published *The Columbiad*—without passing "severe censure on the atheistical principles it contains." Webster wrote sadly:

"No man on earth . . . had so large a share of my affection . . . until you renounced the religion which you once preached & I believe."[38] Though reproachful, Webster retained enough "affection" to suggest spelling changes for later editions of the *The Columbiad* and periodically asked him to send him foreign-language books to use in his lexicographical studies. Barlow's casual attitude toward religion was well known to his contemporaries. Two decades later, William Lee, writing to his daughter from Washington, remarked on a recent arrival of Episcopalian clergymen bent on establishing a theological seminary in the nation's capital to offset the recent consecration of a Unitarian church. The clerics, he wrote, were scheduled to dine tomorrow with the British minister "when I am sure the corkscrew will be in greater demand than the prayer book. But I must stop lest your mother should call me a pupil of Barlow's."[39]

Not surprisingly, Ruth ardently defended her husband against his critics, reacting angrily to the political animosity directed against him. To a friend in Bordeaux in the spring of 1801, she wrote: "You see how they vilify & abuse my husband . . . for supposed crimes in Politicks. I hate the mischief-making word . . . it serves only to blacken characters, separate friends & ruin families."[40] However heartfelt her outrage, Ruth must have realized that her husband was no innocent bystander in the partisan wars of the day and that his critics saw themselves as returning fire for fire. Barlow, for his part, gratefully acknowledged her unwavering loyalty, the one constant in his public life.

In their private lives, their correspondence revealed a growing closeness, especially during Barlow's long absence in Algiers. Their letters, playfully loving at first, gradually took on a sad but stoic tone. While he was still awaiting passage from Marseille in January 1796, Ruth enjoined him to "let me know all your plans & feelings, never conceal anything from me, not even your amours," toward which she promised, "I will be indulgent & only require you love me best when with me."[41] As time went on, she wrote mostly about her daily routine: morning rides in the park, afternoon French lessons, and evenings spent entertaining guests or dining out. She insisted they put her French lessons to good use and write to each other in the "language of love." Within a year she was wielding the subjunctive mood with practiced ease. Breaking the routine of her first year alone, she mentioned attending the Fourth of July bash the Monroes put on for 150 guests and in December reported a welcome visit from

Pierre Skjoldebrand, then en route to England. She chuckled at her husband's recklessness in exposing her to "so dangerous a friend [and] one of the most handsome men I have ever seen." He need not fear a rival for her affections, however. She appreciated Skjoldebrand's obvious fondness for her husband, no less his assurances that Barlow himself was safe from "amours" in a place where the veil put most women beyond temptation.[42]

On learning of the Algerian captives landing at Marseille, Ruth had reason to hope he would complete the Tunisian treaty before winter. The strain of separation was beginning to tell. "Haven't we made enough sacrifices for our country?" she wrote in August but then apologized for her impatience. Lonely but supportive, she insisted he stay in North Africa until he had completed his mission. She admired his sense of obligation under trying circumstances. "You have much more to complain of than I, in that barbarous country."[43] She also knew her husband's rewards were uncertain. In November she quoted Monroe as saying "everyone owes you" but not to expect recognition from an ungrateful public. Her husband, Monroe had told her, could at least take solace in having "done some good for humanity."[44]

Ruth was close to despair when the winter of 1796–97 brought longer intervals between letters. On February 12 she wrote of having received his of November 20, which promised that, pending the arrival of the Tunisian treaty, he would sail for home within twenty-five days. She had not heard from him since. Nearly three months had passed. "Where have you gone?" she wrote, "I have a strong presentiment that I will never see you again," adding that she was not sure she could survive without him. Still, not wanting to alarm him, she apologized for her anxiety, assured him she was in good health and that everyone was treating her kindly. A month later, in March, having learned of the delays, she still feared he might spend the rest of his life in Algiers. "I see no end to this terrible mission," she wrote, though, on the lighter side, she laughed at his account of having returned painfully saddle-sore from a three-day boar hunt with the dey. "I know well that you are bad rider." In April she promised that if she ever got him back, he would never again leave without her. Next time, she vowed, she would follow him everywhere and "brave all dangers."[45]

One of those dangers they both knew was her uncertain health, a factor that always figured in their letters. Unlike her robust husband, Ruth periodically suffered from an array of unspecified illnesses and at some point contracted a persistent case of benign genital tumors. Barlow seldom referred to this affliction by name, but their hope for a cure appears subliminally in the letters they exchanged whenever she was "taking the waters." Over all, the evidence suggests that although Ruth was often sickly, she was seldom seriously ill, her symptoms fleeting and worse in the spring than at other times, suggesting at least a seasonal allergy. Whatever indisposition she reported when they were apart, Barlow seemed to assume she would get past it and showed only a modicum of spousal concern. Upbeat by nature, he preferred to picture her as whole and capable. He may also have sensed an attention-getting quality in her down times. Her chronic health problems certainly drew the bemused attention of William Lee. While staying with them in Washington in 1811, Lee wrote his wife in October that Ruth had just recovered from a fever "contrary to all the expectations of her friends. She suffers greatly and is much to be pitied." Then in mid-December: "Our friend, Mrs. Barlow, is about dying," close enough that Lee had learned the terms of her will. But the following March, he reported happily that Ruth's health "to the great astonishment of every one, is perfectly established; so much so that she is now better than ever."[46]

While in Algiers, Barlow left no doubt he believed Ruth healthy enough to look after their financial interests. Where money was concerned, theirs was a fully shared life. And she, in turn, measured up to his expectations. In April 1797, while boarding with Madame Saint-Hilaire on the rue du Bac, she arranged to rent their house on the rue de Vaugirard (for 13,000 livres a year). She also reported on their holdings of government securities, frequently repeating her decision not to sell, even as their value rose. Not always sure of her judgment, in May 1796 she wrote that if he had been in Paris three months earlier, he might have sold out and cleared a fortune.[47] A year later, still worried at possibly having missed an opportunity for profit taking, she admitted having delayed on Daniel Parker's prediction that government stocks would continue to rise.

Meanwhile, she spoke of investing the interest in real estate.[48] As it turned out, their government securities weathered the slump that preceded Napoleon's takeover in 1799 and rose handsomely in value thereafter. Barlow acknowledged her stewardship in a passage of the will he drafted during the plague. He had made her his sole heir, he explained, because her advice over the years had contributed so much to their financial "competency."[49] And when Barlow did die in the winter of 1812, Ruth was well enough to oversee the day-to-day business of the U.S. legation.

9 Keeping Busy in Paris, Riding out the Political Storm at Home

Barlow never thought of himself as a permanent expatriate and often wrote of plans to return home. And yet, for eight years after returning from Algiers, he kept putting it off. At first he found good reason to stay in Paris. Outspokenly critical of what he believed were Philadelphia's misguided policies toward France, he was understandably put out by the venomous hostility of those who questioned his motives. As noted earlier, he believed his erstwhile friends had fecklessly abandoned their republican principles, an apostasy he took to be a harbinger of worse to come.

But even when Jefferson was elected in 1800, an event that promised a more welcoming reception, at least in Republican quarters, his plans for return remained frustrated. In late August 1802 he seemed to have made up his mind, suggesting to Ruth, then at Plombières-les-Bains taking the waters, that if she felt well enough they might move to Bordeaux before winter and sail home in the spring. He was thinking of selling some of their property, he told her, and was tempted by a "friendly & flattering" letter from Jefferson alerting them to the availability of a hilltop property in the District of Columbia. Perhaps he should ask the president to buy it for them if it was not too expensive. On the other hand, he wanted her to stay at the spa long enough to effect a cure, perhaps until October. Whenever she decided, he would come for her when she called.[1] When Ruth did return to Paris that fall, however, her continuing ill health decided the matter. As he explained to Oliver Wolcott, he felt she was not up to a sea voyage.[2]

Having already put their house on the market, he must have felt some chagrin. Indeed, as early as September 1801 he had identified a potential buyer, a nibble that gave him a certain prideful opportunity to describe the property. He did so in terms that left no doubt he expected it to fetch a good price. It was, he wrote "the best built hotel [town house] in Paris, and one of the most commodious & elegant." It boasted 140 feet of frontage on the rue de Vaugirard and had an acre of garden in back planted with three hundred fruit trees. A visitor approaching the main building would pass through an arched gate into an enclosed courtyard flanked by stables (capacious enough to house twelve horses and five carriages) and enter the building by one of three "superb flights of steps." Above the high-ceilinged drawing rooms on the first floor were twenty-four bedrooms, sixteen with chimneys, and in the cellar enough space to store five hundred casks of wine.[3] If a note of regret crept into this description, Barlow took it for granted that before he and Ruth returned home, they would have to cash in this asset if they expected to live in their accustomed style.

In early 1802, as home buyers failed to come forward, Barlow hit on the idea of touting the property as an investment opportunity, offering title to the buyer in return for an annuity. The buyer he had in mind was Benjamin Jarvis, a wealthy American businessman he had known in Hamburg a decade earlier. "I am going to America early in the spring," he wrote," and I propose to convert the property I have here into Life-rent payable there." If Jarvis obliged him, he could expect to profit from the arrangement in the long run because real properties were currently undervalued, selling at two thirds of their peacetime worth. Such buildings, he told Jarvis, would certainly recover their former market value in the next two years. "If I could wait the two years," he explained, "I would stay & take advantage of this rise, but Mr. Jefferson and his friends are urging me to come home." This last was true, but Barlow's mention of it was surely intended to impress. Meanwhile, he promised not to inflate his asking price and invited Jarvis to come look it over.[4] Six months later, Jarvis having declined, Barlow asked his London banker to advertise it for sale for "only 8000 pounds sterling" and to assure prospective buyers that the property would more than double in value over the next few years.[5] Two years later, Barlow was still in Paris, and by the time he and Ruth finally sailed for home in the summer of 1805, they had decided to keep the house and rent it out. The decision proved felicitous. When he returned as U.S. minister to France in 1811, he and Ruth were glad to settle back into its comfortable and familiar surroundings.[6]

With nothing of importance to challenge him in 1802, Barlow occupied his time puttering around the house, tending his garden, dining out almost every night, and writing letters to Ruth and Fulton, who were spending the summer in each other's company at Plombières-les-Bains, a health spa known for sexual permissiveness and whose thermal baths, not unexpectedly, were believed to facilitate pregnancies. Ostensibly, Ruth was there to avail herself of the curative powers of the baths, and Fulton to keep her entertained while he tested a steamboat model in an artificial pond he had built for the purpose. Whether they also entertained each other sexually, or whether her genital tumors discouraged it, Barlow seemed more concerned with the physical aspects of the "cure" than with their possible intimacy. He urged her to throw as much water "as possible *on to* & *into* the parts affected" and was heartened to learn that her doctor believed this treatment would dissolve the "hard places." She should follow the medic's instructions, and Fulton was to make sure that she did.[7] His own feelings about the relationship surfaced suggestively when, on one occasion, he asked Ruth to "tell Toot I love him more than ever man was loved by man. His goodness to little one will not be forgot. Perhaps I shall owe my wife to him at last."[8] If this passage suggests a complacent or perhaps bisexual relationship, his next letter expressed hope that she and Toot would do nothing "wicked" and that Ruth would be returned to him "cured & fat & handsome."[9] How much of their sex lives was wrapped in fantasy and how much was real remains cloudy. In early June, for example, he recounted a dream in which he saw Ruth asleep. Fulton was also in the dream but, he added, not in her bed.[10]

Was he, perhaps, recalling an earlier scene when Fulton *was* in their bed? They did, after all, have adjoining bedrooms on the rue de Vaugirard. Meanwhile, he warned her not to catch cold from too much bathing and reminded her that too much nocturnal partying had been a major cause of past illnesses. Perhaps she should stay in and have Toot entertain her with "some of his wicked stories."[11]

Whatever triangular sleeping arrangements may have existed, Barlow, the poet, and Fulton, the artist-inventor, were seriously intent on helping each other in their respective enterprises. Fulton, for his part, agreed to illustrate the forthcoming edition of *The Columbiad* and began to send sketches to Paris. In return Barlow did what he could to advance Fulton's latest steamboat project, even making a cross-channel trip that summer to scout out the latest advances in steam engineering. In the long run, neither man quite fulfilled the other's expectations. Barlow ultimately hired a London engraver to illustrate *The Columbiad,* and Fulton would seek more substantial backing than Barlow's resources could supply. For a while at least in the summer of 1802, however, each seemed fully committed to advancing the other's project. Barlow described Fulton's early sketches as "perfect,"[12] but when others failed to arrive in late July, he made no further mention of them. He seemed content to put the illustrations on hold while he dashed off to London to get answers to some of Fulton's questions about cylinders and pistons.

Worried lest the British government still find him undesirable, he took care not to disclose his destination. Should anyone ask about his absence, Parker was to tell them he had gone to Rouen on business. Parker also agreed to look after his house while he was away.[13] Once in London Barlow lost no time in picking the brains of William Chapman, an inventor then working on what would prove to be an unsuccessful rotary steam engine. He relayed enough mechanical data to Fulton to believe that he had been of major assistance and the trip well worthwhile. If Fulton had any further questions, he was to write to Chapman directly.[14] This excursion was not without its perils. Despite his determination to avoid his "democratical friends" lest he draw unfavorable attention from the authorities, government officials did track him down and might have detained him had not the U.S. minister, Rufus King, intervened. Fortunately the British government respected King enough to accept his explanation that Barlow's presence was "of a private & commercial nature." Parenthetically President Jefferson himself valued King highly enough to keep him at his London post until 1803, even though he was a Federalist appointee. Barlow, for his part, was grateful for the minister's cordiality and effective intervention.[15]

His ten days in England energized Barlow to the point of planning out Fulton's next course of action. Eager to offer advice, he urged Fulton to go to England and have Chapman construct a small engine "while you are building a boat of a proportionate size." Once the model tested out, he should take it to the United States for patenting while he ordered a larger engine from England. This progression would allow him to remedy any defects that turned up in the model.[16] Fulton, however, had his own agenda. When the *Clermont* paddled triumphantly up the Hudson five years later, its engine was, in fact, British-built but not by Chapman. Nor was Barlow any longer Fulton's principal backer, having yielded sponsorship to Chancellor Robert R. Livingston, then U.S. minister to France. Apparently, Livingston had first noticed Fulton's genius when the latter built and successfully demonstrated a submarine in the Seine in 1800.

Though fascinated by the so-called plunging boat, the chancellor was far more interested in exploiting Fulton's technical know-how to develop the commercial potential of surface steam power.[17] The result of their collaboration would change the face of waterborne commerce. Fulton's role in this breakthrough was critical, though often misconstrued. He did not invent the first steam engine or the first boat powered by steam, but he was the first to adapt one to the other in ways that made steamboats reliably functional and commercially profitable.

Barlow managed fairly well to conceal his hurt at losing his place as mentor and benefactor; he knew Fulton needed the kind of backing that only a person of Livingston's wealth and political clout could provide. Acquiring patents and monopoly rights were better left to the chancellor's devising. Barlow did, however, play a small part in bringing the two men together. Wary at first, he wrote Fulton that Livingston's assistance in New York "would be powerful, but," he cautioned, "I would not hand too much to him."[18] Two weeks later, however, his doubts resolved, he risked showing Livingston a memorandum Fulton had written describing his work, only to learn that the chancellor had already written its author. What remained was to assure his young friend that Livingston would treat him fairly. "There is no danger of his trying to do the thing without you. . . . He has no tho'ts of it." Rather, he worried about some of the technical problems he knew Fulton faced. For example, he shared Livingston's anxiety that an engine having vertically-placed pistons might pound the bottom out of its carrier. From what Barlow knew about steam engines—and by this time he had acquired a good deal of technical knowledge—he agreed that "it is probably best to lay it horizontal," adding that Livingston's fears about "the strain on the boat from the up & down stroke are not without foundation."[19] As it turned out, the *Clermont*'s reinforced bottom easily withstood the pounding of vertical pistons.

With Europe briefly at peace after 1802, Barlow busied himself with various commercial enterprises and flirted briefly with a potential arms deal. From William Lee, then visiting from his post in Bordeaux, he learned that the Virginia legislature had recently authorized its new governor, his old friend James Monroe, to look into the purchase of French arms. At Lee's urging and hoping "to be useful to our country," Barlow wrote him that Lee could handle the contract negotiations with the French government, and he would use his own influence to secure the necessary export licenses. He foresaw little difficulty at his end. French arms makers, caught by the sudden outbreak of peace, were eager to open new outlets. The government would almost certainly oblige them. And because he still planned to return to the United States shortly, he told Monroe he would be glad to bring samples of the military hardware for inspection. Three days later, he tendered a similar offer to Secretary of War Henry Dearborn, vouching for Lee's ability to obtain any quantity of French weaponry and offering to bring samples for field testing.[20] Whatever became of this proposal, his later correspondence made no mention of it. Nor would he leave Paris for another three years.

Much of Barlow's turn-of-the-century correspondence alluded to renewed ventures in the import-export trade, although the specifics are hard to come by. Some of these letters spoke of money owed him by various failed entrepreneurs and told of his efforts to collect. Though usually hardheaded in such matters, he sometimes expressed sympathy for hapless debtors, as in the case of a man named Thomas Dabney who owed him more than $8,000, money he needed to make the final payment on his house on Vaugiraud. Of Dabney he wrote, "No man ought to be distressed beyond measure for debts he cannot pay, altho he may have been imprudent & even blamable in contracting them." When Dabney fled to Virginia in early 1803, Barlow favored him with a signed certificate that he hoped would help him "take advantage of the bankruptcy laws" in the United States. With his own financial fortunes on the rise, he showed only a mild interest in how much he would get from the sale of Dabney's assets.[21] Other letters of this period suggest that he also tried to protect the financial interests of his friends and associates, warning fellow creditors to take whatever legal action they must to prevent others from pressing claims ahead of theirs.

During these last few years in Europe, Barlow watched the world scene with measures of hope and despair. Napoleon's rise to power, though regrettable, he believed a passing phenomenon, a retrograde blip in humanity's march toward a more rationally ordered future. Like many of the Enlightenment era, he believed that social and political norms would inevitably change for the better, despite periodic setbacks. Napoleon's obsession with military glory had "revived the ideas of false gods which were losing ground very fast, before he came up." But ultimately "moral science" or "the habit of right reasoning" would prevail, he was sure.[22]

Meanwhile, he heaped scorn on the manifestations of Napoleonic idolatry. In August 1802 he wrote Ruth that Paris was celebrating the first consul's birthday: "The bells are ringing & cannon firing ever since sunrise, enough to deafen one [and] more powder burnt than would do to conquer half Europe, & this is to conquer only the French people." The religious overtones of the celebration struck him as particularly specious. Noting that a "mameluke" would be baptized at Notre Dame later that day, he allowed that if Min, their own small dog, "was not a Christian already, I would have him baptized as I have no other offering to make to show my zeal for the cause." Somewhat ambiguously, he added, "this poor Christianity is falling into contempt here faster than ever."[23] As one whose belief system was shaky at best, Barlow doubtless perceived the decline in Christian observances as a welcome harbinger of a more rational world order. Like Jefferson, he too looked to a future that would be hostile "to every tyranny over the mind of man."

For the moment, it was the future of Louisiana that drew his uneasy fascination. Before Livingston and Monroe managed to negotiate the purchase, he worried lest France, then in the process of recovering that territory from Spain, might try to occupy it. The former Girondin, who himself had once offered to lead a French expeditionary force to Louisiana, now recoiled at the thought of a French occupation. If they tried, he wrote Ruth, "We shall drive them into the sea," although on reflection he doubted the French could ever establish more than a weak presence there. Earlier French envoys to Philadelphia, men such as Edmond Genêt and Joseph Fauchet, had, for political reasons, exaggerated the support France would find among the Cajun population.[24] The risks of a French takeover were minimal. But like others, once the purchase was accomplished, he fretted lest it open the way to an expansion of domestic slavery. Echoing

Jefferson's misgivings on this score, he wrote prophetically that slavery "may become the greatest scourge to our country." Now, if ever, might be the time to curb it. Mindful of the ordinance that had banned slavery from the Northwest Territory in 1787, he asked Wolcott whether Congress could not also keep it out of Louisiana, hopefully as a step toward "extirpating" the slave system altogether. Congress would do well, he wrote, to seize the opportunity to banish "by gentle & easy means a most alarming calamity from a great portion of the south," adding philosophically that in the long run "a race of hereditary masters cannot be a race of republicans or of just men."[25]

His antipathy toward slavery reignited when the French legislature in the spring of 1802 relegalized it in Saint-Domingue, in part to get a handle on the rebellion French troops there had failed to put down. As Barlow observed heatedly, some European nations and even some of the United States had refused to outlaw slavery, "but no legislative Body, till the 10th year of the French republic, has outraged human nature so far as to make a law to establish it."[26] Part of the government's rationale, he scoffed, was that French colonies needed a reliable workforce—that "without slavery no colonies, without colonies no navy, no commerce." This was preposterous, he countered. The United States had no colonies, but its commerce was five times greater than France's "in proportion to our internal wealth," and "we have now more sailors than France has had at any time in 50 years."[27]

For all his professed dislike of slavery, Barlow never saw fit to explain how he and Ruth came to purchase a black couple as house servants during their later years in Washington. This lapse from principle, if hypocritical, at least had a compelling context. Like other wealthy Southern homeowners who needed domestic staff, the Barlows doubtless felt they had no alternative but to use black servants. White hired "help" was hard to come by, as Barlow discovered when he tried to find "a good laboring man" to look after his garden and orchard.

Significantly, perhaps, in casting about for a groundskeeper he made clear in a letter to his nephew Stephen that he did not want to employ a "negro" for outdoor work.[28] Whether he hoped this distinction would let him escape the appearance of being a prototypical slave owner, historians agree that house slaves generally led easier lives than those in the field. And one can suppose that, given his humanitarian impulses, Barlow was an easy master. At least he never complained of disciplinary problems and, to his credit, provided for the couple's eventual emancipation. In the summer of 1811, shortly before he returned to France, he sold thirty-six-year-old Richard and thirty-year-old Betsy for $400 to a man named Joseph Wheaton, who by the terms of the sale was obliged to free them at the end of six years, contingent on their "diligence."[29]

Suffice it to say that in the days before the antislavery debate heated up, emancipation was still socially acceptable. Barlow's decision and the terms he imposed were unexceptional.

10 Home at Last: Touting a National Institution of Learning

Sailing for home in the summer of 1805, Barlow could look back with greatest satisfaction on his treaties with the Barbary powers. And for a while at least, the results of his handiwork bore up. It helped that in June 1797 a New Hampshire shipyard launched the thirty-six-gun frigate he had promised the dey of Algiers. Christened the *Crescent*, the gift so pleased the regent that he asked to purchase two more American-built vessels, a request the administration blessed with its approval to show its appreciation for the dey's assisting Barlow during his negotiations with Tunis and Tripoli. Thereafter, maintaining good relations with the Barbary states fell largely to Richard O'Brien, once Barlow's most trusted colleague.

O'Brien arrived in Algiers aboard the *Crescent* in January 1798, bearing the sweeping titles of consul to Algiers and consul general to all the Barbary states. Unfortunately, the old dey died in April, succeeded by a regent whose extortionate demands O'Brien fended off as best he could. At considerable additional expense, he managed to keep the peace. Not so in the case of Tripoli where the newly made consul, James Cathcart, a not-so-well-favored Barlow associate, fought a losing battle against that bey's equally extortionate demands. Cathcart's mission ended when Tripoli declared war on the United States in 1801. Thereafter, relations with the Barbary powers remained turbulent until after the War of 1812, finally sinking to insignificance in 1816 when an Anglo-Dutch naval expedition effectively ended piracy in the Mediterranean with a bombardment that destroyed both Algiers's port facilities and its corsair fleet. Tunis and Tripoli got the message. Throughout these years, the young U.S. Navy played a supporting, sometimes a central, role in bringing a final solution to the Barbary problem.[1]

One item of unfinished business Barlow brought back from Europe was the pending publication of *The Columbiad*, his much-worked-over sequel to *The Vision of Columbus,* soon to be published, first in Philadelphia in 1807, two years later in England, and posthumously in Paris in 1813.[2] Like *The Vision, The Columbiad* has won few admirers. Still, the University of Tennessee Press in 2007 published a full-length study titled *Joel Barlow's* Columbiad*: A Bicentennial Reading*. Summarizing its theme, the author, Steven Blakemore, admits that "history has not been kind to Barlow's work," that it had too many "obscure references and allusions . . . to individuals and characters that only a select few would know or care about." Blakemore insists, however, that *The Columbiad* "engages the core issues and strategies of national self-definition and the creation of a vital republican culture." Barlow would have been pleased. For recognition during his lifetime, however, he had to settle for the likelihood that the honorary degree the University of Georgia awarded him in 1809 was partly to thank him for sending a copy to its president, Josiah Meigs.[3] Still, a ripple effect appears from time to time. Barlow's last "vision" in *The Columbiad*, because it prophesied universal peace, reportedly attracted the attention of French prime minister Georges Clemenceau, who proposed raising a monument to Barlow for having foreseen the creation of the League of Nations.[4]

Barlow also left in France a host of friends and associates. Some, like James Swan, he may have visited in prison when he returned. Swan had refused on principle to pay a relatively small debt and had been sent to Sainte-Pélagie Prison in 1808 where he remained for twenty-two years. Family lore suggests his incarceration may not have been particularly stressful. Reportedly, his wife sent him enough money "to live in a handsomely furnished apartment and give dinner parties in prison to his friends."[5] Having dined with Swan when he was a free man, Barlow doubtless dined with him again.

Others, like Fulwar Skipwith, would not be in Paris when he returned. The longtime U.S. consul left his post in 1809 to join the "revolution" against the Spanish regime in West Florida. There he would become governor of the territory until Madison annexed it by proclamation in 1812. Looking back on his dealings with Skipwith, Barlow would recall gratefully the consul's help in expediting his return from quarantine at a time when Americans were not welcome in the French capital. Nor would he forget that, with the onset of the Quasi-War, Skipwith had joined him in cosigning a memorandum urging the

Directory to end French privateering. Politically congenial, they had also shared an active social life. During Ruth's long "cure" at Plombières-les-Bains, Barlow told of visiting the consul's "new country house," half a mile beyond Montmartre, and later serving as a witness at Skipwith's wedding. Obviously on terms of easy familiarity with the couple, Barlow had teased the bride about her morning sickness, allowing that she should have "chosen a wise man like me." All this to Ruth in the long summer of 1802.[6]

Two others left behind, Robert Fulton and William Lee, ultimately followed the Barlows back to the United States. After spending three years in England, Fulton arrived in New York in late 1806, where he was greeted with considerable acclaim, and shortly thereafter visited the Barlows at their temporary residence in Philadelphia. Barlow at the time was nudging his publisher to get *The Columbiad* into print but on Fulton's arrival dropped everything to accompany him on a steamboat-related mission to Washington. There, it appears, Barlow had no difficulty persuading Secretary of War Dearborn to order an army survey of currents in the Mississippi with a view to determining the river's potential for upstream traffic.[7] While in Washington he also looked over the nearby hilltop estate known as Belair, the property Jefferson had mentioned in an earlier letter and which Barlow subsequently bought and renamed Kalorama. For all their frequent contacts thereafter, Fulton's most recent biographer finds a growing rift in the relationship. Cynthia Philip remarks pointedly that Barlow neither attended the *Clermont*'s historic passage in 1807 nor congratulated Fulton on his achievement.[8] She ascribes some of the cooling to Barlow's envy at Livingston's primacy in Fulton's steamboat enterprises. But she also finds the Barlows unhappy at the prospect of Fulton's drifting away from their supposed ménage à trois. They took it hard, for example, when Fulton, writing from England, half-jokingly threatened to stay there and marry a rich English widow.[9] Good feelings were restored when Fulton on his return married Livingston's niece, Harriet, in early 1808. The Barlows promptly invited the couple to stay with them at Kalorama, a visit that lasted until they moved back to New York less than a year later, she to be near her family and he closer to his center of operations.[10] That Harriet gave birth to the first of their four children while at Kalorama makes it unlikely that whatever threesome may have existed earlier became a foursome.

William Lee returned in 1810, leaving wife and children in Bordeaux and promptly moved into Kalorama where he stayed for almost a year. When Madison named Barlow minister to France, Lee accompanied him as secretary of legation. His long-standing ties with the Barlows dated from 1797 when he first arrived in France as a "commission agent" for the Boston firm of Lyman and Williams. By chance, he stayed briefly at Madame Saint-Hilaire's *pension* on the rue du Bac where in his diary he described one of his fellow "inmates," Ruth Barlow, as "a very amiable woman, wife of Mr. J. Barlow, now negotiating our treaty with Algiers."[11] Except for the misunderstanding noted earlier, acquaintance soon ripened into a friendship so close that Lee and his wife Susan named one of their sons William Barlow Lee. When six-year-old William stayed in Paris with his father in 1811, Barlow talked about him so fondly that Lee wrote Susan, "You would have thought it was Barlow's child instead of mine."[12]

And why no children of their own? Ruth's delicate health, of course, offers the readiest explanation. Or, early in their marriage, they may have decided to postpone starting a family lest they fail to reach a level of socioeconomic security that would assure upward mobility for any offspring. Barlow never forgot that he was the only one of his siblings to earn a college degree and thereby escape a life of manual labor. In the letter warning Fulton not to marry his rich English widow, he recalled that if he and Ruth had had children when they were "young and poor, they might have been brought up to labor,"[13] a reminder that the threat of poverty had hung over them for a long time. He had, after all, spent more than a decade groping for gainful employment—not perhaps as a part-time preacher, but surely as a publisher, lawyer, and land salesman—and had only attained a comfortable living as a cargo broker in 1793 and 1794. By this time, Ruth, close to forty, may have been beyond childbearing. Whatever the explanation, Barlow apparently had no regrets or managed to suppress them. In that same letter to Fulton, he expressed relief, perhaps genuine, at having escaped the perils of parenthood. If Fulton's intended marriage were to produce children, he warned, "daughters will create anxiety to yourself & wife during the whole course of their dependence . . . and sons of the rich inevitably disgrace their parents." For a man who had finally won a secure place in society after years of fleeing the farm, so to speak, he may have found consolation enough in playing uncle to a six-year-old.

Thomas Jefferson was halfway through his second term when Barlow joined the capital's Republican elite. From his vantage at Kalorama, where the nation's power brokers often met to discuss the issues of the day, he enjoyed a wide-angle view of the Republican Party's early years in power, savoring its popularity after the Louisiana Purchase and sharing its satisfaction at the demise of the Federalist Party. Their political opponents, Jefferson had confided earlier, were no longer even a "respectable minority," but rather "the bitterest remains of the cup of federalism, rendered desperate & furious by despair." Though gratified at the time, Jefferson was wise enough to foresee and accept the likelihood of future partisan division, when he noted philosophically, "We shall now be so strong that we shall certainly split again." Barlow, too, understood the recurrent nature of political divisiveness and like Jefferson believed it a sign of healthy democracy.[14] What more immediately concerned him were the challenges the president and his party faced in the realm of foreign affairs. War in Europe was once more taking a toll of American shipping and threatening the nation's ability to remain neutral. By the time Barlow was called back to public service in 1811, Jefferson had left James Madison a legacy of failed efforts to curb the depredations of the belligerents. War with Britain lay in the near future, and war with France was a possibility that would send Barlow back to Paris.

Meanwhile, on the home front, Jefferson and Barlow hoped to harness each other's talents to advance projects close to their hearts and for which each seemed well fitted to help the other. Put simply, Jefferson wanted Barlow to write a "Republican" history of the late and unlamented Federalist decade. Barlow, for his part, hoped the president could help him shepherd a bill through Congress that would fulfill his dream of establishing a great national institution of learning. Jefferson's motives were purely partisan, Barlow's ambitiously nationalistic.

As early as 1802, Jefferson had urged Barlow to come home and write a history that would offset the "electioneering purposes" he was sure would infuse John Marshall's impending publication of his *Life of Washington.* Convinced of Marshall's partisan bias, he wrote that he and Madison were counting on Barlow to "point out the perversions of the truth necessary to be rectified." And as enticement, Jefferson painted a welcoming picture of life in the new capital.

Washington, he wrote, was a fine place to live and do research. "I do not think you could do better than to fix here for awhile." Moreover, only in Washington could a historian gather the "verbal communications," known today as oral history, vital to the enterprise. Jefferson was persistent. Two years later, noting that Federalism was in "its last agonies," he wrote, "we want nothing now but for you to come write its history." Marshall's forthcoming book, he predicted, will be "a libel on republicanism under the mask of a history of Gen'l Washington. The antidote is reserved for you."[15]

Fortunately for the profession, Barlow managed to evade Jefferson's request. Perhaps he and the president decided that Marshall's *Washington* was not so grossly propagandic as to warrant a reply. Or perhaps Barlow foresaw difficulty in depicting events he had only observed from afar. Or, given the heated partisanship of the Federalist era, he may have recalled his earlier decision not to attempt a history of the French Revolution because its events would "scarcely stand a chance of being treated impartially by its friends or enemies."[16] Whatever his reason, historians today can breathe a sigh of relief that their ranks were not joined by a man whose earlier brushes with historiography had consisted largely of parading mythical figures in heroic couplets.

As for Barlow's project, even before settling in Washington he had begun to focus his energies on winning support for the establishment of a national university. Having striven to become America's Virgil, he now strove to be its educator-in-chief by producing an all-encompassing and distinctively American blueprint for accumulating and spreading knowledge. Had he been asked to explain his commitment to education, he would surely have pointed to the benefits he had derived from his Yale degree. But his dedication also mirrored a widely held belief that a republic could survive only if its electorate were well-informed. Barlow went a step beyond. Republican leaders, he believed, should commit resources to that end, a point he had made in 1794 when he chided Wolcott that neither the French nor the American republics had articulated a financial commitment to public education.[17]

His hope to enlist Jefferson's support in this project first surfaced in early 1801 when, ruminating over the likely outcome of the contested presidential election, he wondered what changes a Republican administration would bring. Would Jefferson encourage commerce, "the basis of all our happiness," or turn inward to foster internal improvements and domestic manufacture? Though wary of Jefferson's agrarianism, he hoped the new president would continue to advance the spread of learning as he had when he was governor of Virginia.[18]

Barlow could scarcely have found a stauncher ally. No other founding father wrote so often or so passionately about the need for public education. And though the two men had not yet met on this ground, they had known each other since 1788 when, shortly after his arrival in Paris, Barlow had dined with Jefferson at the U.S. legation. Here, as earlier noted, the conversation had focused mainly on the imminent convening of the Estates-General. After Jefferson left to become secretary of state, however, Barlow had kept in touch, sending him copies of his "Advice to the Privileged Orders" and "The Conspiracy of Kings," and later a copy of his controversial letter to Baldwin. Their correspondence was friendly and mutually supportive.

Barlow's plans to establish a full-blown educational system in the United States may have begun to take shape as early as 1798 when he learned from Ira Allen, a founder of the University of Vermont, that his state had set aside lands to support a public school system, including a university. Public instruction, he wrote Allen, offered the best hope for the nation's future, especially "when applied to a new people, where prejudices are not deeply rooted; where most things are yet to create, & few to uncreate." He clearly relished this opportunity to give advice on how to go about laying the foundations and raising the framework. From what he had seen of European universities during his travels, he told Allen, he had found "very little for us to copy . . . and still less in the mode of elementary instruction." He wished Allen had told him more, but whatever Vermont designed, he believed the state should provide the funding and let its university devise curricula for the lower schools. Already, he was addressing the problems of structure, finance, and function that he would soon write into his "Prospectus of a National Institution." Meanwhile, if Allen asked, he would be glad to send a "general plan" to the Vermont board of trustees.[19]

Barlow had barely landed in New York in August 1805 before he set about making contact with Josiah Meigs, the educator he knew best. Congratulating Meigs on the flourishing state of the University of Georgia, he explained that he and Ruth first planned to take a trip through New England, but when they settled in Washington for the winter, he looked forward to hearing more about the university from its cofounder, his brother-in-law Sen. Abraham Baldwin. Addressing Meigs in terms they both understood, he repeated his faith in public education as "the only means of retaining what we have got & of acquiring more of public happiness, liberty & peace."[20]

Late fall 1805 found Barlow, after accompanying Ruth on a tour of New England,[21] flitting between New York, where *The Columbiad* was nearing publication, and Washington, where his "Prospectus" would reach its readers in January 1806. With Congress about to convene, his timing was flawless. Two months later, George Logan of Pennsylvania introduced a bill in the Senate calling for the establishment of a "National Academy." Not surprisingly, the Logan bill followed Barlow's model fairly closely.[22]

Strikingly, what Barlow proposed resembled nothing less than the world's first modern university—or perhaps its first think tank. His plan would bring teachers and scholars together in a single institution, to be located in Washington with branches of learning throughout the country.

To underscore the novelty of his proposal, he pointed out that Europeans had never thought to use their "associations of learned men" as teachers. Neither Britain's Royal Society nor France's National Institute had links to universities. Rather, the powers of Europe had failed to harness the potential of their great thinkers, leaving them instead to muse in solitude. To remedy this oversight, the United States had a splendid opportunity to celebrate its republican inventiveness by bringing together its scholars and teachers in a showcase institution of higher learning. In a ringing tribute to American exceptionalism, he wrote: "Mankind have a right to expect this example from us; we alone are in a situation to hold it up before them; to command their esteem, and perhaps their imitation."[23]

Barlow's institute lacked nothing for inclusiveness. He would have its trustees establish "printing presses, laboratories, libraries and apparatus for the sciences and the arts; and gardens for botany and agricultural experiments." It might even take custody of the military academy, the patent office, and the mint. And while he was at it, he foresaw its printing and distributing "vast quantities" of low-cost primers to elementary schools across the country. In short, he seemed to envision an educational octopus that would wrap its benign tentacles around nearly every intellectual and practical aspect of daily life.[24]

When he came to conceptualizing the relationship between scholars and teachers, he pictured a subordinate role for the professoriat. Rather, it was the institute's scholars, acting as trustees, who would dominate the operation, presumably providing fodder for professorial lecturers who, in turn, would carry their newfound wisdom to the far corners of the republic.[25] Understandably, for reasons of time and place, he did not foresee the possibility that university teachers might engage in research or even imagine that someday their very livelihood would depend on the academic dictum of "publish or perish." Moreover, by authorizing the institute's chancellor to hire and fire faculty at will, he shifted far to the future any notions of faculty tenure or self-governance.

As for cost factors, he hoped to head off economy-minded congressmen by voicing certainty that "opulent" citizens who, like members of Congress, cared for "the nation's unity and welfare" would surely step forward to endow the institute and cover its operating expenses. Also on the side of economy, he reminded members that they need pay only the salaries of the professors. Prestige and honor would adequately compensate the scholars. Moreover, he personally would be satisfied with a small beginning. Congress, he observed, need not carry his "system . . . into immediate practice in all its parts." He asked only that it grant a charter. The institute's trustees, once they had a clearly defined mission, could begin to tap financial backers. And as an enticement not to dawdle, he suggested the trustees might recruit "several men of science "in time to hold the institute's first lecture series the following winter.[26]

The Logan bill, when it appeared in print in March 1806, lacked the finer points of Barlow's advocacy but retained the central idea of combining scholars and teachers, albeit with a start-up faculty of only three. Mostly the bill altered his terminology. It called for a "national academy" instead of a "national institute" and substituted the phrase "members" for Barlow's "trustees." Otherwise the bill pretty much followed his design: the president was to appoint the academy's first chancellor and the first cadre of its fifteen "members," who would also serve as a "board of visitors" and elect future chancellors, as well as more visitor-members. Like Barlow's proposal, the bill gave the board control of the academy's funds, permission to appoint additional faculty, and the authority, shared with the chancellor, to fire them. Again following Barlow's design, faculty would be appointed in "the arts, sciences, literature, and agriculture," and the board could establish "printing presses, libraries and laboratories." Perhaps recalling Washington's suggestion a decade earlier, the bill also visualized the academy becoming the forerunner of a more traditional university with which it would coexist.[27]

Much to Barlow's disappointment, and despite President Jefferson's putting in a good word, the Senate bill died obscurely in a House committee sometime in the spring of 1807. Earlier, in his annual message, the president had tried to keep it alive. Alluding to "the present consideration of a national establishment for education," he suggested that if financing were a problem, Congress might endow it with a "donation of public lands."[28] This suggestion, though it foreshadowed the land-grant colleges of the future, fell on deaf ears. All things considered, congressional inaction was not surprising. For one, Jefferson's Republican followers were grimly attached to a small-government philosophy and frowned on nearly every item of public expenditure. They had, after all, won office at least in part by denouncing their Federalist predecessors as tax-and-spenders. Perhaps more importantly, by early 1807 Congress was distracted by a series of foreign policy crises brought on by mounting seizures of American shipping. This was the year its members would end by enacting Jefferson's desperate counterstroke, the soon famous embargo. In this darkening scene, agenda items of lesser importance stood little chance of passing.

Barlow as educator also took a personal interest in adding to the store of science and technology. Like many of his contemporaries, he felt an obligation to make known to the scientific community whatever he discovered by way of useful knowledge. Accordingly he kept an eye peeled during his travels for anything new or different his countrymen might use to their advantage. While in Algiers, for example, he speculated that American farmers might profit from planting a North African variety of wheat. Because it fetched a high price in Europe, he believed it might be of "superior quality." Suiting action to thought, he asked Captain O'Brien to deliver "five measures of Barbary wheat" to the Agricultural Society next time he put in to Philadelphia. Significantly, because he knew that exotic plants could produce unintended mischief, he warned the society to cull out whatever "pernicious" weed seeds the shipment might contain.[29] And later, during a lull in his mission to Paris, he took time to send Wolcott a packet of indigo seeds, noting vaguely that the French seemed to like them. And in the same letter he promised to send a new machine called a "stocking loom."[30] In this instance, whether he realized it, he was contributing in a small way to the transatlantic "technology transfer" that would jump-start American industry.

Among the sciences, Barlow foresaw an especially bright future in the study of minerals. Just where such studies might lead seemed to elude him, but in 1801 he promised Josiah Meigs he would bring him "a little cabinet of lithology."[31]

He was proud enough of his rock collection to mention it in a letter to Meigs's brother, Col. Jonathan Meigs, a month later. Addressing the latter as an "old revolutionary acquaintance" and knowing him to have figured prominently in western settlements, he asked the colonel to look after any of his nephews who might come to take up the Ohio Company lands he still owned. These were Aaron's sons, he explained, Aaron having died and their property in Connecticut lost to debt. At this point, perhaps to curry the colonel's favor, he mentioned having collected "a cabinet of minerals for his brother and his university."[32] Presumably, this collection of minerals, along with a copy of *The Columbiad* and a set of French literary classics, reached the University of Georgia sometime after the Barlows returned home.[33]

If Barlow found satisfaction in contributing to the natural sciences, the poet in him found inspiration there as well. His notebook of 1802 shows him groping for updated similes and metaphors. From his familiarity with electrical experiments, for example, he wondered what human scenario might be compared to "the frog tortured after death by galvanizing?" Or what "moral" comparisons he might make between the production of maple and cane sugar: "the one made by freemen, the other by slaves—the one in winter, the other in summer." Nor among his jottings could he resist coining new hyphenated adjectives, splices such as "heaven-reflecting flood," "wine-crested hills," and "snow-fed torrents." His quest for poetic imagery seldom rested.

11 Nurturing Nephews, Defending a President

Barlow's life at Kalorama, except for its proximity to the nation's political center, did little at first to prepare him for his forthcoming mission to France. His correspondence touched occasionally on the administration's economic warfare against the offending belligerents, but most of it dwelt on family matters, beginning with news of his older brother's death, which had reached him in Paris in 1800. Aaron Jr., who brought the news, confirmed the worst: the family's iron works, indeed all of his father's property, had been lost to creditors.

Barlow's immediate response was to offer Aaron's sons the only asset he could readily lay hands on—his lands in the Ohio Valley.[1] To that end he notified the Ohio Company directors that he was vesting power of attorney in his five oldest nephews and asked that they be furnished with all the "deeds & documents" relating to his three shares. As nearly as can be determined, none of Aaron's sons took up the offer, perhaps because, despite his apparent generosity, Barlow intended to keep the title. As he explained to the company directors, he planned to sell the lands later, either to the nephews or other buyers.[2] To Stephen he explained regretfully that he wished he could have made an outright gift, "but I am too poor for that. I am not in any profitable business & never shall be. Indeed I never had a talent for getting money. And I must depend in some measure on the sales of those lands." Whatever half-truths leaked out of this explanation (Barlow was far from poor by that day's standards), he might be forgiven for not wanting to relinquish a potentially valuable asset. Still, the opportunities of the frontier intrigued him. In the same letter, he suggested to Stephen, whose law practice was languishing, that he might find the Ohio Valley a better place to hang his shingle than Fairfield, Connecticut.[3]

On his return from Europe, Barlow took particular pains to advance Stephen's career prospects, partly out of a sense of obligation he felt for Aaron's youngest son, Thomas, barely a teenager, whom Stephen had taken under his wing. Caring for Thomas's welfare, even by proxy, roused paternal instincts he clearly relished. His first order of business, however, was to test his connections in high places to see if he could improve Stephen's situation. Kalorama was, after all, only "a short half mile from the President's house." Unfortunately, his earliest lobbying effort—an attempt to get his nephew a customs house job—ran afoul of Jefferson's high-minded decision, initially at least, not to remove federal office-holders except for gross misconduct. He had discussed other appointive offices with the president, he told Stephen, but even if a vacancy fell open, he believed his nephew would be thought too young to qualify.[4] Little more than year later, however, he succeeded in persuading Postmaster General Gideon Granger to give his nephew a postmastership in Saugatuck, Connecticut.[5]

By this time Barlow had become obsessed with grooming thirteen-year old Thomas for a life of upward mobility. His questions and advisories to Stephen were endless. Was Tommy being well schooled? Did he mind his manners? Did he speak grammatically? He paused only occasionally to apologize for doubting that Tom had mastered these "accomplishments," because he was sure Stephen already knew their value.[6] After nearly four years of sending books, reading lists, and exhortations—along with the occasional cash donation—Barlow turned to the serious matter of selecting a college. He had some fairly strong opinions on the subject. "I have been thinking of Dartmouth," he wrote Stephen in March 1808. "There is none this way worth a farthing & those your way are not much better—Princeton, Newhaven & Cambridge are governed by tories—[but] I should prefer Newhaven among those three."[7] With Yale the final choice, he enjoined Stephen to "wind up" Tom's ambition to make sure he became "a superior scholar . . . and a gentleman in his manners & sentiments & language." And to make sure Tom met the "right people" in New Haven, he furnished him with letters of introduction; Yale President Timothy Dwight was the exception. "As for their President," he told Stephen, "I have nothing to say to him. I regret indeed that such a bigot & tory should be placed at the head of such an important school, but," he cautioned, "it is best not to give Tom any unfavorable ideas of him . . . for on some accounts he is doubtless respectable."[8] Partisan passions died hard.

Some months earlier, hoping to improve on Stephen's postmastership, Barlow suggested he put in a bid to build some of Jefferson's famous gunboats. If what he had learned was reliable, building gunboats would yield a handsome profit. Against the government's contract price of $4,000, a friend had estimated construction costs at $3,280. He was not sure, however, whether this figure factored in "contingency" costs for anchors and spars. In the end, Barlow's proposal came too late. In a follow-up letter, he said he "should have struck a month sooner." To be sure, Congress had authorized construction of 188 gunboats, but only 100 contracts had been let, and all had been spoken for. Moreover, Connecticut already had its share. Ten were scheduled to be built at Middletown, another four or five at Norwich. But if bids were put out for the remaining 88, he would let Stephen know.[9]

Mulling over other entrepreneurial possibilities, Barlow accurately prophesied the rise of New England's shoe industry but fell short in predicting the length of Jefferson's embargo. Writing in January 1808, he assured Stephen, "the embargo of course cannot last a great while [it would last more than a year], but war or no war there are always some supplies wanted for troops. I should suppose that in a country full of cattle and hides like yours, shoes & boots could be made cheap, belts & cartridge boxes, perhaps woolen stockings, salted beef & pork, &c. I mention these things at hazard for you to think of, should occasion call for any thing that you can furnish."[10] Whether Barlow intended to back any of these enterprises with hard cash, he expected a return on his investments. As payback for shouldering the bulk of Tom's tuition, for example, he expected to hear regular progress reports from Yale. When Tom's correspondence lagged, he supposed his nephew had "grown lazy . . . which is a bad sign." He wondered if his nephew was becoming "an indifferent scholar" but asked Stephen not to tell him he said so. "It is impossible that a father should be more anxious for his prosperity than I am."[11] A year later he told Stephen he would continue to pay for Tom's tuition, "always provided that he behaves well." He thought highly of his nephew's writing style—just wished he would write more often. In all, Barlow laid out almost a thousand dollars for Tom's college tuition, more than twice what his own had cost, he grumbled. Nor was he altogether enthusiastic about the quality of a Yale education: "I think on the whole it is as good a college as any, & that is not saying much in its favor." And reports he received during Tom's junior year raised suspicions that his nephew was coasting on "a disposition to rely too much on genius & too little upon application," though he admitted that he did not know Tom well enough to judge his character.[12] Whatever doubts he harbored, his nephew dispelled them when in Paris he gratified his uncle by plunging eagerly into the city's educational and social opportunities. "Tom is doing well," Barlow later assured Stephen. "He is steady as a clock and learns well." Besides lessons in dancing, fencing, and French, he was taking courses in chemistry, natural science, and astronomy at three different colleges.[13] Barlow was clearly pleased with this investment.

His relations with Stephen, meanwhile, hit a bump in December 1807, when he asked his nephew to send him a "good laboring man" to look after Kalorama's thirty acres of fields and gardens.[14] When Stephen wrote back that he had identified a hard worker named Adams, Barlow told him to put the man under contract for a $100 a year and "send him on." Before this instruction reached Saugatuck, however, Adams had left for Washington without a contract. Barlow was chagrined. Without an agreement on wages, he chided Stephen, he would be at the man's mercy. He foresaw Adams playing the "old Yankee trick of refusing to put a price on what we have to sell" as in "What will you take for your horse? I don't know. What will you give for it?"[15] Whatever the ultimate wage agreement, Barlow found Adams only moderately satisfactory, "a good fellow to work at common farming," he told Stephen, "but he is a sloven, careless, & not the neat intelligent watchful overseer which I want." He would probably let him go at the end of the year.[16] In a land of opportunity, however, Adams made his own choice. A year or two later he left Kalorama and opened a grocery store near the Navy Yard. His departure, if nothing else, underscored the difficulty of retaining free white labor in the antebellum South. Whether Barlow subsequently hired a black groundskeeper he did not record.

Meanwhile, his tireless efforts to improve Stephen's financial situation finally bore fruit in late 1810. "More lucrative than building all the gunboats in the country," he gushed, were the profits Stephen could earn by placing bank notes among borrowers on the frontier. The Bank of Washington, he explained, "wishes to circulate its notes in the western country, that is, exchange them for other banknotes & specie." As chairman of one of the bank's committees, Barlow had prepared a three-year contract for an agent to place up to a million dollars. With a 2 percent commission "on all the notes he put out," both he and Stephen stood to make a sizable sum. If the bank accepted his proposal, "I shall claim the contract for you & and offer myself as your guarantee, for which," he added, "I should expect a portion of the profits, say a third." He estimated the venture might ultimately clear them as much as $30,000.[17] Three days later, the bank having tentatively approved the contract, he counseled Stephen to move swiftly. If I were you, he wrote, "I should not hesitate an instant." Stephen was perfectly free to say no, of course, "without any regard for my own emolument," insisting that his nephew's best interests were his primary concern. But as a token of support that also enhanced his claim to a share of the profits, he told his nephew that he was prepared to post bond of $40,000. If Stephen accepted, he should take the next stage to Washington. "Then, if all is settled, you can go back to take a few days for the disposal of your affairs, & set off for the grand expedition."[18]

In his enthusiasm, Barlow could hardly have foreseen that the country would soon witness its first major era of wildcat banking, a speculative bubble that would burst in a shower of worthless banknotes in 1819. By that time, fortunately, Stephen Barlow had completed his contract and escaped the consequences.

On learning that the bank directors had adjourned without approving the contract, Stephen postponed his departure. Barlow, however, reassured him that when the directors reconvened, they would raise "no serious objection."[19] He was right. By the end of October, the contract approved, he again urged Stephen to waste no time coming to Washington. The delay, he explained, arose from a quibble over the amount of the bond he should post. Newly set at $80,000, he promised to find a co-guarantor, if necessary. "The sooner you are here, the sooner you will be on your way." And if the agency fell through, he and William Lee would find "another project for you, which would be much better than any thing you can do in Connecticut."[20] Stephen agreed. By late December he was in central Pennsylvania, his financial operations apparently well under way. In the weeks that followed, Barlow kept a watchful eye on his nephew's accounts, dispensed advice, and assured him the bank committee was pleased with his returns.

Over time, however, despite Stephen's substantial remittances, it became clear the directors thought he could do better. In mid-February 1811, responding to Stephen's latest deposit of $2,500, Barlow told him that "this will be somewhat discouraging to our gentlemen" and warned him that his contract "has enemies & its friends are not as sanguine as they were at one time."[21] Office politics being what they often are, Barlow may have worried too much. Just before he sailed for France in August, he wrote Stephen that he had left the directors "in very good humour with you and your affairs." To keep it that way, he identified several directors whose goodwill he should cultivate.[22] Later from Paris he revealed how warily he had moved behind the scenes. As Stephen wound up his final accounts, Barlow instructed him to deposit a quarter of the profits in his account but not tell anyone about the money or his involvement in the agency. He may have feared criticism for having shared in his nephew's commission. His parting advice to Stephen, however, lacked any hint of hypocrisy. He urged his nephew "to be sure to give satisfaction to the board, whatever else you do. I have always found that a reputation for honest honorable inflexible integrity is a fortune, & a fortune a thousand times more to be relied upon than a great deal of money without it."[23]

Other family matters were more stressful. In March 1807 Barlow was in Georgetown laying the groundwork for the purchase of Kalorama when he learned that Ruth's brother Abraham had died.[24] He stayed in Washington only long enough to arrange for the senator's funeral and file his will for probate, telling Ruth he expected to return to Philadelphia shortly. Added to his keen sense of loss, however, he developed a fever, and a full week passed before he was well enough to head back.[25] Ruth, equally stricken, took to her bed. Her health and state of mind improved considerably, however, when Fulton came down from New York to offer his condolences.[26]

At the other end of the year 1807, Barlow and Noah Webster renewed a correspondence that revealed how tenaciously these two middle-aged nation builders continued to pursue their efforts, each in his own way, to define the new republic. Before the year was out, Barlow would publish *The Columbiad,* his epic poem celebrating America's past, present, and future. And Webster, now selling more than 200,000 copies of his "spelling book" a year, boasted of his progress in adapting the English language to a distinctive American usage. "I have had it in view," he wrote, "to detach this country as much as possible from its dependence on its parent country."[27] True to his word, he would leave his imprint, even if it seemed only to mean that Americans thereafter would spell "flavor" and "candor" without the "u" and music and public without the terminal "k." He later thanked Barlow for having mentioned his dictionary in a postscript to *The Columbiad*, praised the poem's illustrations, but grumbled at its price. He gave no indication that he had read it.[28]

On the Fourth of July 1809, Barlow delivered an oration that proved to be a major highlight of his homecoming years. Hailed by a biographer as "one of the best things he ever wrote,"[29] it was heard by an audience who described themselves as "the Democratic Citizens of the District of Columbia." The published version identified neither where he spoke nor the number of persons who heard him, but the message was vintage Barlow: visionary, patriotic, and relentlessly optimistic.[30]

Thematically he addressed the question of whether "representative democracy on a large scale" could survive as Americans grew in numbers and spread across the continent. He was not the first, of course, to voice concerns as to whether demographic and territorial expansion might adversely affect political institutions. Two decades earlier, James Madison in his "Federalist, No. 10," had weighed the prospect of population growth against the ever-present threat of factional divisions, concluding, however, that a growing population would spawn so many factions that they would cancel out each other's mischief. Or, as Madison put it, "a greater number of citizens and extent of territory . . . [will] render factious combinations less to be dreaded."[31] Barlow, for his part, chose to focus on the centrifugal or separatist forces likely to be unleashed by a rapidly expanding frontier. To keep the union from flying apart, he argued, Congress should take an active role in funding "public improvements and public education." Roads, bridges, and canals, he contended, would not only prosper Americans' commercial activities, but also would "hold them together as one people."[32] If, as anticipated, the U.S. Treasury produced a surplus, he continued, Congress had a grand opportunity to apportion monies to the states, according to population, to build those roads and canals.[33] Again, his proposal was not original. He knew, of course, that Jefferson's signature on the Cumberland Road bill three years earlier had already set a precedent for the federal government's investment in infrastructure. But he also knew that constitutional objections and tightly held purse strings were likely to slow any further investments. To keep up the momentum, he appealed once more to American "exceptionalism," a popular notion then (and still?) that, having sloughed off the corrupting influences of Europe, Americans were capable of greater and nobler achievements. Our federal government, he observed, need not imitate those European monarchs who wasted vast sums on wars and glory. Rather, it stood fair to embrace the splendid alternative of spending its revenues to improve and unify an empire in peace and prosperity. To underscore his argument, he estimated the British government could have built 30,000 miles of canals for what it had spent fighting the American Revolution.[34]

Equally forceful was Barlow's renewed advocacy of publicly funded education, "incontestably one of the first duties of the government." Summarily, he dismissed the often-heard arguments against public funding: "Some say the people have no need of instruction; they already know too much; they cannot all be legislators and judges." Others contend that those who work for a living "need no other knowledge than what is sufficient for that purpose." Or that education is a parental concern, "the state has nothing to do with it." These arguments, he exclaimed, were "preposterous." Why? Because "every citizen is a voter" who must distinguish between the "characters" of the men he elects. Otherwise, "he becomes both an object and an instrument of corruption, . . . an injury to himself and a nuisance to society." Mindful perhaps of how easily his earlier proposal for a "national institution" had been shipwrecked, Barlow hesitated to prescribe the details of a federally funded system or how it might be administered. But he believed it would not be expensive "if properly arranged and wisely conducted."[35] Once again, however, his vision outstripped his times. The land-grant colleges still lay in the future, and local governments would continue to be the sole sponsors of education.

Having painted fair skies for the future (that is, if Congress followed his advice), Barlow felt obliged to call attention to the clouds that gathered over the Atlantic whenever Europe was at war. As long as Americans depended on Europe for manufactures, warring nations would interrupt commerce, their country's "only point of contact [with] the unjust governments of Europe." And because the United States did not yet have sufficient naval force to ward off such predators, it must find "another mode of defense."[36] Seizing the opportunity, Barlow put forward the possibility that Americans might use submarines to defend themselves on the high seas. Not much thought had been given to it, he admitted, but he could not let the moment pass without expressing his "private opinion that the means of submarine attack, invented and proposed by one of our citizens, carries in itself the eventual destruction of naval tyranny." With this bow to Fulton and waxing more eloquent as he drew to a close, he predicted that submarine warfare "might rid the seas of all the buccaneers both great and small that now infest them; it might free mankind from the scourge of naval wars, one of the greatest calamities they now suffer; and to which I see no other end."[37] Nor did he foresee—although it might have occurred to him—that America's enemies, too, might someday discover submarine warfare.

Not until 1811, the year Madison sent him to Paris, did Barlow reveal how closely he had followed the unfolding of foreign policy issues. He made known his familiarity with the details that year when he published *A Review of Robert Smith's Address to the American People,* a rebuttal of Smith's criticism of the Madison administration's policies. Madison had appointed Smith secretary of state at the outset of his administration, hoping to win political favor with his powerful and obstreperous brother, Sen. Samuel Smith of Maryland. Robert, however, proved to be woefully incompetent, reportedly showing so little talent for the business of his office that Madison had to rewrite or at least edit many of his official papers. Worse, Smith was disloyal. He almost certainly leaked confidential cabinet information to his brother's antiadministration forces in Congress, as well as to the British minister in Washington. To be rid of him while allowing him to save face, Madison had offered him the post at St. Petersburg. Smith at first accepted and then declined, perhaps recognizing it as the exile Madison's loyalists hoped it would be. Instead, from retirement he published an *Address to the People of the United States,* a vengeful, second-guessing critique of Madison's recent foreign policy decisions. Barlow's "review" of this tract took it apart piece by piece. In the process, Barlow showed a grasp of foreign policy issues that doubtless commended him for the mission he would soon undertake.[38]

The foreign policy crises that ultimately brought Americans to war with Britain—and near-war with France—had begun shortly before Barlow returned to the United States in the summer of 1805. In May Nelson's defeat of a Franco-Spanish naval squadron at Trafalgar had foreclosed the likelihood that Napoleon could defeat England by invading it. Thereafter, for lack of naval capacity, the French emperor took aim at Britain's vital export trade, hoping to weaken, if not destroy, his enemy's economy by closing the ports of Europe to British commodities. For Britons whose motto was "export or die," Napoleon intended to hasten the latter. Soon known as his "Continental System," such closures, matched by British countermeasures, took a predictable toll in captured American ships and cargoes, and led Congress to enact a series of economic reprisals.

Curiously it was the British who fired the first round—a fact the French often pointed out to American diplomats—when in May 1806 London announced its intention to blockade all of Europe's channel ports between Brest and the Elbe River.[39] Lacking enough warships to interdict so lengthy a stretch of coastline, Fox's Blockade, as it was called, clearly violated the dictum that to be "legal," a blockade must be effective. Napoleon responded to the affront but not immediately. Not until November did the emperor strike back. By this time his victory over Prussia made it feasible for him to contemplate port closures on a continental scale. In a decree issued from Berlin, which only hinted at his larger purpose, Napoleon blithely declared a blockade of the entire British Isles.[40] Although his Berlin Decree appeared to be an absurd gesture of defiance—one paper blockade deserving another—it did provide a pretext for French corsairs to seize American vessels caught entering or exiting British ports. Predictably, American protests began to march in lockstep with the offenses both belligerents were soon committing against the presumed right of neutral vessels to trade in wartime to any port not effectively blockaded.

Retaliatory measures escalated in late 1807. In November a British order-in-council required neutral vessels bound for Europe bearing such "colonial" cargoes as sugar and coffee to stop first at a British port, pay a transit tax, and purchase a license.[41] These levies were intended, in part, to assure that Frenchmen would pay more for these commodities than would Englishmen. Napoleon, now in Milan, responded briskly and on point. He decreed fair prize any vessel that submitted to British search, touched at a British port, or "paid any tax whatsoever to the English Government."[42] Congress, by now thoroughly fed up with shipping losses, passed its memorably famous Embargo Act of 1807, a self-protective lockdown that forbade American vessels to leave port except for coastal trafficking and put the latter under heavy bond to keep them from slipping cargoes across the Atlantic.[43] Combined with an earlier Non-Importation Act leveled against Britain and given the lack of any significant commerce with France, the embargo ostensibly effected a complete trade stoppage. Except, of course, that it leaked, especially when American shipowners managed to warn their captains still at sea not to return. Neither Britain nor France was particularly impressed.

In March 1809 a disillusioned Congress gave James Madison an inaugural do-over when it replaced the Embargo Act with the so-called Non-Intercourse Act, a piece of legislation designed to relieve the distress of American shipowners while retaining the coercive intent of the previous law. The Non-Intercourse Act reopened commercial contacts with all trade partners *except* Britain and France, toward whom the law promised a renewal of commerce if London rescinded its orders-in-council or Napoleon his Berlin and Milan decrees.[44] It soon became apparent, however, that "non-intercourse" posed fewer obstacles to commerce than had the embargo. American shipowners, forbidden to clear for either French or British ports, simply sent their vessels to neutral ports, principally in the Caribbean, where, in effect, they swapped cargoes with their former trade partners. Parenthetically, it might be noted, Britain drew greater benefit from these circuitous transactions because France never had much direct trade with the United States to begin with. Meanwhile, diplomatic probes on both sides of the Atlantic failed to elicit from either belligerent an unconditional willingness to ease its strictures.

In May 1810, after nearly three years of failed experimentation with trade sanctions, Congress abandoned all pretence at activism. It scrapped the Non-Intercourse Act and opened trade with all parties, while challenging the belligerents to take their own initiatives. Macon's Bill No. 2, as it was called, held out the lure that if one belligerent revoked its strictures and the other did not, the United States would reinstate sanctions against the holdout. Madison, for one, hoped each belligerent would view this latest enactment "not as a coercion or a threat to itself, but as a promise of attack on the other."[45] As he waited for either London and Paris to respond, he predicted (correctly) that Napoleon was more likely to take the bait. France, he reasoned, had more to gain from a cutoff of Anglo-American trade, even if poorly enforced, than it would lose from a revocation of the Berlin and Milan decrees. Supporting this likelihood, though unbeknownst to Madison, Napoleon was already preparing to accomplish the purpose of those decrees by instituting a ship-licensing system. At the cost of a modest breach in his Continental System, he began to license French and American carriers to import those commodities France most needed. To keep intact the exclusionary feature of his system, he required incoming carriers to bring with them a French consul's certification that the cargo was not of British origin. Between licensing and certification, the Berlin and Milan decrees were fast becoming superfluous.

Napoleon bore out Madison's prediction when, in August 1810, he ordered his foreign minister, the duc de Cadore, to send a letter to the U.S. minister, John Armstrong, announcing that as of November 1, the Berlin and Milan decrees "will cease to have effect." The Cadore Letter contained two either-or conditions, however. The first was straightforward but unlikely. It required that Britain first agree to renounce its "new principles of blockade"—that is, revoke its orders-in-council. Or, failing that—and here the wording became belligerently Napoleonic—the United States must "cause their rights to be respected by the English."[46] Did this ominous phrase mean that he expected the United States to declare war as well? From Madison's standpoint and on its face, Macon's Bill merely promised no more than to reinstate trade sanctions against Britain. Believing this to be enough to satisfy Napoleon that Americans were causing their rights to be "respected," Madison accepted the terms of the Cadore Letter, and Congress endorsed his acceptance in February 1811 when it reimposed trade sanctions against Britain.

From here on, Madison's problems began to multiply. First, he had to live with Napoleon's refusal to make a formal announcement that his decrees had actually been revoked. This element of uncertainty lingered on into the spring of 1811 and cast doubt on the president's wisdom in having accepted the Cadore Letter in the first place. Second, Madison's critics, Robert Smith among them, pointed out that in his eagerness to accept the Cadore Letter, the president had failed to stipulate that Napoleon restore the American vessels recently detained in Spanish ports under French control.[47]

Writing in Madison's defense, Barlow took obvious delight in picturing Smith as an inconsequential cabinet figure who had a bad memory and couldn't keep his facts straight. Smith, he wrote, "contents himself with the merit of finding out faults when too late to amend them, and foreseeing events after they have happened."[48] But if Barlow relished poking fun at Smith's delusions of certitude, he also felt compelled to address the questions Smith had aimed at Madison's dealings with France—specifically, how to explain Napoleon's refusal to clarify the status of his decrees and why the president, in accepting the Cadore Letter, had neglected to negotiate at least a partial restoration of American property. Barlow tackled the first by asserting a double negative—that is, that Smith had "no evidence . . . that the decrees were not repealed,"[49] implying that Americans must assume that they had been. Mindful perhaps of the weakness in this line of argument, he warned against taking any action that might question Napoleon's compliance. If Congress, for example, now rescinded the sanctions it had levied against Britain, it would "risk national honor by breaking a contract on doubtful ground." Here Barlow adopted Madison's own view that his acceptance of the Cadore Letter constituted a contract that could not be broken without definitive proof that Napoleon had defaulted.[50]

Barlow found it easier to defend the president's apparent negligence in failing to secure the return of vessels recently seized in Spain. Macon's Bill, he pointed out, required only that Napoleon revoke his decrees; it said nothing about restoring captured property. Similarly toward London, Congress had required only that Britain revoke her orders-in-council; it made no reference to restoring American property. From this narrow construction, Barlow took his argument a step further by drawing a distinction between the status of ships captured at sea, clearly in violation of U.S. neutral rights, and those interned after they arrived in French ports. The United States could rightly demand indemnification for violations of its maritime rights, but American vessels detained for violating French domestic law fell into a different category. Their being condemned on arrival surely evinced ill will, he admitted; they might even be the victims of decrees retroactively enforced. But however France chose to treat them was within her sovereign powers. "We might reproach such an exercise of sovereignty," he wrote, but "we could not in strictness arrange such municipal spoliations under the head of violations of our *neutral* rights."[51] In sum, he drove home the point that Smith was wrong to suppose a link between the recent seizures of American vessels and Napoleon's offer to repeal his Berlin and Milan decrees. What Barlow soon discovered, however, was Madison's determination to pursue Napoleon relentlessly to secure indemnification for both categories of property loss. The instructions he received shortly before he left for France left no doubt on this score.

12 Watching the Worsening Relations with Britain and France

In many ways, Barlow was a logical choice to undertake a mission to Paris. His long years in the French capital assured that he could move easily among its officials, many of whom he had known socially, and his treaty successes in North Africa promised to put his formidable diplomatic talents to good use. Moreover, he had the confidence of both the president and the new secretary of state, James Monroe, who knew him to be an articulate advocate, confident, persuasive, and above all tenacious. Viewing the near impasse in relations with both belligerents, they doubtless believed that if anyone could deal effectively with Napoleon, it was Joel Barlow.

When the new minister sailed for France in August 1811, Congress was less than a year from declaring war on Great Britain. And when it did, the Senate came within two votes of provoking war with France as well. What, if anything, Barlow could do to prevent a worsening of relations with Paris remained to be seen. But like other American diplomats before him, he soon realized how limited his options were in the face of hardened French and British maritime policies. Simply put, Paris had long made clear it would not back away from its abuses of American shipping unless London retreated first, and the latter was equally insistent that France make the first move. By mid-1811, without clear proof that Napoleon had in fact revoked his decrees, the British government stood firm on its orders-in-council.

But it was Britain's other offenses that go far to explain the subsequent vote for war. Weighing the relative mischief of the two belligerents, most Americans had long perceived Britain to be the more incorrigible. By way of confirming this view, shortly after Barlow sailed word reached Washington that a British judge had condemned another eighteen American vessels for attempting direct trade with France. Such persistent provocation assured that Americans would continue to focus their anger chiefly on Britain. And while Barlow jousted with Napoleon and his ministers, he would have to keep an eye fixed on London to determine to what extent his own diplomacy might be affected by the further unraveling of Anglo-American relations. Those relations, it should be noted, had not been consistently bad. Jay's treaty of 1794, despite its flaws, had resolved enough issues relating to boundaries and claims to usher in what one historian has called the "first rapprochement."[1] And because Jay's treaty was also the proximate cause of their Quasi-War with France, Americans were able, however briefly, to view Britain as the enemy of their enemy who had become their friend.

Whatever goodwill these factors generated in the late 1790s ended abruptly in May 1805, when a British judge upheld the seizure of an American ship, *Essex*, on grounds that it had violated a rule the Admiralty had set down in 1756 during the Seven Years' War. Under this rule, Britain had banned neutral-flag vessels, on pain of confiscation, from carrying to Europe cargoes originating from colonial ports that were closed to them in peacetime. Now, half a century later, because Britain was once more at war with both France and Spain, and because the latter needed neutral carriers to service their Caribbean ports, Americans had been lading "colonial" cargoes in ports where in peacetime only French and Spanish carriers were admitted. Besides losing scores of vessels under the impact of "the *Essex* decision," what Americans particularly resented was that for the previous five years the British had allowed them to circumvent the Admiralty's rule, offering no objections, provided the Caribbean cargoes were first landed at a U.S. port before being "re-exported" to Europe. This landing and re-shipping, known as "broken voyage," ostensibly conferred U.S. "origin" on such cargoes, permitting their export to Europe under the dictum that nations may always trade with one another in commodities of their own "production." Clearly, however, conferring U.S. citizenship, so to speak, on bags of Caribbean-grown sugar and coffee simply because they had been routed through a U.S. port had become by 1805 an absurdity up with which the Pitt ministry would no longer put. With the *Essex* decision of that year, the Rule of 1756 came back into play.[2]

Congress, hoping to force a return to the profitable permissiveness of broken voyage, took a halfhearted swing at economic retaliation. The spring following the *Essex* decision, it passed an act forbidding the importation of British goods, except, pathetically, those items Americans really needed, such as cotton goods to clothe their slaves. Nor did non-importation take immediate effect. Rather, Congress intended the delay to give the British time to consider restoring the good old days of "broken voyage."[3] When the diplomatic scene shifted to London, the American negotiators—William Pinkney and James Monroe—found the Fox-Grenville ministry unwilling to negotiate under threat of a punitive deadline. Contingent on their withdrawing this threat, however, they did manage to extract a partial return to the pre-*Essex* status quo, only to have Jefferson decline to submit their treaty to the Senate because it failed to address the issue of impressment.[4]

Another anger-provoking issue, impressment was the name given to the British naval practice of kidnapping seamen from American merchantmen on the pretext of recovering deserters. Many of those recovered *were* deserters, British tars who had fled bad food, low pay, and heavy discipline for more comfortable and better-paid berths aboard American merchantmen. But many others—perhaps as many as seven thousand by 1812—were native-born Americans whose forced servitude constantly reminded their countrymen of British bullying and whose release posed a stubborn problem for American diplomats. Sensitivity to this issue reached a climax in the summer of 1807 when the British frigate *Leopard* broadsided, boarded, and then proceeded to remove four alleged deserters from the crew of an American naval vessel shortly after it left Norfolk. This attack on the USS *Chesapeake*, clearly an insult to national honor, might have brought war had Jefferson opted to call Congress into session. Instead he hoped to parlay Britain's certain acknowledgment of its wrongdoing into a blanket renunciation of the practice. Jefferson only half succeeded. London finally did apologize for attacking and boarding a U.S. Navy vessel but made clear it would not forgo its time-honored right to recover deserters wherever else they might be found.

Added to these grievances was the suspicion, bordering on conviction, that British provocateurs operating out of Canada were behind recent Indian raids along the Ohio frontier. Barlow was well settled in Paris when, in November 1811, British-made firearms were reportedly discovered after Gov. William Henry Harrison of Indiana laid waste a supposedly hostile Indian village at the confluence of the Wabash and Tippecanoe rivers. Ironically, later evidence suggests that

British authorities in Canada were trying to restrain rather than provoke their Indian allies.[5] After the Battle of Tippecanoe, however, an increasing number of Indian raids, plainly retaliatory, strengthened the popular perception that the frontier would never be safe until the British were driven from Canada. How easily a sense of grievance could mutate into a rationale for conquest became clear when a small but vocal group of Republican congressmen, whom their Federalist enemies dubbed "War Hawks," made the conquest of Canada one of their war aims.

In a sense Barlow's mission to France afforded Madison an opportunity to force London's hand in the only way he knew how. The president clearly counted on his emissary to win enough visible concessions from Napoleon for him to be able to demand that London do likewise. A hopeful sign, frail though it was: the emperor had recently released a few American vessels. If Barlow could persuade him to release more, pay for those he had confiscated, and publicly announce the revocation of his decrees, Madison believed he would have enough leverage to wring similar concessions from London or, failing that, go to Congress with a strong case for war.

As Barlow soon discovered, however, Napoleon was not about to fall in with Madison's stratagem. He much preferred to keep Americans and Englishmen on a path toward war, mindful that any concession he made to the United States, if matched by London, might mend Anglo-American relations. Accordingly, despite the best efforts of American diplomats, Barlow among them, Napoleon would yield only enough to make sure Congress remained focused on Britain's more outrageous behavior.

The situation Barlow would face when he reached Paris had entered a critical phase in August 1810, when, as noted earlier, U.S. Minister John Armstrong received a letter from the French foreign minister, the duc de Cadore, promising the recall of the Berlin and Milan decrees contingent on the U.S. reinstatement of non-intercourse against Britain. Armstrong had returned home that fall, believing the Cadore Letter had opened the way to a lasting settlement. What he left behind, however, was a cluster of unresolved maritime claims that Napoleon showed no sign of settling. Indeed, the likely fate of those claims became all the more bleak when the emperor announced—ironically on the same August date as the Cadore Letter—that he would pocket the proceeds from the sale of the American vessels he had confiscated the previous March under his Rambouillet Decree. Since that time, the monies obtained from selling these vessels had remained in the *caisse d'amortissement*—that is, in escrow. Now, with a flourish, his Trianon Decree ordered those funds transferred from escrow directly into the French treasury, thereby burying a category of spoliation claims so deeply that American shipowners would have to wait more than a quarter of a century to be indemnified. Both the Rambouillet and Trianon decrees spelled out the same justification. Both alluded only to those American vessels detained between May 1809 and May 1810, dates bracketing the time period during which France had allegedly suffered losses from the operation of the American Non-Intercourse Act. In both decrees, Napoleon singled out Article 3 of that act for having threatened the seizure of any vessel—British or French—entering a U.S. port while the law was in effect. It little mattered that no French vessel had actually been confiscated under Article 3. For Napoleon, the threat itself, plus a generous dollop of greed, was enough to warrant retaliation.[6]

A full year passed before Barlow replaced Armstrong. In the interim an American consul named Jonathan Russell had charge of the U.S. legation. On the plus side, Russell brought to the post a wide range of expertise. Well versed in maritime issues from his recent consular duties in Hamburg, he also had experience as a successful businessman actively engaged in transatlantic commerce. In sum, he knew the issues and what it would take to sustain American interests in the face of Napoleonic game playing. As chargé d'affaires, however, he lacked the stature Barlow would bring as a fully accredited envoy. When, for example, Russell asked for a one-on-one meeting with the emperor, the word came back that Napoleon did not want to see him until a general "diplomatic audience," at which time he could present his credentials.[7]

Russell's most frustrating problem was to extract assurances that Napoleon had unconditionally revoked his Berlin and Milan decrees. When Madison's acceptance of the Cadore Letter was known in Paris, Russell held it up as reason enough for such assurances. Through the early spring of 1811, however, he met with the off-putting rejoinder that Congress had yet to affirm Madison's acceptance by breaking off trade with Britain. Until then, he was told, Americans would not have fulfilled the requirements of the Cadore Letter. When news arrived that Congress *had* acted, Russell tried again, this time bracing Napoleon's new foreign minister, the duc de Bassano. He voiced hope but some misgiving, and, as he feared, Bassano was quick to point out that, contrary to the emperor's expectations, Congress had not closed down trade with Britain completely.[8] While the so-called Eppes Bill prohibited British imports, it had put no restrictions on American exports to Britain. Moreover, Bassano complained, the Eppes Bill permitted vessels departing Britain before the law's enactment was known to land their cargoes. Basically, however, the impasse reflected a lack of trust on both sides. Congress, for its part, had declined to cut off both legs of British commerce because a majority of its members suspected that while Napoleon may have suspended his decrees (no word had come of recent seizures), he had not declared them revoked and might still resurrect them.[9]

Napoleon, for his part, hesitated to swear off his decrees entirely lest Britain follow suit and thereby patch up relations with the United States, but also because he believed British and American commercial interests to be so closely linked as to defy telling them apart. French port authorities, he knew, could not be certain whether incoming American ships, crews, and cargoes were, in fact, what their captains claimed them to be. Such vessels, he knew, often presented forged registries and submitted cargo manifests that belied the origin of their cargoes. Moreover, the owners of such vessels might, in fact, be British subjects or Americans acting on behalf of British commercial houses. As for the American crewmen who came ashore speaking the enemy's language, he was sure Britons were among them.

Napoleon's wariness, though well grounded, also contained an element of calculation. As Russell soon noted, the Berlin and Milan decrees, irrespective of their official status, were not being enforced. American vessels were no longer detained in their name, he concluded, because Napoleon intended this lapse in enforcement to calm the American shipping community while at the same time depriving American diplomats of the hard proof they needed to persuade the British ministry to recall the orders-in-council. In London, William Pinkney was making as strong a case as he could for their recall. Unfortunately at one point Pinkney mistook Russell's reports of non-enforcement to mean that Napoleon had, in fact, revoked his decrees. The confusion thickened when, in December 1810, Bordeaux port officials—apparently unaware that they weren't supposed to—seized an American vessel, the *New Orleans Packet,* openly citing it for violation of the Milan Decree. The *Packet* certainly filled the bill. It had sailed from the British port of Gibraltar and been twice visited by British warships. Alarmed, Russell promptly sent Bassano a written protest. When to his dismay his note was published in the Paris press, Pinkney was furious. How could he persuade the British to recall their orders-in-council if Russell was hinting that Napoleon still enforced his decrees? Russell explained ruefully to Madison that he had not expected his "remonstrance" to be published. Moreover, he heatedly denied having suggested to Pinkney that nonenforcement had signaled revocation. In the end, the president expressed sympathy for Russell's dilemma. In June the *Packet* was released from custody, and in London a disgruntled Pinkney continued to butt heads with the foreign office.[10]

By late 1810 it became clear why Napoleon could afford to let his decrees become inoperative. He was already enforcing what remained of his Continental System by licensing French (and neutral) vessels to provide France with the imported goods it most needed. As long as French consuls abroad certified the non-British origins of incoming cargoes, licensing upheld the original purpose of his "system." Better still, revenues derived from selling these "*permis*" made a welcome addition to his treasury, and because licensing was administered under domestic law, he no longer offended maritime neutrals by making captures at sea. Licensing was not without drawbacks, however. Lest importing without exporting cause a serious outflow of specie, licensed importers were required to lade export cargoes equal in monetary value to those they had brought in. Unfortunately this requirement seriously delayed departures when bureaucrats in Paris took their sweet time determining the relative values of import and export cargoes. Moreover, some of the required export items, like silks, became so unmarketable that their captains later claimed to have thrown them overboard.[11]

Licensing also widened the fissures in Napoleon's much-vaunted aim of choking off Britain's access to European markets. His application of the "system" became increasingly asymmetric. On the side of harsh enforcement, to be sure, he annexed the Netherlands in June 1810, ousting his brother from its throne largely because Louis had been unable, or perhaps unwilling, to shut down a brisk cross-channel trade in contraband. And two years later he would invade Russia in part because Czar Alexander refused to close his ports to British commodities.

Still, as early as April 1809, he deliberately licensed a limited number of vessels for direct trade with Britain itself. Historians, puzzled by this willingness to trade with the enemy, speculate that at this juncture Napoleon was acting on impulse to relieve French grain farmers temporarily burdened with bumper crops and falling prices by taking advantage of a simultaneous grain shortage in Britain.[12] Begun as an ad hoc expedient, licensing soon expanded to become a major feature of France's external commerce. Later, from his exile on Saint Heléna, the emperor lamented what he called its "mischievous" results and blamed the British for starting it.[13] He was right on this score. By 1809 the British government had discovered how richly rewarding it was to sell licenses to neutral shipowners who gladly paid for the privilege of sailing unhindered through British blockades on their way to ports in Europe. By the end of 1810, London had sold more than eighteen thousand licenses.[14] Still, blaming the British for originating the "mischievous" practice belied Napoleon's reasons for following their example. For both belligerents, selling licenses was a highly profitable source of revenue.

American officials at all levels reacted negatively. When French licensing first gained prominence in the spring of 1810, John Armstrong registered objections. Procuring a license, to be sure, offered American vessels a means of escaping detention, but he saw problems with their being bonded by the French government to make round trips to and from specified American destinations. Not only would the British surely confiscate any vessel caught sailing under French bond, but the licensing requirements, he noted, were not all that different from the onerous controls London itself had imposed.[15] For several months, Armstrong's protests registered strongly enough in Paris to delay American participation, but as opportunities multiplied, American shipowners took their own initiatives, snapping up licenses whenever they became available. Not only did licenses offer an escape hatch for their vessels, but also assured that return cargoes would be admitted without question or the risk of detention. All they had to fear was British capture.

Back in Washington, meanwhile, the administration echoed Armstrong's objections and set its face sternly against having anything to do with this latest wrinkle in French maritime policy. Monroe repeatedly warned the newly arrived French minister, Louis Serurier, that the administration already took a dim view of French consuls certifying the non-British origin of outgoing cargoes. Now those consuls, newly charged with overseeing the American end of a French licensing system, not only violated U.S. sovereignty by conducting their official operations on American soil, but also infringed on the right of Americans to carry cargoes wherever they pleased.[16] Predictably, such protests carried little weight with Paris or, for that matter, with those Yankee entrepreneurs who then, and even now, seldom allow their government's disapproval to stand in the way of profit taking.

Jonathan Russell took up the case against licensing where Armstrong had left off. In October 1810, on the job only a few weeks but armed with hard evidence, he asked Cadore if he was aware that neither French nor American vessels were being allowed to depart without a license. The foreign minister breezily assured him that Americans were free to leave whenever they pleased and, besides, only French-flag vessels were being licensed. He lied on both counts. American clearances were few and far between, and Cadore was already telling Serurier that plans were afoot to license some thirty American vessels to bring in cargoes from Charleston and New York.[17]

Russell was not altogether deceived. And like Armstrong, he questioned the anomalies of the licensing regime. Much to Cadore's irritation, he asked pointedly how such controls over neutral commerce differed from Britain's equally obnoxious maritime practices. And how could Americans defend against British capture if they accepted such controls? He aimed his sharpest rebuke at Napoleon's continued licensing of trade with England. How, he asked, could France insist Americans not trade with Britain when she herself continued to license that traffic?[18]

Not surprisingly, he received no answers to these questions. And once Paris made clear it would sell licenses to Americans, he found himself fending off sea captains who sought his help to secure them. To his credit and apparently without exception, he refused their requests. He assured Monroe he would do whatever else to secure the release of American vessels but would take no action that would make the U.S. government a party to French maritime policy. He also reported turning away officials who wanted him to single out captains who, if licensed to bring in American grain, would help ease a temporary food shortage.[19] Meanwhile, Cadore's capacity for deception remained unabated. In January 1811, mindful of Russell's objections, he referred vaguely to what he called "changed circumstances" and hinted that France might abandon its licensing regime in the near future. Knowing that Russell would report the good news to Washington, he told Serurier not to take it seriously. The emperor had no plans to forgo a profitable source of revenue.[20] Licensing still had a future.

Barlow, when he arrived in Paris, adopted a more relaxed view. Having once engaged in transatlantic commerce, he appreciated the entrepreneurial spirit of those who risked much to make a profit and seemed less troubled that, in this instance, they operated under the aegis of a foreign power. As his mission unfolded, he even hoped to fine-tune the licensing regime in ways that might be shaped to compensate shipowners for their earlier losses. And because his instructions stressed the importance of securing indemnification, tweaking the licensing system became one of the ways he sought to serve that end. But that, too, lay in the future.

13 Beginning the French Mission—with Lively Exchanges

By August 1811 neither France nor Britain had shown an inclination to renounce the policies and practices Americans so bitterly resented. Napoleon, to be sure, had released a few vessels but under a licensing regime the administration found humiliating. And though not enforcing his Berlin and Milan decrees, neither had the emperor offered enough evidence of their revocation to give London a reason to recall its orders-in-council. William Pinkney returned home empty-handed that month, convinced of Britain's settled ill will.

Toward France, meanwhile, the administration's complaint remained largely directed at Napoleon's refusal to countenance the claims of American shipowners who believed their property had been wrongfully confiscated. That said, demands for French indemnification lacked the immediacy of the growing outrage Americans felt toward what they regarded as Britain's far more numerous and hurtful injuries. Congress a year later might toy with the notion of declaring war on both offenders, but by that time complaints against France had been drowned out by even louder outcries against London. Britain's insults were not only unremitting; they also struck closer to home. Seafaring Americans might be stranded in faraway France when their vessels were detained, but off the Virginia capes they were being kidnapped and put to forced labor. And in the back country, British provocateurs were suspected of inciting Indian attacks and later would appear to be playing on the secessionist predilections of disaffected New England Federalists. Echoing this drumbeat of hostility, the Dover packets, arriving biweekly, continued to bring reports of more ships and cargoes lost to British court decisions, constant reminders of how cavalierly London disrespected Americans' right to carry cargoes to any port not effectively blockaded. Nor was relief in sight on this score. Indeed, Barlow was only six days at sea when, as noted earlier, news broke that a British judge had condemned the American vessel *Fox* and eighteen others for violating the 1809 order requiring vessels bound for Europe to stop first at a British port.[1]

Pinkney's failed diplomacy in London had its counterpart in Washington where a newly arrived but hopelessly instructed British minister made clear that an Anglo-American rapprochement was not nearly within Madison's reach. Not only did Augustus John Foster insist on solid proof that Napoleon had revoked his decrees, but he also laid down the preposterous condition that London would rescind its orders-in-council only if the United States compelled the emperor to open his European ports to British ships and cargoes. Madison was outraged, and Monroe asked Foster whether London seriously meant to hold the United States responsible for securing British access to French ports and thereby force France to trade with her enemy. Reporting to Paris, Louis Serurier exulted at the furor Foster's "insolence" had caused and wondered how much longer Americans would tolerate such treatment. Congress, he noted, was due to meet soon, five weeks earlier than scheduled, and some expected it would declare war.[2]

Madison's message, dated November 5, disappointed that expectation.[3] After dwelling at length on the critical state of relations with both belligerents, the president ended by calling on Congress, not to declare war, but to take measures of preparedness and raise more revenue for troops and naval construction. Toward Britain, he touched on the bizarre nature of Foster's latest demand and then reviewed the cumulative damage done by the orders-in-council for which, he noted, no "redress" had been promised. As for the attack by the USS *President* on HMS *Little Belt* the previous May, he made no apology. A naval inquiry had confirmed that the British warship had fired first. He would send Congress the findings of that inquiry, along with "correspondence evincing Britain's suspected 'interposition'" in the Floridas. Had Congress convened a few weeks later, he might also have chalked up the Battle of Tippecanoe as more evidence of British hostility. Rather, he simply noted that troops had been sent into the Ohio Valley to deal with Indian unrest. As between the two belligerents, there was no mistaking that Madison's call for military preparedness was aimed at the likelihood of war with Britain unless diplomacy resolved some serious issues.

Toward France, he calibrated his critique somewhat more finely. He accepted as fact the revocation of the Berlin and Milan decrees but found no evidence that France intended to restore, or indemnify Americans for, property seized under those decrees or under subsequent measures. Though the most recent detentions of American vessels did not violate any precept of maritime neutral rights, they "were nevertheless founded in such unjust principles that the reparation ought to have been prompt and ample." Madison also parsed the licensing issue. If France continued to restrict trade by admitting only those goods brought by licensed carriers, Congress should consider imposing similar restrictions on imports from France. Meanwhile, it should at least enact legislation to prohibit Americans from accepting those licenses.

But while finding both belligerents guilty of wrongdoing, Madison hinted that France might be open to a settlement. Unlike Britain's "hostile inflexibility," he voiced the hope that "our minister plenipotentiary lately sent to France" would report back what would be required for such a settlement. Without mentioning Barlow by name, he told Congress he would keep it informed of the minister's progress.[4] Some, like Louis Serurier, soon took it as an article of faith that if Barlow sent a favorable signal—even an inkling of French goodwill—Congress would move more swiftly toward war with Britain. Much, he believed, rested in Barlow's hands.

Whether from the prospect of seasickness or the magnitude of the task ahead, Barlow boarded the USS *Constitution* on August 1 with a keen sense of foreboding. The ship was clean and the crew well disciplined, he wrote Fulton: "But my heart is heavy. I have left my country, possibly and why not probably forever. . . . I go with an ardent wish but without much hope of doing good, —and with the full intention, tho' with a feeble hope of living to return." As usual, his depression was short-lived. Five days later, the sailing smooth, his stomach settled, and his spirits revived, he wrote Fulton he expected to make a "fine passage." He just wished his "prospect of success in this mission were as good."[5] The dispatch boat took back two other letters that day, one asking Monroe to send some books he had left behind, and the other, to Stephen, reporting cheerfully how well their party had taken to shipboard life. Ruth and her half-sister, Clara Baldwin, were well and healthy and sent their love, and young Tom was so high-spirited, Barlow feared he might "fall in love with the sea."[6] Once clear of the capes, strong westerlies and a following sea made for a swift and relatively comfortable passage. After thirty-four days at sea, the *Constitution* dropped anchor at Cherbourg, and within two weeks Barlow and his entourage were in Paris. He and Ruth, he wrote, were glad to be back in their "old elegant & convenient house" on the rue de Vaugirard, "the best I ever inhabited."[7]

William Lee, who made the passage with them, took major credit for re-orienting Barlow to the Paris political scene. At least that is what he told his wife Susan, who wanted him back in Bordeaux. He explained to her that as secretary of legation and having been in Paris more recently, he felt obliged to stay and introduce the new minister to various officials. He assured her these meetings and courtesy visits were "tiresome," but Barlow "cannot get on well without me."[8] Ruth chimed in helpfully, assuring Susan that her husband was eager to be with her, "but my husband thinks nothing can go right if Wm. Lee is not at his elbow. Indeed, we could not have got along without him."[9] This picture of ministerial helplessness, while intended to reconcile Susan Lee to her husband's absence, belied the fact that Barlow's diplomatic mission hit full stride from the moment he arrived in Paris on September 19. Though disappointed to learn Napoleon had left for Holland that same day, he responded eagerly when the duc de Bassano invited him to call at the foreign office at four o'clock on the 21st. Because Bassano was due to leave shortly to join the emperor, they met again the next day and talked for two hours.[10]

Each left extended accounts of their early meetings. Barlow's report to Monroe was somewhat guarded and for good reason. He was already planning to finesse his instructions, which focused almost exclusively on securing indemnification, and negotiate a full-fledged commercial treaty. His mercantile background doubtless told him that if Americans were ever to be reimbursed for past property losses, it would have to be in the context of a treaty that would so handsomely expand Franco-American commerce as to reduce indemnification to a minor issue. Suspecting the administration might not approve of this indirect approach, he told only of having unloaded some "new ideas" on Bassano, who showed enough interest to ask that they be put in writing and promised to convey them to the emperor in a favorable light. Otherwise, Barlow reported generalities unrelated to indemnification. He and Bassano had, for example, explored the possibility of establishing a regular packet service so that Americans could get their news of Europe directly rather than through the filter of British interpretation. They also discussed whether American vessels might be employed to transport and supply French forces sent to liberate Spanish America. As a quid pro quo, Barlow held out the possibility that Napoleon might reset the western boundary of Louisiana at the Rio Grande.[11] To his friend Wolcott, he wrote: "The minister has received me with fair words & good promises as to public concerns, & personally with flattering attention. This is all right, but untill business begins, I cannot tell how it will end."[12]

Bassano, writing to Serurier from Amsterdam, struck a deliberately upbeat note. Barlow now understood that the Berlin and Milan decrees no longer operated against American vessels and the few most recently seized had forfeited their neutral status by accepting British convoy. As for others detained for having visited a British port, their disposition was still pending. In the future, however, France would "immediately release" any American vessel, even those that had touched at British ports, as long as the British had not prevented them from reaching their French destinations. In sum, Serurier was to spread the word that France was now more welcoming of American vessels and that the emperor had warmly received Barlow as the harbinger of better relations. The American minister's eagerness to expand commerce was a subject he expected to explore more fully when he and the emperor returned to Paris.[13]

In retrospect Barlow's decision to push for a broad-based commercial treaty put him at a tactical disadvantage because it allowed Napoleon to dicker over details and thereby delay bringing negotiations to a head. Nor, it bears repeating, was the emperor particularly keen to reach an accommodation. Putting Barlow on hold would give Americans more time and perhaps additional motives to declare war on Britain, even though he had no illusions as to their value as cobelligerents. Whenever the United States caught his fleeting attention, he typically reacted with either disgust or irritation, having long since concluded that Americans were a hopelessly sorry lot, ignobly driven by commercial greed, too cowardly to take up arms against their British oppressors, and too unwarlike to make much difference if they did. As an irritant, American grain ships provisioning the British forces he was fighting in Spain roused his anger long enough in the spring of 1812 to dispatch a naval squadron to intercept and burn them at sea, news of which reaching Washington explains why

Congress nearly declared war on both belligerents. Meanwhile, absent a crisis, Napoleon could afford to string out negotiations, tantalizing Barlow with the prospect of minor concessions, while he occupied himself with the more glorious prospect of invading Russia.

Whether or not Barlow realized he was being toyed with, he clearly felt he had no choice. Had he begun his mission with a flat-out demand for indemnification, as instructed, he might as well have gone home. Napoleon was not about to admit liability for any wrongdoing, much less pay for it. Barlow knew this intuitively but hoped to offer enough enticements on issues beneficial to both parties that compensation for property losses, or at least the promise of compensation, could be worked into a final draft.

When Bassano left Paris to join the emperor, he turned Barlow over to Jean-Baptiste Petry, former consul in Charleston who now ranked as the foreign office expert on all things American.[14] As he and Barlow ranged over problem spots in Franco-American relations, Petry manfully defended the emperor's maritime policies while at the same time hoping to give Bassano a clearer understanding of where Barlow was coming from. At their first meeting, he did his best to cool the American envoy's enthusiasm for a commercial treaty, arguing that the time was not right and too many of its articles would have only short-term effect. Undaunted, Barlow rejoined that a treaty of amity and commerce would demonstrate France's good intentions and have a salutary effect on British policy and confound the pro-British party in the United States. Moreover, the resulting increase in trade would benefit both parties.[15]

Petry, however, repeated what soon became the official party line: if France were to be more welcoming of American vessels, the British would simply seize more of them as they came and went. Could France, he asked, allow this to happen while Americans continued to trade freely to British ports? From what this question implied, Barlow said he must assume that "the Berlin and Milan decrees have not been repealed" or, he grumbled, perhaps they had been succeeded by other measures equally destructive of the law of nations. From this exchange, Petry concluded that wherever their subsequent talks might lead, Barlow would hold fast to the principle that neutral-flag vessels had a right to trade to any belligerent port not effectively blockaded. When, for example, he asked if the United States could prevent its grain ships from supplying British troops in Spain, Barlow replied that if all parties observed the principle of "free ships," it mattered little whether the grain was landed at Cadiz or transshipped there by way of Liverpool. Wryly Petry warned Bassano that on his return, he could expect to be lectured extensively on the law of nations.[16]

Having heard enough on that subject, Petry hauled back and took a well-aimed swing at the Eppes Bill. He pointed out that this halfway compliance with the Cadore Letter, by allowing Americans to export goods to Britain while banning return cargoes, had led to widespread smuggling. He estimated that British goods worth half a million pounds were already in Halifax and would soon reach their American destinations. Barlow replied somewhat lamely that insofar as the law was intended to operate, it forced British buyers to pay for American cargoes in hard cash. Thus enriched by an outflow of British specie, Americans would use it to buy French manufactures, thereby reversing the unfavorable trade balance France had long suffered in its commerce with the United States. Petry was unpersuaded. Did Barlow truly believe the British would pay cash or that Americans would accept it when both parties could profit from spiriting cargoes out of Britain and landing them at such entrepôts as Halifax, Bermuda, or that notorious smugglers' den at the mouth of the St. Mary's River in Florida? Having exhausted this topic, they moved on to France's licensing system. Barlow questioned why France needed to license importers when French consuls were already certifying the non-British origins of incoming cargoes. In response Petry observed mildly that French port authorities needed to know more precisely where imported goods came from.[17]

Mulling over what Barlow's mission portended, Petry noted significantly that "in all my conversations with this American minister, he never once pronounced the word *war.*" Nor had Barlow hinted that any favors from France would have that result. From this, Petry believed Washington had sent him merely to play for time, hoping he could negotiate a treaty reaffirming the maritime rights of neutrals while delaying any further action toward Britain. Congress had been called into session five weeks early, he noted, and appeared to be waiting to hear news from either France or England before taking its next step.[18]

Despite his negative tone, however, Petry believed the time had come for France to step forward and announce its "intentions in a most decided manner." Like Serurier, he believed that with French encouragement, Congress would be more inclined to take up arms. Until now, he remarked, that body had sought to avenge the property damage done by both belligerents by imposing a series of sanctions that fell short of war. "If we persist in our [present] course, it will recur to other half-measures."[19] How France might motivate Congress at this juncture Petry did not spell out, but if a show of good "intentions" succeeded, France stood to reap both short- and long-term advantages. The emperor could not, of course, look for strong military or naval support, but Americans at war would put an end to British smuggling and seek out France as an alternate trade partner, a commerce made safer because the British would be forced to spread their naval forces more thinly on both sides of the Atlantic. Commerce, he reminded Bassano, was Americans' life's blood, producing the tariff revenues their government needed to survive. To be sure, war would deprive them of the revenue they derived from duties on British goods, but they could make up the losses from levies on the cargoes of an increasing number of French arrivals. That Petry accepted the possibility of this trade-off clearly showed Barlow's influence on his thinking. So, too, the positive aspects of bringing the United States into the war. He knew from talking to Barlow that Americans were certain to attack Canada, compelling the British to reinforce their garrisons there. And American shipowners who turned to privateering would wreak havoc on British shipping. "By amicable measures on our part," he concluded, Americans could be led to war, although again he left those measures to Bassano's devising. He warned, however, that France's window of opportunity would remain open only as long as London refused to recall its orders-in-council.[20]

Despite Petry's efforts to deter him, Barlow promptly drafted a broad outline for a commercial treaty. This draft dated November 10 he personally delivered to Bassano shortly after the foreign minister returned to Paris. Bassano, in turn, asked Petry to review it, and then forwarded his own opinion to Napoleon on December 5. The emperor's formal reply, bearing the date December 27, challenged most of Barlow's premises but signaled a willingness to begin negotiations.

Barlow sent Monroe two copies of this November 10 note—one in English, the other in French—explaining that Bassano did not read English and he distrusted the foreign office to make an accurate translation. He also enclosed an account of his first audience with Napoleon four days earlier. He had to admit that he came away from this encounter with mixed feelings. Although the emperor had greeted him graciously and joined in his hope for better commercial relations, Barlow had winced at the familiar qualifier that "you on your part must defend your dignity against my enemies." This jab at Americans for their supposed knuckling under to British abuse struck Barlow as symptomatic of "the same ambiguity which has so long continued." He hoped Monroe would not disclose it to the press lest their "animadversions" in print make his mission more difficult. Otherwise, he assured the secretary, he was determined to forge ahead.[21]

His November 10 note began by comparing the feeble state of Franco-American commerce with the robust future he envisioned for it if only the two parties made changes obviously beneficial to both. American vessels still languished in French ports, he observed, no longer held for violating the Berlin and Milan decrees, to be sure, but victims of "municipal orders & regulations which equally exclude their commerce, or sequester it." France, he believed, was also mistaken to limit her imports to a few licensed vessels. Were she to open her ports to all comers, he calculated as many as two thousand ships a year would come and go. Arrivals were few, he believed, for a number of reasons. Besides shipowners' reluctance to cope with the "multiplicity & changing nature of French municipal regulations," they had to cope with French authorities who had no "fixt rule" for distinguishing their ships and cargoes from those of the British. And in seeking return cargoes, they had met with the absurd requirement that they lade silk goods up to 2/3 the value of the whole. "All the silk looms in France," he scoffed, "would not be able to furnish the quantity necessary." But if the requirement were dropped, Americans, cut off from trading with Britain, would carry away French cargoes worth many times the value of silks. Finally, American importers were shy because they saw little hope of finding markets in France for goods that were dutied at 400 percent of their value. Whatever the emperor may have intended when he decreed his Trianon tariff in August 1810, it had proven to be prohibitive.

To sweep away these strictures, Barlow had in mind a treaty based, he hoped, on France's willingness to open its ports, lower its import duties, and of course, release the American vessels now detained on various pretexts. Failure to accomplish these ends, he warned, might force Congress to reopen full commerce with Britain. Like Petry he reminded Bassano that Americans "must have a commerce & an extensive commerce," not only because they needed Europe for its manufactures, but also as a market for their raw materials and because their government depended on import duties for more than 90 percent of its revenues. This said, Barlow counted up the benefits France stood to gain were she to embrace the free and unfettered commerce he envisioned.[22]

Curiously, perhaps for reasons of national pride, no French official saw fit to point out to Barlow that his flight of imagination flew in the face of the frustrating reality that Britain, more industrially advanced, had long outstripped France in the production and variety of exportable manufactured goods and had nailed down overseas markets not easily breached. Since the 1790s French consuls in America had lamented France's inability to compete with Britain in the production of cheap cotton fabrics, household furnishings and ordinary hardware. Barlow had to admit that American consumers had long preferred to buy their manufactures from England. But, he argued, if France were willing to adjust to American tastes and preferences, she could create new buying habits for French goods and establish a permanent clientele not only in the United States, but also in Spanish America where British manufactures were already gaining a foothold. Again, the question arises: how could Barlow have expected France to will into existence a more diversified export economy or mobilize the necessary resources quickly enough to make a difference? For him to suggest that a largely pre-industrial French economy could suddenly rise to the challenge of breaking Britain's grip on the overseas markets for manufactured goods clearly said more of his optimism than his grasp of reality.

Barlow took another unlikely tack when he tried to link his free-trade argument to Napoleon's vigorous naval building program, recently undertaken and well under way. This bid to challenge Britain's sea power, he pointed out, would require a great many newly trained seamen. The emperor, he told Bassno, "is building ships in such numbers & capacity as could scarcely now be equipped by all the seamen in the world," adding the grace note, "French bravery alone is not enough to win naval battles." But on the bright side, he pictured seamen as a fluid labor pool; they "flow with the tide of employment & seek their level." He gave as an example American crewmen left unemployed by the embargo who had flocked to the British maritime service. "The fact is," he wrote, "& there is no harm in saying it, there are at present more American seamen who seek that service, than those who are forced into it." Having thus skirted the difference between impressment and voluntary employment, he predicted that as Franco-American commerce grew in volume, market forces would increase the number of French merchant ships engaged in it, thereby training enough seamen to man Napoleon's new navy when the time came. Again, one might ask: did Barlow truly believe the emperor would divert his shipyards from building warships to building a larger fleet of merchantmen? Fortunately, in the end—and especially in London one could hear a sigh of relief—Napoleon's fateful invasion of Russia put an end to his naval construction program.[23]

Drawing his November 10 note to a close, Barlow called on France to restore all American property then in custody and permit American vessels to depart. From this reasonable request, he moved into the thicket of past spoliations, proposing a "separate convention" by which France would agree to indemnify Americans whose property had already been confiscated and sold. Given the opposition he knew to expect, he was deliberately vague on how such a convention would operate. To cap these gestures of goodwill, he invited France to sign a sweeping commercial treaty, fully "reciprocal" with respect to customs duties and permitting the freest possible trade in agreed-upon commodities. Finally, to assure French port officials that incoming vessels and cargoes were certifiably American, he would agree to any system of "marks, signals or other measures."[24]

Barlow gave no sign of foreseeing how bleakly his proposals would be received on both sides of the Atlantic. He seemed not to realize that Napoleon would need more than the promise of an expanded commerce if he were to lower his tariffs, give up licensing, and admit enough guilt to be willing to indemnify Americans for earlier property losses. And on this last point, he could only hope that Madison and Monroe would not insist on a more material recognition of French liability than a convention promising recompense at some future date. Still, he hoped for a prompt and favorable reply and had told Bassano he would hold the *Constitution* in readiness to convey it.[25] Instead, he was greeted by the first in a series of delaying tactics when the foreign minister assured him that the emperor had read his note repeatedly and had found his reasoning "just" and his conclusions "undeniable." But . . . whether his proposals could be reconciled with the Continental System "presented difficulties."[26]

As he waited for a response, Barlow did more than talk to Petry about the specifics of Franco-American commerce. He also found occasion to try at least to disabuse Napoleon of two of his more prideful mind-sets: first, that his Continental System was working just fine, and second, that, unlike Frenchmen, Americans were too cowardly to stand up to the British. On hearing Napoleon's boast that his system had "crippled" British commerce, Barlow took statistical exception. Although it may have cost Britain six million pounds a year in lost European markets, he told Bassano, she had more than doubled that figure in the value of her exports to the West Indies, Spanish America, and, until Congress had enacted non-importation, to the United States. Indeed, Americans' most recent sacrifice in closing off British imports had just begun to make the Continental System feasible. Moreover, it might have occurred to the emperor that Americans' willingness to suffer this loss belied the charge of supineness.[27] Even more pointedly, when Bassano alluded casually to Americans not making their flag respected, Barlow shot back that the administration had just won "entire satisfaction" for the *Leopard*'s attack on the *Chesapeake* three years earlier. Bassano, abashed at having Napoleon's rhetoric thrown back in his face, said he intended no "reproach" but merely meant to observe that British cruisers routinely picked off American vessels entering and leaving French ports. From there the conversation turned vaguely to the possibility of convoying.[28]

Petry's gloss on Barlow's note of November 10 revealed a remarkable readiness to conciliate.[29] At one remove from the emperor's wrath, Petry apparently felt he could bounce ideas off Bassano with relative impunity, although he was careful not to cross any lines that might bring a rebuke. The Continental System, for example, he knew was sacrosanct. He could, however, empathize with some of Barlow's complaints about the high costs of insurance, tonnage fees, and harbor dues, and the financial drain of feeding crewmen aboard vessels whose departures had been delayed. To speed up the turn-around time, Petry suggested no longer requiring that incoming and outgoing cargoes be of equal value. He also believed the American envoy had made a reasonable case for reducing the silks requirement. But lest he be seen to have fallen completely under Barlow's sway, he reported holding the line on the Trianon tariff and had reminded Barlow that a sudden reduction of duties would destroy the value of the inventories held by French merchants who had bought at the earlier high rates.[30]

He also gave Barlow little hope for indemnification. The American envoy, he wrote, refused to distinguish between the status of property seized before and after November 1, 1810—the date Madison had accepted the Cadore

Letter. To no avail, he explained why the threat to French shipping posed by Article 3 of the Non-Intercourse Act had justified the earlier seizures and why any settlement of those losses would have to be "negotiated." He was not about to utter the word "indemnification." He could only assure Barlow that since November 1 no vessel, except the *New Orleans Packet,* had been held under the Berlin and Milan decrees, and she had been released. As for those still held on other pretexts, Petry urged Bassano they be released.[31]

Petry then echoed Barlow's prediction that Congress would almost certainly re-open full trade with Britain unless France gave American carriers freer access to her ports and those of Europe under her control. If, however, France agreed to speed the turn-around time for American carriers, drop the equal import-export requirement, and gradually lower her tariffs, she would give Congress a powerful reason to persist in non-importation. In short, Petry not only bought Barlow's recommendations, but also saw them as a means of keeping Americans on the path to war.[32]

Unfortunately, the duc de Bassano did not warm to either Barlow's or Petry's description of what was wrong or needed to be put right. Reporting to Napoleon, he summarized the American minister's complaints and dismissed them one by one.[33] Contrary to Barlow's reading, for example, France had made no recent changes in her "municipal regulations." American shipowners had no reason to be uncertain on that score. And although high duties may have diminished the number of customers for imported goods, the resulting price increases fell largely on buyers of colonial produce that, he noted, Americans had been privileged to bring in, and not on commodities of U.S. origin. Bassano did admit that vessels were often delayed in meeting the equal import-export requirement but termed it "a nuisance, not an obstacle."[34] Nor would French silks glut the American market unless—an unlikely event—a great many more American vessels turned up in French ports. Even Barlow had to admit that if France attracted more vessels, the British would become more active in seizing them. Their few numbers lay not in how France received them, but rather in Britain's success at intercepting them. In words he had learned from his master's lips, he assured Napoleon there would be no end to this problem until "the United States undertakes to make England respect their flag."[35]

Short of the kind of "respect" that meant declaring war, however, the foreign minister pointed to a possible ameliorative. Barlow had hinted that Congress might agree to put American vessels under armed convoy. For Bassano, this was the only bright spot in the Barlow-Petry talks, and he wished Petry had pushed harder to get a commitment, something "more positive than a fugitive conversation" on the subject. As a follow-up, he told the emperor, he would instruct Louis Serurier to find out what the administration thought about convoying.[36] Barlow's vagueness, he may have suspected, stemmed from the precept of international law that vessels sailing in convoy forfeit whatever rights they might otherwise claim as maritime neutrals. Barlow had, nonetheless, ventured to Petry that if Franco-American commerce took on the dimensions he hoped for it, Washington would almost certainly provide for its protection.[37]

Bassano did accept Petry's premise that Americans must have "commerce at any price," but he doubted they would scrap non-intercourse and restore full trade with England if France failed to offer what Petry called "effective concessions." This was not what he was hearing from Serurier, who pictured Congress standing firm on non-importation, bent on war unless London rescinded its orders-in-council, and needing only a show of support from France to take the fateful step. Bassano doubted this, as well.[38] Some minor concessions, he speculated, might strengthen the hands of the pro-war forces in Congress but not enough to assure their ascendency. Neither set of "either-ors"convinced him. From Petry, it was either grant concessions or risk a renewal of full-bodied Anglo-American commerce. From Serurier, it was either make concessions or Americans won't have the guts to take on the Brits. His man in Washington, he concluded glumly, was mistaken to believe that any favors France offered would move Congress to declare war. Nor had Barlow predicted "such a result," he reminded Napoleon. France could expect little, he concluded, "from a nation that is always ready to sacrifice its independence and its dignity to its commercial interests."[39]

Low expectations aside, however, Bassano recommended that talks with Barlow continue. Granting a few favors along the way would at least serve to keep congressional hostility focused on Britain. Already France had released nearly all the American vessels taken since November 1, 1810. Other minor points might be conceded. Indeed, Petry had led him to believe that Barlow no longer expected to negotiate a full-fledged commercial treaty and would be "satisfied with effective concessions."[40] Perhaps the promise of a treaty, if not its fulfillment, would serve French purposes.

14 Outlining a Treaty, Waiting for a Response

The year was drawing to a close when Bassano sent the emperor's formal reply to Barlow's note of November 10. It addressed only two issues and in language that reflected Napoleon's fixed perception of Americans' shortcomings. With no mention of the problems Americans had encountered in French ports, Bassano repeated the emperor's formulaic explanation that few vessels arrived because the Americans had shamelessly allowed the British to intercept them. Nor should Barlow complain. Those that evaded British cruisers had profited enormously from selling their cargoes. And "if the American flag were respected," they would come in greater numbers and reap even larger profits. In short, the United States, not France, was to blame for the moribund state of Franco-American commerce. In response to Barlow's complaints about the high tariff levies, Bassano denied they were prohibitive and pointed out that, unlike American tonnage duties, which discriminated against foreign vessels, the Trianon duties fell equally on all importers, French and American alike. Notwithstanding these misperceptions, Bassano notified Barlow that the emperor had authorized him to negotiate a new commercial treaty "on the principles of perfect reciprocity." Such a treaty, he hoped, would satisfy the United States and might even inspire Americans "to assure the independence of their flag."[1]

Despite its unpromising tone, the mere offer to negotiate galvanized Barlow to action. On December 28, the day after he received the note, he called on the foreign minister armed with "interim proposals" he hoped might precede a full-scale treaty and lend an air of goodwill to the enterprise. Specifically he urged that the emperor release the vessels he still detained and hereafter require no more of new arrivals than that they show clearance papers signed by

American port authorities and a French consul's certificate of origin. In other words, be more welcoming of American vessels and show good faith by dismissing the charges against those still in custody. Pressing for an early breakthrough, he urged Bassano to sign a statement endorsing these proposals. The foreign minister demurred, however, assuring him that a written statement was unnecessary because "every one of those principles was adopted by the emperor and would enter into the Treaty." Barlow persisted. A signed agreement, he argued, would restore confidence among American shipowners. Bassano, however, was not about to act without authorization but promised to forward his request to the emperor and get back to him.

Two days later he relayed Napoleon's view that it was not "proper" to sign such a document but that Barlow could notify his government that these "principles are adopted and from this day forward they will be in operation." Orders had been issued to expedite the legal proceedings against the vessels still held, and incoming cargoes would need only a consul's certification, except in the case of colonial products, which, because of the difficulty in determining their origin, must remain under license.[2] Barlow seemed unfazed by how small a dent he had put in the armor of French maritime policy or, for that matter, how summarily Bassano had dismissed his arguments on other points. When, for example, he questioned the need for licensing imports, Bassano replied that if Barlow could suggest a better means of keeping British products out of Europe, the emperor would gladly oblige. And when Barlow suggested France should abandon privateering with all its attendant evils, Bassano simply "acknowledged that something ought to be done."[3] William Lee, then in Paris, was puzzled by Barlow's optimism. Given earlier expectations, he wrote Madison, he found Bassano's note disappointing.[4]

For Serurier's benefit, Bassano spelled out the major elements in the emperor's game plan for dealing with Barlow. Most of it was a blueprint for delay. He told of having swept aside most of the American minister's complaints but urged Serurier to assure the administration that the emperor had received its envoy as "a man of great capacity, seemingly well acquainted with the interests of his country & showing good faith in discussing them."[5] Also on a happy note, Serurier was to spread the word that American vessels now "arrive without inquietude in our ports." He was to point out, however, that more would arrive if Americans took steps to safeguard them from British depredation.

This brought Bassano to his major point. Convoying, he wrote, "is the only thing that can effectively protect the commerce of the United States, inspire in England the fear of initiating a new war . . . & dispose France to treat the United States with still more marked favor."[6] Serurier was to sound out the administration on this possibility, he continued, while he and Barlow explored what "new facilities" France might extend to American commerce. The emperor had authorized a treaty negotiation but primarily as a show of goodwill. Under cover of this negotiation, he would listen to Barlow and perhaps offer concessions if the American envoy had anything to offer in return. If their discussions touched on maritime claims, however, he would turn a deaf ear. And so should Serurier.[7] In sum, Barlow was to be held at arm's length until Congress either provided armed protection for American vessels or declared war. By implication, Serurier should not expect the kinds of concessions he believed would tip the balance.

Meanwhile, the French minister should make known that no American vessel, licensed or unlicensed, had been turned away since November 1810. Some, having been visited by British men-of-war, might have been detained, but the Berlin and Milan decrees no longer applied. Most had been allowed to depart, and when Barlow had complained of delays, the emperor had interceded to speed them on their way. Indeed, the emperor had even released some of the vessels taken in retaliation for the Non-Intercourse Act. The remainder of the pre-November confiscations, however, were a fait accompli. Serurier should avoid discussing them and focus instead on France's "benevolence" toward American shipping during the past year.[8]

The ink was hardly dry on these initial exchanges before Barlow was jotting down treaty articles, pausing only long enough to realize he might be "embarrassed" if he began to negotiate without having more detailed instructions. Eager to suggest how those instructions might read, he singled out tariff reduction as the most promising way to expand commerce, provided both parties agreed to it. And because lowering tariffs would require congressional action, he knew the administration would need good arguments to persuade it. The advantage, he believed, lay with the United States. If he could also persuade Napoleon to afford tariff relief, he foresaw American exports to France doubling in value and thereby offsetting the losses Americans traditionally suffered in their unfavorable balance with Britain. "The aggregate benefit," he told Monroe, "would be manifestly on our side." Revenues lost from reduced levies on French imports could be written off as insignificant because at present the American market for French products was meager.[9] As that market expanded, revenues would grow. Though Barlow was sincerely committed to a freer exchange of goods, he must have had doubts. Neither Petry nor Bassano had given him reason to believe Napoleon would lower French import duties. And he would soon hear from Monroe that Congress, preparing for war, was more likely to raise tariffs than lower them.

Determined to omit nothing of consequence, Barlow sent Bassano a draft treaty in mid-January crammed with more articles than seemed likely to be accepted. As a seasoned negotiator, however, he may have planned to bargain away some of the lesser items in order to save the essentials.[10] Thirty articles in all, they addressed nearly every ill that had afflicted American commerce with France in the past half-dozen years. And as he embarked on treaty talks, he may have sensed this would be his last service to his country: to see it through the final paroxysms of a world conflict that had raged intermittently for nearly two decades, knowing that if it declared war on Britain, he might at least make France a benevolent and supportive cobelligerent. Much rode on the outcome: his country's best interests, his reputation, and even, he hoped, a better future for maritime neutrals in time of war. The visionary as diplomat approached the starting line.

Sixteen of his draft articles were cribbed from the boilerplate of the Franco-American Convention of 1800; the most important would resurrect and renew a commitment to the principle of "free ships, free goods." Among the other fifteen, he announced immodestly, there "may be one or two which are strangers to all treaties & will be new in the law of nations," but he added righteously that they were not at odds with "the law of public justice." Most particularly, he meant to do away with the concept of contraband, arguing that because the United States did not export arms or ammunition, for which the narrowest definition of contraband should obtain, he and Bassano should agree that American vessels not be visited, searched, or harassed on that account. Nor should they be detained on arrival for any reason other than presenting "false papers" or breaching a "legal blockade." And to solve the problem of forged ships papers, he proposed to have the two parties agree on the "private marks" they would use to validate a ship's ownership and registry. As to blockades, he borrowed from the Convention of 1800 that a blockade to be deemed legal must "invest" a port so tightly as to pose a "manifest danger" to merchant ships that tried to cross them. To this he added the novelty of his earlier proposal: vessels approaching a blockade unknowingly should not be subject to seizure unless they tried to enter a second time. Finally, recurring to his free-trade impulse, he proposed that France and the United States cap the duties they levied on each other's imports at 20 percent ad valorem. And in the name of reciprocity, he even offered to do away with the discriminatory tonnage fees Congress had long imposed on vessels of foreign registry, so that incoming French carriers would pay no more than American vessels of like displacement.[11]

While he waited for a response, Barlow began to realize that tariff reduction, his favored means for expanding Franco-American commerce, was almost certainly a lost cause. Not only had French officials signaled every intention of retaining the high levels of the Trianon tariff, but he now learned that Congress, intent on preparing the country for war, had no choice but to increase this major source of revenue. Accordingly he told Monroe he would not pursue tariff reduction as long as no other obstacle stood in the way of completing a treaty. Indeed, he seemed convinced that by forgoing the 20 percent cap on imported goods, he could clear the way for a quick signing. Agreement on other issues would pose no problem, he ventured, and told Monroe he would hold the *Hornet* to convey the good news.[12]

Unfortunately, the foreign office failed to share his sense of urgency. Nearly a month passed before Bassano got around to summarizing Barlow's treaty proposals to Napoleon. Moreover, he suggested that if the emperor decided to proceed, a negotiator be appointed. The foreign minister clearly had no wish to enmesh himself in the lively give-and-take that treaty talks with Barlow was certain to entail, especially at a time when he was wholly occupied with rounding up allies for his master's planned campaign against Russia. Moreover, he pointed out, the American envoy not only hoped to sign a commercial treaty; he also wanted to talk about maritime claims and conclude a new consular convention. By implication, dealing with Barlow would be a full-time undertaking.[13]

As noted before, Barlow had a tendency to overreach, and in this instance his overloaded docket made it all too easy to invite counterproposals. And as he would soon realize, even getting to the table would take time. Almost three months elapsed before the emperor took Bassano's advice and appointed a well-briefed councillor of state to begin face-to-face talks. In the interim, although minister and envoy met informally, Barlow complained that Bassano often cancelled their appointments. He was not surprised. Aware of the bustle in the foreign office, he had no choice but to accept the latter's explanation that preparations for the Russian campaign were all-consuming.[14]

While Barlow continued to nudge Bassano for a substantive response, he also hoped to hear encouraging words from Washington. Because winter crossings were infrequent, however, not until April did he learned the administration's reaction to the diplomacy he had set in motion in mid-January. Madison and Monroe did not respond favorably. Even before the secretary of state had a copy of Barlow's treaty project, he found enough in the envoy's early dispatches to realize how far he had strayed from his instructions. The administration, he wrote back, had no present need for a commercial treaty, especially one that proposed to cap tariffs at a time of rising revenue needs.[15]

Worse was to come. Later, with Barlow's specific proposals in hand, Monroe took particular aim at the envoy's failure to nail down indemnification. Extracting a promise from Paris to settle maritime claims at some future date was simply not acceptable. Unless his treaty promised a formula for immediate settlement, he warned, "you may be sure that it will not be ratified." With barely suppressed irritation, Monroe went on to criticize seven of Barlow's treaty proposals either for their imprecision or lack of reciprocity.[16]

Unaware of how bleakly Washington would greet his efforts, Barlow turned to other matters, not least the uncertainty surrounding the Berlin and Milan decrees. Writing to Monroe in mid-March, he was pleased to report that Napoleon had alluded to the American exemption in a speech to the Senate the day before. Bassano, however, had warned him that American vessels might once more be targeted if Congress permitted the importation of British goods whose purchase had been contracted for before the passage of the non-importation law had been made known. Barlow reported having tried to explain that Congress intended no loophole but simply to uphold the sanctity of contracts, but, he added, "I have since heard that the Emperor is not well satisfied."[17] Worse, Bassano himself muddied the waters when he, too, addressed the Senate, staunchly defending the decrees in all their punitive aspects but failing to mention the American exemption. Barlow immediately jumped on this oversight as certain to give the British the pretext they needed to justify retaining their orders-in-council.[18]

In a broader sense, what particularly frustrated him and, for that matter, vexed all Americans concerned with Europe's transgressions, was the persistent interface between French and British maritime policy. Although Americans' exemption from the Berlin and Milan decrees remained uncertain, France had made no captures in their name since November 1810. As a result, except for American demands for indemnification, Franco-American tensions had subsided to the point where the British orders-in-council remained a major grievance and the issue most likely to lead Americans to war. Thus, while Bassano apologized to Barlow for failing to mention the exemption and told Serurier to portray it as an unfortunate oversight, it remained in France's best interest not to give Britain a pretext for recalling its orders.[19]

On these exasperating realities Barlow's diplomacy seemed to have run aground. London, he chided Bassano, would surely interpret the foreign minister's failure to mention Americans' exemption from the decrees to mean that they had not been. He was proved right when on April 21 a ministerial pronouncement, soon known simply as the Prince Regent's Decree, specifically cited Bassano's omission as reason enough to believe the decrees still operated against American vessels and therefore justified not recalling the orders. While rebuking Bassano for his "unaccountable reserve," Barlow nonetheless glimpsed in this latest British pronouncement an opportunity to press for a formal renunciation of the French decrees. The Prince Regent's Decree had stipulated that if Napoleon were to "publish an authentic act expressly and unconditionally repealing the Berlin and Milan decrees, the Orders in Council, including that of January 7, 1807, should be wholly revoked." Barlow sensed an opening, but to put Bassano off guard he expressed doubt the British would actually fulfill this promise. Rather, they would surely cast about for some other, less convincing pretext for continuing their depredations. The emperor, however, could do much to unite Americans against a common enemy, were he to announce the exemption "in as formal a manner as we have promulgated our law for the exclusion of British merchandize." The emperor need only "publish an authentic act, declaring the decrees, as relative to the United States, to have ceased in November 1810 . . . [and] have not been applied in any instance, since that time, and shall not be so applied in future."[20]

Whatever Barlow may have expected at this juncture, events in May and June of 1812 altered the diplomatic scene so drastically as to confront him with an entirely new set of problems. Within this two-month period, Napoleon pretended he had long since recalled his Berlin and Milan decrees, the British did in fact recall their offending orders-in-council, and Congress, unaware of London's retreat, declared war on Britain anyway. With France and the United States now cobelligerents but not allies, it would be up to the American envoy to milk this relationship for whatever advantages it might offer, while continuing to press for a commercial treaty neither side particularly cared for.

This sequence began to unfold when Bassano surprised Barlow with a document that claimed Napoleon had definitively ended the enforcement of his decrees against American shipping a full year earlier. However welcome the news, the so-called Saint-Cloud Decree, bearing the date of April 28, 1811, was an obvious fabrication. Although Bassano insisted he had sent copies to both Russell and Serurier at the time, Barlow found no file records of Russell's having received it and told Monroe he was certain the decree had been "created last week expressly for the purpose and in consequence of my note."[21] And in Washington, Serurier lamely suggested to Monroe that his own copy must have been intercepted at sea.[22] From a documentary standpoint, it might noted, had this decree been promulgated at Saint-Cloud on April 28, 1811, the *procès–verbal* the next day would surely have mentioned it. It did not.

More puzzling is why Napoleon, after months of refusing to clarify the status of his decrees, suddenly affirmed that they had long been void against American shipping. By claiming to have lifted them a year earlier, of course, he avoided the appearance of having yielded to American pressure. But why retreat at all, when obfuscation had served so well to keep America off balance in their relations with London? Groping for an explanation, Barlow suspected the emperor had acted out of calculation. He supposed that Napoleon, about to leave Paris for his Russian campaign, had thrown this sop to Americans, convinced that an Anglo-American rupture was inevitable and that Washington, inflamed by the intransigence of the Prince Regent's Decree, had already declared war or would do so before American diplomats would have an opportunity to use his concession to patch things up with the British. Believing this to be the explanation, Barlow eagerly leapt at the opportunity to show that Napoleon had miscalculated. He immediately sent word to Jonathan Russell, urging him to act quickly, to snatch peace from the jaws of war by holding up the Saint-Cloud Decree, despite its dubious provenance, as proof that Napoleon had met London's requirement for withdrawing the orders-in-council.[23] This done, he told Monroe he had done his best to keep the peace. And when on June 23 the British ministry announced its suspension of those orders-in-council, he was sure his resourcefulness had been rewarded. Somewhat smugly, he wrote the secretary: "I am gratified with a result far more favorable than I expected . . . more complete than could have arisen from the more successful war."[24]

To his chagrin, Barlow soon discovered that he had been wrong on both counts. The Saint-Cloud Decree barely registered as a causative factor in the ministry's explanation of its retreat. Neither the press nor the ministry gave it credence at the time. Rather, historians agree, the orders-in-council were jettisoned largely because Britain's mercantile community, badly hurt by a sharp economic recession, persuaded the ministry they could no longer afford to be cut off from the American export market. Barlow was wrong, too, to believe his initiative had played a role in preserving peace.[25] News soon arrived that Congress, unaware of its diplomatic victory in London, had declared war on Britain five days before the ministry's announcement. The fallout from these events left the international scene strewn with ironies. Napoleon now had a cobelligerent whose worth he never appreciated. Britain had a new enemy toward whom she could ill afford to divert her military energies. And Americans had a war for which they were badly prepared and for reasons that had all but disappeared from their list of grievances. What remained of the latter was the vain hope of annexing Canada, or at least forcing Britain to renounce impressment, which to this day she never has. In the outcome, the United States was lucky to survive with its northern boundary intact.

This newly reordered wartime scene inevitably complicated Barlow's mission. Now in addition to completing his long-sought-after commercial treaty, he had to pry from France the right of American privateers to dispose of the British prize vessels they would soon be bringing into French ports, while bending every effort to secure the repatriation of the increasing number of American seamen, some found impressed aboard those vessels and now stranded in French ports.

15 Sorting Out the Issues in Franco-American Cobelligerency

Since April, Barlow had had Monroe's warning that his treaty would be rejected unless it included an iron-clad pledge to indemnify Americans for their maritime losses. At the time Barlow could scarcely contain his chagrin. Injecting spoliation claims at this point, he wrote back, would be "dull work, hard to begin and difficult to pursue." Nor was he apologetic. Even without a claims commitment, he noted defensively, a treaty with France would have undercut London's rationale for its orders-in-council or, failing that, bolstered American resistance to them. In a backhanded rebuke, he added cryptically: "I am not certain, since the receipt of your letters . . . that I shall consent to any treaty that they are likely to give me, and yet I have little doubt that their intention is to offer me one that, under all circumstances, I should think ought to be accepted."[1] This plaintive dispatch was on its way to the *Hornet* when Barlow received a cordial letter from Bassano announcing the emperor's appointment of an experienced councillor of state who was authorized to negotiate with full powers to conclude a treaty. To catch the *Hornet* before it sailed, Barlow sent a second dispatch dated the same day, telling Monroe of this promising development.[2]

One thing was clear by mid-April 1812: Bassano had persuaded Napoleon to shore up relations with the United States before he left for Russia, or at least go through the motions. In a long report dated the 17th, he reminded the emperor that Barlow had expected treaty talks to begin the previous December.[3] Since then, he had done his best "to satisfy the impatience of that minister" who had found "this long incertitude all the more painful," he explained, because the Franco-American Convention of 1800 had expired three years ago, leaving American commerce without treaty protection. To underscore the urgency of appointing a negotiator, albeit belatedly, Bassano picked up on what Barlow, Petry, and Serurier had been telling him for the past four months: whether Congress could bring itself to declare war on Britain might well depend on its receiving some sign of goodwill from France. Without it, Serurier had recently warned, "the Federalist or English party" would gain strength in Congress at a time when its Republican majority seemed seriously intent on bringing its quarrels with Britain to a head. That majority was angry at the Prince Regent's Decree, London's recent defense of its orders-in-council, and even more recently incensed by rumors of British-inspired secessionist activity in New England. Congress, he believed, was on the brink of declaring war.[4] News that France had actively engaged Barlow in a treaty negotiation might well tip the scales. His wariness cloaked in prolixity, Bassano wrote: "The moment seems to me decisive, & if your Majesty sees no inconvenience in it, I shall have the honor to propose to him one measure, suited at least to prevent the discouragement of the party which pronounces itself against England." Having dared to suggest a negotiation, he went on to propose assigning it to Alexandre Lanouette, the comte d'Hauterive, formerly a French consul in New York, who, he assured Napoleon, had been well known and well liked in America. He characterized Hauterive as a reliable foreign office factotum who would keep within whatever bounds the emperor might set, the right person to conduct negotiations especially if the emperor decided he did not want "immediate results, should circumstances change.[5] Despite Bassano's preference, and for whatever reason, Hauterive was not appointed. Rather, three days later he informed Barlow that the emperor had named the duc de Dalberg, a councillor of state who had been active on the French diplomatic scene for more than a decade.[6]

To win favor on the other side of the Atlantic, Bassano also primed Serurier to spread the good news. Besides announcing the onset of treaty negotiations, he was to assure the administration that all was still well on the maritime front, that no American vessel had been seized under the Berlin and Milan decrees since November 1810, and that Americans now enjoy "more favors in French ports than the vessels of any other nation." And should the United States declare war on England, he could promise the emperor's bestowal of still more favors on their commerce.[7]

Bassano added a cautionary note, however. If the administration showed impatience with the pace of the negotiations, Serurier should point out that Barlow's unexpected "innovations" were likely to "impede the course of this important business." The message was clear: blame Barlow for prolonging the negotiation, but also be aware that the emperor's absence from Paris would cause further and not unwelcome delay. By implication France was still in no hurry to reach an accord, at least not on Barlow's terms. Bassano then explained in great detail why the American envoy's two most controversial aims—obtaining indemnity and lowering tariffs—were nonstarters. The emperor, he wrote, had no intention of indemnifying Americans for ships and cargoes he had taken prior to November 1810; these were just reprisals for the threat posed to French vessels by the Non-Intercourse Act. Accordingly, he had instructed Dalberg to "put off claims questions with M. Barlow as long as possible" and Serurier to refrain from discussing them, although, if pressed, he was not to "close the door" to future adjudication.[8]

Nor was Barlow's case for lowering tariffs acceptable. American arrivals were sparse not because of high duties, but because British cruisers continued to pick them off in transit. Moreover, Bassano pictured Barlow's tariff proposals as a thinly veiled bid for commercial domination. Americans carrying goods from one European port to another would be the principal beneficiaries of any tariff reductions. They already had the advantage of numbers. American vessels were everywhere, he wrote. "Their flag is the best known, the most commonly used on our seas." Any lowering of tariff "would give still greater activity to their commerce." France, he concluded, had to be "circumspect" in such matters and look to her own interests. Serurier was also to point out that except for raw cotton, imported goods of American origin were virtually untouched by the Trianon tariff. Finally, Barlow could hardly argue for tariff reduction if, as had been reported, Congress had recently raised its own tariff by 50 percent.[9] By Bassano's reading, then, the subtext to the Barlow-Dalberg negotiations was that France would show only enough goodwill to keep Americans on the path to war with Britain.

The duc de Dalberg made a good first impression. Writing to Monroe on May 12, Barlow described the councillor as "an amiable, intelligent man, well disposed but bound very straight by his instructions. I believe that a treaty may be got out of him that will be worth accepting." Ten days later, having broached the subject of indemnification, he had reason to hope for a positive response.[10] But not soon. Bassano had just left for Warsaw, and despite his promise to respond promptly to Barlow's communications, distance would be a delaying factor that meshed comfortably with what he had told Serurier: the emperor was in no hurry to conclude a treaty.

Chastened by Monroe's insistence on an indemnities clause, Barlow told Dalberg that a French commitment to compensate for damages done to American shipping must "precede or accompany" the signing of a treaty. This was Monroe's word-for-word condition, and Barlow dutifully made it his sine qua non. Marshaling his arguments in a long analysis dated June 5, he explained precisely how France had violated Americans' neutral rights and why justice required her to pay for the resulting property losses.[11] To begin, seizures under the Berlin Decree, which had declared a French naval blockade of the entire British Isles, were totally unjustified. The foreign office had assured John Armstrong at the time that American vessels were not its target. Moreover, under the prevailing terms of the Convention of 1800, it violated the principle of "free ships, free goods," and finally, Britain's two-thousand-mile coastline "could not possibly be subjected to a naval blockade by France, when she had no ships at sea." In sum, France owed reparation for vessels seized in the name of a non-existent and therefore illegal blockade.

Moving to the Milan Decree, he expressed dismay that the emperor could order American vessels confiscated for having submitted to a British warship's visit and search. An unarmed merchant ship, he observed, could no more avoid being boarded by a warship than he himself could "avoid being crushed by a millstone falling on my head from a hundred feet in the air." The emperor must surely see the injustice of punishing shipowners for yielding to a procedure they had not the means to resist. Moreover, the law of nations had long established the right of belligerents to conduct visits at sea, "for how else can the registry, cargo, and destination of a vessel be determined?" And why else would sea captains carry ship's papers, if they did not expect to be visited? Nor could France justify the seizure of American vessels "for having made a voyage to England [or] having paid a duty in England." Shipowners had a right to put into any unblockaded port they pleased, and once there they had no alternative but to pay certain fees and duties. On this last point, he carefully avoided mentioning the somewhat less than "neutral" conduct of Americans who bought British licenses in order to facilitate their commerce with the continent.[12]

Taking aim next at Napoleon's Rambouillet Decree, ostensibly an act of reprisal for the alleged threat to French shipping posed by Article 3 of the Non-Intercourse Act, he noted that Congress had given French and British shipowners eighty days' advance notice not to enter American ports on pain of confiscation. But more to the point, the penalty had never been imposed because neither belligerent had violated the law: "[N]o property was ever arrested under the law. It was never complained of as a hostile measure, a breach of neutrality or in any manner offensive to his Majesty." And yet, inexplicably, a full year after its enactment, the emperor had seen fit to begin reprisals, seizing vessels that were otherwise accustomed to coming and going freely. Because the rationale for the decree was baseless, France had a clear obligation to indemnify its victims.[13]

Harking back to April 1808, Barlow also called for redress of seizures resulting from the Bayonne Decree, so named because Napoleon was then in that city on his way to oversee his Spanish campaign when he learned of—and reacted to—news of the U.S. embargo. This "singular" decree, Barlow reflected, falsely assumed that because the law locked down American vessels in their home ports, others still at sea and claiming U.S. registry "must be english property." In fact, Barlow estimated, close to two thousand vessels were at large when the embargo took effect, and because the law did not require them to return home, they continued to trade from one foreign port to another "till many of them fell into the hands of french Cruisers." As for the twisted logic behind this decree, he wrote: "We had not engaged french privateers to help us execute our embargo law."[14]

While still drafting his rationale for indemnification, Barlow kept a close eye on other treaty-related issues. The dizzying events of June and July complicated but ultimately brightened his unflagging passion to free up and expand Franco-American commerce. Once London had suspended its orders-in-council, of course, he could no longer contend to Bassano that a friendly French treaty would inspire Congress to declare war on Britain. Given a choice, however, he preferred a peaceful outcome, as witness his intended use of the Saint-Cloud Decree. And when Britain's retreat signified an easing of tensions, he smoothly reversed fields and tried to impress on the foreign minister the even greater need for a treaty to regulate the burgeoning commerce that was sure to follow once British cruisers no longer preyed on American shipping. With British depredations presumably a thing of the past, he pictured a splendid opportunity for France and the United States to expand their exchanges of goods, especially if they were to write lower tariffs into a treaty. Once more he voiced the belief that given the stimulus of freer trade, France would soon outstrip Britain in supplying the American market. Even as Barlow finished this letter, however, came news that Congress had declared war. This turn of events, he assured Bassano in a hastily written postscript, lent even greater urgency to the need for a commercial treaty.[15] Peace or war, his impulse to negotiate never flagged.

Bassano, meanwhile, anticipating Barlow's claims for indemnification, marshaled the counterarguments Dalberg should throw back at him. Assuring his negotiator that France could readily justify the seizure of American ships and cargoes prior to November 1, 1810, he proceeded to revisit the timeworn rationales, beginning with the Berlin Decree, which he characterized as a righteous "municipal" measure unrelated to American maritime rights and therefore not a basis for claims. How an announced blockade of the entire British Isles could fall under the heading of municipal lawmaking he did not explain, but his rationale for its sequel, the Milan Decree, made more sense. The latter, he declared, properly punished Americans for their unneutral submission to British maritime policies, for submitting to British cruisers' visits and searches, and for paying British taxes and fees in order to smuggle cargoes of British origin to the continent. He was not deceived on that count. And lastly, the Rambouillet Decree fittingly exacted reprisals for the threat posed to French vessels by the Non-Intercourse Act. Dalberg was to reject all claims relating to these decrees, but, he added, "without altogether refusing claims that are just." He could, for example, agree—at least in principle—to "examine" claims based on the detention of American vessels since November 1810, a number so small the foreign minister doubtless saw it as a manageable liability.[16]

Bassano also prepped Dalberg on how to respond to each of Barlow's thirty-one treaty articles. About to leave Paris to join the emperor, he apparently realized that if the negotiations were to go forward, his agent would need to be instructed as fully as possible. France, he began, could agree to renew most of the provisions of the Convention of 1800 with a few minor changes—but not Barlow's "new" proposals, either because they conferred too much favor on Americans, lacked reciprocity, or advantaged the emperor's enemies. Abandoning the concept of contraband, for example, by agreeing not to seize weapons of war found on board American carriers would not keep the British from seizing arms bound for France. Nor need Dalberg be reminded how assiduously Americans had armed insurrectionaries during France's failed effort to subdue Saint-Domingue a decade earlier. As for Barlow's call for lowering tariffs and equalizing tonnage fees, Bassano repeated what he had told Serurier: Americans would benefit disproportionately. Their vessels already "carry more commerce than any other neutral nation." Moreover, France could not grant such concessions without according the same benefits to others with whom it had most-favored-nation agreements.[17]

Not to appear entirely hostile, Bassano grudgingly identified a few points Dalberg might concede. Recovering American deserters, for example, was a matter reasonably left to U.S. consuls; France had no stake in the outcome. Nor would the emperor object to restoring to their owners American vessels retaken from a common enemy in wartime or prevent Americans from selling vessels to French buyers, although in neither instance would the United States likely be called on to reciprocate. Also lacking in reciprocity, because U.S. embargoes were less frequently imposed, was Barlow's suggestion, which Bassano curtly dismissed, that France pay a per diem to American captains whose vessels were detained by French embargoes for more than ten days. Dalberg was to reject this one outright. Americans would have to take their chances. Still, he was open to Barlow's so-called transit proposal—that is, to allow American importers who failed to find an immediate market for their cargoes to store them for a period of six months on payment of a 1 percent transit duty. Bassano thought 1 percent was probably too low and expressed some concern that the subsequent marketing of these goods elsewhere in Europe might undersell French competitors. He nonetheless authorized Dalberg to write a schedule of transit duties into the treaty if it met with the approval of the comte de Sussy, France's minister of commerce.[18] In the ensuing three-way correspondence, Sussy said he foresaw no problem in permitting Americans to store cargoes in transit, and by imposing duties up to 5 percent the French treasury would net a modest but welcome return.

Bassano ended his lengthy instructions with a word of tactical advice. Barlow, he warned, would not be deterred from putting forward his "innovations," and Dalberg should avoid making "a positive refusal" to any of them. Rather, if dissuasion failed, he should tell the American envoy that he would seek new instructions. Meanwhile, he and the emperor had confidence in Dalberg's "dexterity" to keep the negotiations alive.[19]

On May 28 Dalberg reported his first meetings with Barlow. Predictably, the American envoy had touched on the issue of indemnification, but mostly he had complained of France's continued ill treatment of American shipowners, some hassled by French port officials on arrival, others facing loss of their vessels to the uncertain application of the Berlin and Milan decrees. He could move the negotiations forward, he believed, but only if the emperor at this point met Barlow's insistence that the captains of French corsairs be notified that they no longer applied to American vessels. As long as complaints persisted on this score, Barlow had assured him, Americans would have no confidence in dealing with France.[20]

Bassano's response, dated June 9, was snappishly dismissive. He himself had assured Barlow that no American vessel had been seized under the color of those decrees since November 1810. How could the American envoy possibly doubt this was true? Heated though it was, Bassano's defensiveness proved short-lived. Even as he scoffed at Barlow's disbelief, Navy Minister Denis Decrès was writing to tell him that French corsairs, in fact, still operated as though the decrees were still in force because, he explained, "no change in instructions to corsairs has been ordered by His Majesty, and they believe they have the right to stop Americans as when these decrees had truly and nominally all their vigor." Should the emperor wish to change these instructions, Decrès remarked equably, he would, of course, "transmit" them.[21] Bassano never raised the issue again, and whether the captains of French privateers were ever notified became irrelevant when, shortly thereafter, the United States entered the war. Franco-American cobelligerency finally laid to rest the protracted uncertainties surrounding the status of the Berlin and Milan decrees. Claims relating thereto Barlow added to the tally.

Bassano was equally defiant in responding to Barlow's generalized complaint about American vessels being badly treated on arrival in French ports. Remind the American, he told Dalberg, that cargoes of American origin were freely admitted to all the ports of the empire and that Americans were the only foreigners privileged to bring in colonial goods. Remind him, too, that France had bestowed these and other favors, even though the United States had not fully lived up to the conditions of the Cadore Letter; it still permitted its citizens to export cargoes to Britain. And as for the indemnification issue, Bassano brushed aside his negotiator's suggestion, doubtless planted by Barlow, that France might agree to compensate those Americans whose vessels had been taken before the decrees were known, or were found in fact not to have violated them, or had been given assurances of immunity by officials in Naples, Holland, or Spain. Bassano would hear none of it. He repeated what he had told Dalberg at the outset: France had solid grounds for denying property claims prior to November 1810. And as before he told his negotiator to steer Barlow away from talk of maritime claims and focus on commercial matters.[22]

On this score Dalberg made clear he hoped to tie commercial clauses into some sort of political commitment. His May 28 report, doubtless influenced by Barlow's thinking, dangled the possibility that if they could devise a treaty that would expand Franco-American commerce to the point where France replaced Britain as a major trade partner, thereby assuring the U.S. government of the tariff revenues it needed to survive, Americans might agree to close their ports to all British traffic as long as France and Britain remained at war. The alternative, Barlow had cautioned, was grim. Without such a treaty, and without the prospect of an alternate source of tariff revenues, he feared Barlow was right to predict Americans would once more "throw themselves into the arms of England."[23]

If Dalberg was uneasy about treaty prospects, Jean-Baptiste Petry saw an even bleaker outcome from what was transpiring off the coast of Spain. He told Bassano how angrily Barlow had greeted the latest reports that more American grain carriers had fallen victim to the French naval squadron operating in those waters and how sternly he had demanded that France indemnify the owners and punish those responsible for burning these vessels. What especially concerned him was Barlow's prediction that Congress, on learning of these latest outrages, would find it difficult to continue down the path to war with Britain and might even back away from the warlike measures it had already taken. And on hearing of Barlow's stalled treaty negotiations, it might retreat even further for want of the sort of French support that would make war with Britain a feasible course of action. So believing and as one who had had firsthand experience of American politics, Petry hoped Bassano would heed his warnings.[24]

Petry, it might be noted, had gradually thrust himself forward to become a significant figure in the negotiations as the summer wore on. Apparently he felt Bassano and Dalberg lacked some of the context underlying Barlow's steady outpouring of complaints. Although his familiarity with the American political scene was somewhat dated, he did scan the *National Intelligencer* whenever he could get a copy and projected the air of being well qualified to read Barlow's stance on various issues. During their frequent meetings, he listened patiently to the American minister's grievances, rebutted them when he could, or tried to minimize their importance in the larger sphere of common interests. Indeed he was so attentive to Barlow that one historian suggests he may have been angling to replace Dalberg as chief negotiator.[25] If so, Dalberg seemed unaware of the challenge and sometimes used him to convey messages. When on one notable occasion Sussy relayed the emperor's promise that if Americans declared war, he would accord them "all the commercial advantages they could desire," he asked Petry to tell Barlow the good news. In this instance, Napoleon's qualifier was not well received. Tired of being toyed with, Barlow replied heatedly "under that condition there will be no treaty."[26] When Congress *did* declare war, of course, he was quick to remind Petry what the emperor had promised.

Not all the month of June was spent jousting with Dalberg and Petry, however. When Ruth and Clara went junketing that month, he wrote of having ridden out to Malmaison to call on Josephine. He went to put in a good word with the onetime belle of Martinique on behalf of William Lee, who hoped to import two or three million pounds of sugar from that island and believed the former empress might be able to secure him permission. Whatever the outcome of the visit, Barlow's letter to Ruth ended with more than the usual endearments, in this instance offering her advice on how to avoid a French kiss. Amid strains of diplomacy, he still managed to retain a lighter side. "Give Clara a little dry kiss for me," he wrote playfully, "with the outside of the lips. Don't bite & don't open the mouth."[27]

Personal moments like these soon became fewer. In late June the diplomatic scene came alive with a vengeance when news broke that London had removed a major American grievance by suspending its orders-in-council. Jean-Baptiste Petry made the first move, hoping to stave off the Anglo-American rapprochement that seemed certain to follow. The British ministry's retreat, he explained to Bassano, was contingent on the United States agreeing to restore full commercial relations. The bad news was they would likely comply. On the bright side, however, he believed the British government's announcement was flawed insofar as it had not explicitly suspended Fox's Blockade of 1806. If, as he hoped, Americans had the wit to reject the olive branch on this account, France should look to how else it might revive their war spirit. In a worst-case scenario, of course, it might keep Americans in line by threatening to re-activate the Berlin Decree, which, he reminded, had been the emperor's specific response to Fox's Blockade.[28]

To his credit, Barlow knew what was afoot, and had he been conversant with modern-day put-downs he might have muttered, "Nice try, Petry, but not this time." Two days after Petry wrote Bassano questioning the recall of the 1806 blockade, Barlow sent the foreign minister copies of three letters from Jonathan Russell, which together conveyed Foreign Secretary Lord Castlereagh's assurance that Fox's Blockade had indeed been among the suspended orders.[29] And for the moment at least, until news of war arrived he was pleased to parade London's retreat as a victory for Americans' stalwart defense of freedom of the seas. No longer, he wrote Bassano, could the emperor accuse them of not "vindicating the independence of their flag." And as mentioned earlier, he proceeded to regale the foreign minister with the golden possibilities now open for Franco-American commerce if France were to negotiate a commercial treaty.[30]

By the end of July, even with news of America's entry to the war, the principal players on the international scene were not sure what it meant. Dalberg, for one, feared that London, having met America's major grievance, might try to abort the impending hostilities or that Congress itself might think better of its war declaration. He could only hope the situation had become irreversible, that Americans were already attacking Canada and sending out scores of privateers.[31]

Petry, alarmist as usual, feared that Americans, having summoned up the resolve to make war on Britain, might lash out at France, as well. Their anger had united them against Britain, he warned, but they were also sorely displeased with France for what he bluntly described as "our spoliation of their commerce, the hauteur and contempt with which we receive their remonstrances, and above all for having burned their vessels at sea." Congress had already warned that "if the pending negotiations with France do not completely terminate differences in an honorable manner, the American Government will adopt toward France the same measures that were adopted against England." He estimated that sometime in the next six months, Congress *would* declare war on France unless the emperor acted to resolve those differences. At the top of the administration's grievances, he continued, were the unsettled maritime claims. Thanks to the publication of "live" diplomatic correspondence routinely submitted to Congress, Petry was able to verify that Washington had looked coolly on Barlow's initial draft treaty because it lacked a firm indemnities pledge. This explained why in recent weeks the American envoy had dwelt so single-mindedly on this issue.[32]

Careful not to raise the claims question himself, Petry recounted having discussed other ways to relieve tensions. Now that France and the United States were cobelligerents, he and Barlow had revisited a familiar array of possible French concessions, but he also drew from Barlow a sense of how France might win favor by playing a benevolent role in Madison's apparent designs on Spanish Florida. The emperor, he reflected, would do well to oblige the administration by recognizing its recent annexation of West Florida. Americans had long claimed the panhandle as part of the Louisiana Purchase, and because no one had ever precisely defined the boundaries of Louisiana, the point was not worth contesting. The future of East Florida presented a somewhat different but not unwelcome scenario. The United States obviously had no valid claims to the peninsula, but the fact that American forces were even now marching toward St. Augustine was certain to complicate Anglo-American relations in the future, especially if London continued to support the Spanish junta. Accordingly, he urged the emperor to acquiesce in the de facto takeover of West Florida and take satisfaction from the Anglo-American enmity certain to be generated over the ultimate disposition of East Florida.[33] Finally, because American privateers would soon be bringing in British prizes, he forwarded Barlow's request that they be permitted to sell off both captured ships and cargoes, requiring only that they lade cargoes equivalent in value to the prize goods they disposed of. He called this the sort of "hospitality one owes to one's friends."[34] Two weeks later Barlow seconded Petry's call for greater wartime "hospitality" but thought it inappropriate to burden privateers with the equal-value export requirement.[35] The conversation over how France would receive American prize-masters was just beginning.

What particularly concerned Barlow, when word of war reached him, was the fate of the swelling number of American crewmen found on board captured British vessels. Some were unquestionably U.S. citizens, either forced into service if the prize were a British warship or seamen who had voluntarily signed on to a British merchantman. French officials, unable or unwilling to distinguish one nationality from the other, were locking them all up as prisoners of war. The plight of these Americans, he wrote Bassano, smacked of wholesale injustice. Those forced into British service might already be deemed prisoners of war, but France, instead of freeing them on arrival, had imprisoned them along with their former captors. Once locked up they lacked the resources of the British prisoners who received a daily money allowance from charitable subscriptions in England, thus were deprived of the sustenance that allowed their cell mates to enjoy "a certain degree of comfort." In sum, he wrote, the American captive "suffers all the calamities of a British prisoner, without sharing his advantages; and to add to the horror of his situation, he has before his eyes the despair of ever being exchanged." London, he noted, had made clear that French and British exchanges of prisoners would not include Americans. The minister of war, he told Bassano, would confirm this wretched situation, and if the latter were to release these Americans to his custody, he promised to establish their bona fides and ship them home on the next available American naval vessel. As an added incentive, he predicted that many of them would enlist in the U.S. Navy and join France in wreaking vengeance on the power that was now "our common enemy."[36]

In this instance, Barlow's plea did not go unheeded. By early September Bassano had arranged for the war and navy ministries to release Americans taken from captured British vessels, on a case-by-case basis. Barlow's success in repatriating them thereafter depended on his being able to document an individual's nationality to the satisfaction of French authorities.

16 Brainstorming a Solution to the Indemnities Issue

During the second week of August, Bassano and Dalberg exchanged assessments of the ongoing negotiations. The foreign minister, for his part, was quick to blame Barlow for having created the current impasse, recalling acerbically that when the American minister had first presented his treaty proposals in February, maritime claims had been "accessory" to commercial issues and that he had seemed satisfied to postpone them. Since then, however, the American minister had inexplicably thrust indemnification to the fore, deliberately reviving "past resentments" and blocking the way to rapprochement.[1]

Clearly annoyed, he told Dalberg not to send him any more of Barlow's complaints; he resented their "sharpness" of tone and would not respond. Remind Barlow, rather, that no American vessel had been seized under the Berlin and Milan decrees since November 1810 and that he had already been told why all claims prior to that date were nonnegotiable. Remind him, too, that the British had been the first to offend against the rights of neutrals, having touched off the cycle of spoliation with Fox's Blockade, followed by taxing American vessels and often using their flag to smuggle goods through the continental blockade. Satisfied that he had made a no-fault case for France's negotiating position, he advised his agent to stick to his original instructions—that is, agree to renew most of the Convention of 1800 and promise the emperor's bestowal of more commercial advantages as soon as he was no longer occupied with other important matters. He ended with the customary qualifier that Dalberg might allow "but always verbally and without committing that the business of indemnities will not be lost to view & that legitimate claims will be examined."[2]

Dalberg's assessment, unlike Bassano's, sounded a note of desperation. He was alarmed by the threatening passages Barlow had read to him from his most recent instructions. They pictured Washington, already frustrated by its envoy's inability to win a claims settlement, now furious at the burning of American grain ships. Dalberg was shaken. War was almost certain, he warned, unless France put an end to this source of grievance and agreed to indemnify. And like Petry, he speculated that even if the United States did not declare war on France, it might be forced to make peace with Britain. Were this to happen, Barlow had warned him, the administration would turn on France; Madison was sure to "rupture relations." Given the urgency of the situation, he told Bassano he had taken what he believed was a necessary initiative: he had sent the American minister a counteroffer listing the treaty articles he hoped would signal the emperor's good intentions and slow the slide toward war.[3]

Not surprisingly Dalberg's proposals prefigured no major change in commercial policy. France would still license imported colonial goods, require certificates of origin, and insist that incoming and outgoing cargoes remain equal in value. But as long as both remained at war with Britain, he proposed to add some of the quasi-alliance features he had hinted at earlier. He hoped, for example, they could agree to protect each other's merchantmen, offer convoy when convenient, and permit the sale of prize vessels in each other's ports. France, he allowed, might also permit Americans to store cargoes "in transit." Beyond this, he merely proposed to renew the Convention of 1800, most of its articles having to do with property rights, salvage, ships' papers, and consular duties.[4]

Barlow promptly accepted all of Dalberg's proposed articles and added a few of his own by way of amplification. Clearly eager to make a beginning, even a small one, he still left no doubt that he expected the final document to provide for indemnification. "This being adjusted," he wrote hopefully, "would produce a great and salutary effect" when their treaty reached Washington. Dalberg deftly sidestepped the indemnities issue and applauded Barlow's willingness to proceed with a scaled-back list of treaty items. He cautioned, however, that the emperor would have to approve whatever they agreed to, and because the latter was occupied with "the greatest operations of war," more delay was inevitable.[5]

By the end of August, Bassano seemed ready to take his own initiative. Barlow's reminding him that Americans were now joined against a common enemy appears to have softened his reflexive tendency to say no to anything the American minister proposed. Barlow's barrage, coupled with Dalberg's dire forebodings, apparently persuaded the foreign minister that the time had come to put forward at least a few wartime concessions he hoped Napoleon would find acceptable. Wary of approaching his master without backup, he turned to the comte de Sussy with a question. Would the minister of commerce subscribe to his recommendations that Americans be permitted to sell off British prize vessels and their contents, allow them to store for re-export any goods of British provenance, and not require them to lade cargoes of equal value?[6]

Sussy's response made clear he thought Bassano had overreached. Despite earlier signals that he looked favorably on cultivating American goodwill, Sussy balked at his colleague's generosity. The emperor, to be sure, had reason to welcome the increasing number of American privateers in European waters (Barlow estimated that three hundred were already at sea), but he saw no reason to grant them greater rights than were accorded to French prize takers. The emperor might, however, permit Americans to store prize cargoes pending re-export unless their contents were forbidden entry. Sussy also drew the line at forgoing the equal-value export requirement, although he would offer the captains of privateers a full year to comply with it.[7] How this time line would oblige the captains of small armed sloops whose cargo-carrying capacity was minimal seemed to escape him.

Clearly Napoleon's prolonged absence meant that French officials could only guess how the emperor might rule on the treatment of American privateers when they arrived in French ports with prize vessels in tow. Barlow was quick to suggest, however, that for lack of explicit instructions, they should adhere to guidelines set forth by the Convention of 1800. As early as August 8, he asked Bassano to make sure U.S. consuls were permitted to oversee the process, as authorized by Article 24 of that document.[8] His efforts began to bear fruit when, in mid-September, Bassano confirmed that the maritime prefect at Brest had acceded to the request of the American consul there to dispose of a British prize brought in by the privateer *Decatur*.[9] Haltingly other concessions followed. Thanks to Barlow's unremitting insistence, French officials seldom challenged the right of U.S. consuls to sell off captured vessels and their cargoes, unless the latter were of British origin. Under Sussy's rule, such goods were "sequestered" pending a decision as to their disposition. Not until April 1813 did Napoleon decree that

American captors might re-export goods not lawfully permitted entry. Considering that such goods were ordered burned when brought in by French prize masters, the emperor's concession in this instance ranks as one of his few gestures of goodwill toward his American cobelligerents.[10]

While the wheels of compromise ground slowly behind the scenes, Barlow continued to chafe at the prospect of further delays. During a meeting in late August, he harangued Petry on how shabbily France had treated his mission. On its face, his distress seemed genuine, although he may have overdone it deliberately, hoping to signal that his patience was running out and that he might end the negotiations unless France picked up its pace. He knew he could count on Petry to relay his impatience to Bassano, and sure enough, Petry wasted no time. While the American minister's words were still fresh in his mind, he quoted him directly. Barlow had begun, accusingly: "I have had nothing from the Minister for four months, nothing (he told me) but a single letter on the subject of a blind seaman about whom I had written so long before that I had forgotten about him. He promised me back in January in the most positive manner that the treaty would be made within a few days and the indemnities disposed of to our satisfaction. Now six and a half months have passed and nothing is finished—not even the appearance that anything will be done for a long time now—I am always criticized for complaining—but can I see our vessels detained, our vessels burned, our seamen imprisoned, prevented from taking service on board our ships or employed aboard yours . . . without making representations? What opinion would they have of me in America, and here even, if I stay silent? . . . Has not the Emperor told me *that if we declared war, he would accord all that we would ask, all that we would desire?*" Petry reported having tried to persuade Barlow that only Bassano's absence in Wilna (today Vilnius, Lithuania) and the emperor's being even further afield stood in the way of completing a treaty. Barlow was unmoved. "'War is declared,' said he, 'a decision is soon given and transmitted.'"[11]

Except for one more jab at how badly France had treated his countrymen, this sullen response more or less marked the end of Barlow's summer of frustration. A more hopeful era was about to open, but meanwhile in a bitter letter to Bassano dated September 4, he recounted the ironic saga of four American seamen who, having been forced to serve on board a British frigate, had subsequently been assigned to a prize crew put aboard an American dispatch boat the frigate had captured. Acting with laudable initiative, the four had assisted the captain and crew to retake the vessel and had brought it into a French port where, Barlow remonstrated, they had been seized and imprisoned. So now, he exclaimed, "they find a prison on land instead of a prison at sea." They should be released at once, he told Bassano, inasmuch as William Lee had conclusively verified their citizenship. Nor was this the only instance, he added, in which American seamen, impressed through no fault of their own, had been locked up indiscriminately with British prisoners of war.[12]

For all his sense of outrage, Barlow would soon discover how difficult it was to single out the "true" Americans captured with English-speaking crews. Whereas American sailors often took the precaution of carrying papers attesting to their U.S. citizenship, they were not required to, and those who had them sometimes sold them to British deserters, relying on their shipmates to verify that they were native sons if French officials came asking. Some were lucky, others were not. Barlow, to his credit, never flagged in his efforts to repatriate those he could honestly identify as his fellow countrymen—either that or find berths for them aboard French or American privateers. Not surprisingly, he spent much of his time in the weeks that followed looking after the interests of American seamen, either stranded or wrongfully imprisoned.

How Joel Barlow finally managed to resolve the indemnities issue, helped by his old friend Daniel Parker, makes for a fascinating tale of persistence and ingenuity. When he boarded his carriage in late October and set off for Napoleon's headquarters in Wilna, he brought with him both a commercial treaty and a maritime claims convention—drafts of which Dalberg had agreed to and Bassano had promised the emperor would sign.

A breakthrough began on August 26 when Barlow, having just returned from a visit with Parker at the latter's country estate, called on Dalberg to tell him that he and Parker had discussed various ways France might satisfy American maritime claims. Although Barlow declined to discuss details, Dalberg must have sensed an opening. The next day, clearly hoping to prepare Bassano for whatever full-bodied proposal might materialize, Dalberg put the situation to him in stark terms: he was certain there would be no treaty unless France agreed to settle all maritime claims, not just those arising since November 1810. Barlow had just repeated his instructions on this point, and the collateral evidence was conclusive. Madison's recent message to Congress, Monroe's letters to Barlow, and what Petry had gleaned from the Washington press all pointed to the centrality of the indemnities issue. Dalberg made clear he believed the time had come to stop contesting the validity of those claims and find a way to meet them. Whatever plan Barlow came up with at this point, he hoped Bassano would agree that France could find no better "intermediary." Here, after all, he wrote, was a man "who owns a house in Paris, writes poetry that is more read here than in America," and "is reproached at home for his fondness for France."[13] His implication was plain: if no treaty with Barlow, then with whom?

Barlow, for his part, having piqued Dalberg's curiosity, indulged a playful show of reticence. Holding back on his plan, he urged the Frenchman to use his imagination: surely there were ways France might devise to compensate American claimants and, yes, at little expense. Or, if Dalberg were to listen carefully, he might hear some of the indemnification proposals then circulating among members of the American business community.[14] Why Barlow tried to distance himself from his own plan, at least at the outset, remains uncertain. He may have hoped Dalberg would be more open to proposals if he believed they came with widespread support, that they reflected a consensus, and were not something he and Parker had cooked up on their own, although almost certainly they had. Dalberg, his curiosity aroused, pressed for details, but again Barlow told him there was an easy solution if he would only give it some thought. Puzzled as to how France could arrange to compensate Americans claimants at little cost, he speculated that perhaps Barlow meant to resurrect earlier proposals to have the United States indemnify its own claimants by selling off public lands in territories it did not yet own but might acquire, if France were to press Spain to cede East Florida or retroactively saw fit to expand the western boundaries of Louisiana. Having researched the foreign office archives, he knew such proposals had surfaced from time to time.[15] Otherwise, he was at a loss to fathom Barlow's hints at a cheap and easy way out. And when he probed again, and Barlow once more replied that it was not up to him to propose a solution, Dalberg was so affronted by his "brusque" behavior that he refused to continue the conversation and told Bassano he intended to find out what Barlow was up to by "other means."[16]

Whatever those "other means," when Dalberg wrote again to Bassano in early September, he enclosed a two-page outline of a very explicit indemnity proposal. In light of Bassano's incurious response, perhaps it was only a summary. It was undated, unsigned, and bore no reference to its provenance.[17]

The author of this "plan" estimated U.S. claims against France at a total of 20 million francs (roughly $4 million) based on the seizure of an estimated two hundred vessels since 1806. For compensation purposes, these claims were to be split evenly between what France was believed to owe for the seizure of one hundred ships and cargoes between November 1806 and July 1809—that is, between the Berlin and Rambouillet decrees—and what she owed for the other hundred confiscations since 1809. To satisfy claimants in the earlier category, France was to give Barlow thirty licenses, which he in turn would sell to American captains, permitting them to import native products from the United States subject to the tariff levels that had obtained at the time their property was seized. Guaranteed to profit from these lower tariff rates, the licensees would, in effect, indemnify themselves for the property losses they had suffered prior to July 1809—that is, if they were still active as importers. Separately Barlow would use the proceeds from the sale of the licenses to establish a fund to pay off those whose property losses also predated 1809 but, presumably, were no longer in business.

To satisfy the hundred claimants in the second category, Barlow would sell another thirty licenses to American importers of colonial products but subject to current tariff levels. Here the compensatory factor lay in the licensees' having the exclusive right to import and sell these products for a period of eight months. And again, proceeds from the sales of these licenses would go into a fund to indemnify others whose property losses postdated 1809.[18]

Bassano showed only mild interest in the plan, but Petry, when he learned of it, exploded in outrage. Barlow, he wrote, had proposed a disgraceful means of bestowing immense profits on those Americans currently engaged in the import trade. Worse, the 20 million francs he proposed to derive from the sale of the licenses would not come close to indemnifying other American claimants. Barlow, he charged, had hatched a speculative scheme so discreditable as to warrant his recall. If it were known in America, he would certainly be recalled. France should have no part of it.[19]

He went on to explain how claimants in both categories stood to rack up enormous profits. First, because no point of origin had been specified for colonial goods, licensees in this category would likely smuggle them in from England. By dint of lower freight and insurance costs, they would undersell their French competitors to the latter's great disadvantage. As for the thirty licensees authorized to bring in American products, they could expect even larger rewards. He took cotton as an example. Over the course of several voyages, thirty vessels, each lading three hundred tons of cotton, could net profits as high as 56 million francs—this after duties were paid and Barlow had set aside a measly 20 million francs for other claimants. Cotton cargoes aside, he went on, whatever the imported articles and whatever the duties imposed on them, these licensed "speculators" would profit greatly, causing losses to the imperial treasury and contributing little to the overall well-being of Franco-American commerce.[20]

Petry was clearly shocked at Barlow's readiness to hand a windfall to one set of claimants and shortchange others. In his later correspondence, he showed a certain fondness for the American minister and openly mourned him at the time of his death, but in this instance he was livid. This scheme, he wrote Bassano, comes from an "impure source," from a man whose "speculations in France during our revolution" should not be forgotten. Just as Barlow had bilked Frenchman during the Scioto fiasco, he now stood ready to betray the financial interests of a sizable group of his own countrymen. It was "a villainous affair."[21]

Bassano responded rather vaguely to what may have been only a summary of Barlow's plan. His answering letter referred without comment to what he understood to be a proposal to license Americans to import goods from America at former tariff levels and colonial goods at current levels. Whatever its details—and he seemed not to want to know—the plan nevertheless struck him as being "very delicate," something Dalberg should discuss with Sussy, whose ministry had oversight of licenses and tariffs.[22] Once more passing the buck, Bassano was, in this instance, perhaps merely deferring to his colleague's overlapping brief, but also, one suspects, he shrank from voicing opinions that might come back to him wrapped in Napoleonic wrath. His safest course respecting indemnities was to stand by what he knew to be the emperor's prevailing dictum, that Americans had no basis whatever for maritime claims. Accordingly he seemed quite content to let others talk of settling them. Turning to treaty-related matters in general, he struck a more positive note, observing that Barlow's scaled-back response to Dalberg's counterproposal had swept away "a large part of the difficulties." Problems remained, of course, as to what Americans might be permitted to export or re-export, but aside from these and other unresolved issues—most of them negotiable—the foreign minister conveyed the impression that the only obstacle to a signing ceremony was the emperor's preoccupation with "far-flung military operations."[23]

Far from reassured, Dalberg sounded a note of panic. He had, as instructed, referred Barlow's indemnity plan to Sussy but had received no response. Meanwhile, the American minister had repeated his warning that a refusal to settle maritime claims would almost certainly lead to war. The indemnities issue had become so critical that his being forbidden to discuss it had made his mission "more delicate and more difficult." Unless the emperor were indifferent to the outcome, he must "consent to some arrangement" and do it quickly.[24]

By late September, apparently weary of dealing with Dalberg, Barlow cast about to hasten his mission by reaching out to prominent figures in the French political establishment. In this he was fortunate to have in hand a recent letter from Madison that underscored the possibility of war with greater authority than he alone could muster. Written on August 11, at a time when the president still hoped for an early end to hostilities with Britain, Madison had warned that "in the event of a pacification with G.B., the full tide of indignation with which the public mind here is boiling will be directed ag'st France, if not obviated by a due reparation of her wrongs. War will be called for by the nation almost *una voce*."[25] Barlow not only read this passage to Dalberg; he also made its contents known to persons who, he hoped, would persuade Napoleon that war with the United States was imminent unless indemnification were forthcoming.

Those whom he sounded out reacted differently. The comte d'Hauterive stiffly reminded Barlow of Dalberg's primacy in the ongoing negotiation, and Talleyrand, whom he twice approached, told Barlow he had no authority to receive any overtures. More receptive was Jean-Jacques-Régis de Cambacérès, the arch-chancellor of France and its de facto ruler in Napoleon's absence, who ventured optimistically that once the emperor realized the gravity of the situation, he would surely move swiftly to settle all American claims. Cambacérès added helpfully that Talleyrand, though not in a position to help, also shared this view.[26] Dalberg, for his part, took these violations of protocol in stride. Barlow, he remarked wryly, might also have written directly to the emperor If his American friends had not dissuaded him.[27]

Petry, always alert to what Barlow might be up to, learned of his back-channel activity when authorities intercepted a letter he had written to Madison on September 26. Some of its passages were encrypted, but others made clear the American envoy had actively sought and, in some instances, won a sympathetic hearing from prominent figures. Petry sniffed disapprovingly at the irregularity but was quick to reinforce Barlow's assessment of how dangerously Franco-American relations had deteriorated. The warning signs from Washington, he noted, had steadily escalated ever since Madison had made his case to Congress for a declaration of war against Britain in June. That same presidential message had also denounced France for her "outrageous" treatment of American shipowners and her refusal to recompense them for her "extensive spoliations." Now, in addition to the president's letter to Barlow—the one openly threatening war unless France agreed to indemnify—a similar threat from Madison had appeared in the *National Intelligencer.* With Barlow standing firmly on the same ground, Petry put the crisis squarely to Bassano: "The question is therefore, do we desire a rupture with the United States, or do we not desire it?" If France were to avoid war, he wrote, "there is no time to lose to prevent it." Though pleading ignorance of what might be the emperor's "grand designs," he had to believe that if United States did declare war on France, Britain would be the principal beneficiary.[28]

Whether Napoleon was persuaded by the cumulative impact of these warnings or the certainty of war expressed in Madison's August 11 letter, he must have decided he had nothing to lose by inviting Barlow to Wilna, luring him with the promise that he would sign both a treaty and a claims convention. Bassano sent the invitation on October 11, and Barlow left for the emperor's winter headquarters on October 26.[29]

Before he left on what would be his final mission, Barlow busied himself with ministerial duties that in some instances set the tone for the near future of Franco-American relations. His efforts to spring American seamen from detention, for example, intersected fortuitously with the wartime need to man an increasing number of French and American privateers. Except for the duels at sea in which American frigates covered themselves with glory, privateering produced one of the brighter spots in an otherwise lackluster war effort. Shipowners, seizing the moment, hastened to mount guns on small vessels and sent them swarming across the Atlantic where they sometimes captured outbound British merchantmen still within landfall.

Barlow, to his great satisfaction, found himself well positioned to lend support to one of the unsung heroes of this enterprise, a swashbuckling individual named Nathan Haley who had once served in the French navy and would soon be known as the "scourge" of British shipping lanes. Because the captains of privateers, like Haley, lost much-needed deckhands whenever they put a prize crew aboard a captured vessel, the two men found common ground. Haley needed the extra crewmen for a sixteen-gun sloop he was fitting out at Brest, and Barlow believed he had a means to oblige him. The day he set off for Wilna, he sent ahead to Bassano the names of seventy-seven American detainees who, he wrote, were eager to serve their country and who, if released and put under Haley's command, would serve the cause of both nations.[30] He continued to lobby for their redeployment when he reached Wilna, assuring Bassano that Haley was "a mariner of great courage & experience, not unknown to the French marine, having been formerly for a while an officer in your naval service." Bassano repeated this description word for word when, two days later, he commended Haley to his colleague, the duc de Feltre, minister of war, urging that he be allowed to recruit the fifty-four American detainees who, Barlow had told him, were being held at Cambray, Arras, and Valenciennes.[31] Indeed, Barlow himself might have written this letter, beginning with its expressed dismay that these men had been imprisoned in the first place. They were Americans, Bassano parroted, taken from captured British vessels, persons whom Barlow could certify as U.S. citizens, and who, as further proof of their American citizenship, had been denied British subsistence or inclusion in prisoner exchanges. Ever since the United States had entered the war, Americans had invariably freed their countrymen whenever they found them pressed into British service. France, he believed, could do no less: "What they themselves do, it seems natural and just they be able to obtain from the French government."[32]

There followed a predictable back-and-forth between the war and navy ministries, but once assured of the emperor's approval, the duc de Feltre ordered the prisoners released to Haley's custody. The process was not without delays, however. Feltre insisted on making sure that none of those released had received charitable aid from Britain during their detention and required that the U.S. legation positively verify their U.S. citizenship. Only if they had satisfied these "formalities" would he hand them over to Captain Haley.[33] Fortunately Consul Isaac Cox Barnet already had their affidavits in hand and promptly satisfied the ministry that Haley's recruits were what they claimed to be.[34]

Pleased with the outcome, Barlow assured Bassano that Haley would put the former detainees to good use. "His promise of returning two English prisoners for each American that he receives from France, may resemble the premature sale of the Bear Skin," he admitted, "but I have little doubt that he will keep his word."[35] In the aftermath, Haley did not disappoint. He sailed from Brest in March 1813 on the first of three highly successful voyages. Ultimately, his *True Blooded Yankee* sent back captured British ships and cargoes worth an estimated $400,000. When the British finally caught up with him that fall, Haley had sent ashore so many prize crews that his full complement of two hundred had been reduced to twenty-three. They and Haley spent the rest of the war in a Gibraltar prison.[36]

While Americans taken from captured British prizes had to prove their citizenship, the fate of crewmen whose vessels the French had been detaining since 1806 were only slightly better off, left to fend for themselves often with little hope of employment or repatriation. During Armstrong's watch, French authorities had sometimes allowed them to stay on board while their vessels were undergoing adjudication, their captains permitted to sell off parts of their cargoes in order to feed them.[37] This stopgap more or less fell into disuse once American privateers in need of deckhands began putting into French ports. Offered the prospect of prize money and ultimately a trip home, those who had despaired of their situation now flocked to sign on. Others, however, sick, disabled, or simply stranded without hope of employment, turned to U.S. consuls to feed and house them. Fortunately, by tradition consuls were charged with caring for "distressed seamen" until they could be repatriated. Barlow made sure they did. Writing from Wilna a month before he died, he assured Monroe that he had met all his consuls' claims for reimbursement in these instances and promised to send a complete accounting when he returned to Paris.[38]

Another ministerial chore—one that kept Barlow busy, even as he wrestled with Dalberg over treaty matters—was to keep a watchful eye on the wartime activities of his consuls. Most were self-starters who needed no guidance and who, rather than trouble Barlow, brought their problems directly to various French ministries. As early as the previous March, for example, on hearing of congressional preparations for war, his friend William Lee had suggested to the duc de Feltre that the U.S. government might agree to swap masts and ship timbers for thirty or forty thousand French-made muskets. Lee had to wait more than a month while Feltre consulted with both the foreign and navy ministers. The answer, when it came, was "no." As the minister of war told Bassano, all newly made firearms were being shipped to Poland where, considering Napoleon's problems on the Russian front, they would obviously be put to more urgent use.[39] Even so, Feltre worried that wily Americans might get their hands on French weaponry and urged port officials to supervise the loading of American privateers whenever they put in to replenish their supplies of powder and shot.[40] Barlow, when he reached Wilna, followed up on Lee's proposal, asking Bassano whether the emperor would allow the exportation of perhaps as many as thirty thousand muskets. If Lee managed to ship them out of Bordeaux before the end of December, he noted, they would have "less risk of capture in the season of long stormy nights [and] arrive in the United States before the opening of the [spring] campaign." Contingent on the emperor's approval, he also asked that firearms be permitted to substitute for wines and brandies under the equal-value/return-cargo requirement.[41] In light of Napoleon's crumbling military fortunes, Barlow must not have had much hope for a positive response.

Other consular officials, especially those stationed along the English Channel, tried to keep track of freewheeling American entrepreneurs whom they suspected would trade with the enemy if they could. One such instance caught the attention of Isaac Cox Barnet, the longtime consul at Le Havre, whose vice consul at Caen had reported an imminent departure. The day Barlow arrived in Wilna, Barnet was writing to Bassano urgently requesting permission to detain an American captain named Baker and four of his crew who, after their vessel had been confiscated, had loaded another with a Prussian cargo and were about to leave for England. Because French officials in Caen had refused to detain the vessel, Barnet hoped Bassano would persuade Decrès to let him take all five into custody.[42] What became of this request is less significant than what it said of Barnet's aggressive style. As more American prize-masters began to arrive in the channel ports, Barnet quit his post in Le Havre and opened an office in Paris. Knowing that legal proceedings in prize cases invariably ended up in the French capital, he clearly intended to profit from being near the scene of their disposition. Predictably his collecting fees from litigants touched off a bitter quarrel with David Bailie Warden, the named consul to Paris. With good cause, Warden fumed at the intrusion and later charged Barnet with having gone so far as to advertise himself as *the* U.S. consul for Paris.

Barnet's trespassing was only one of Warden's grievances. French officials also wanted their cut. The previous December, before Barnet appeared on the scene, Warden had returned to Paris after a brief leave of absence to find that Council of Prizes officials would no longer grant him access to the documents he customarily used in his efforts to assist American litigants. A gang of French lawyers, he was sure, had conspired to shut him out and take whatever fees they could from cases that were properly his. In this instance, Barlow tried to help. Three times he wrote Bassano requesting that Warden's access to documents be restored. The answer, long in coming, was negative: Prize Council policy no longer afforded this privilege to foreign consuls.[43]

Warden felt even more abused when, in June, he suspected Barlow's legation staff were invading his territory. The fees they were taking in prize cases, he charged, were costing him "some thousand francs per annum."[44] Barlow, somewhat annoyed, felt obliged to set Warden straight on the relative responsibilities of consuls and ministers and the differences between the fees consuls charged for "commercial business" and those they charged in prize cases. If Warden could prove his secretaries were profiting from commercial transactions, he promised to "correct the abuse." Otherwise he reminded Warden that, as U.S. minister, he alone had the authority to decide how prize cases were dealt with. Until recently he had followed his predecessors' practice of referring litigants to the Paris consul, offering his "diplomatic representation" only if needed. Recently, however, so many captains had sought help from the legation that rather than see them suffer loss, he had agreed to represent them. He had even hired an additional secretary to handle the case load. "But you must not suppose," he wrote, "it was for my own pleasure or emolument."[45] Nor, he insisted, had his secretaries ever taken fees from Americans, but only from French officials who needed certain documents stamped with the legation's seal. He told Warden to continue to take on any prize cases he could handle, but as he later explained to Monroe, the legation would continue to take the lead because the Council of Prizes, while denying documentary access to consuls, still permitted his own staff to examine its papers.[46] Unfortunately Warden remained resentful, and six months later he would visit his bitterness on Ruth Barlow in the days following news of her husband's death.

17 Failed Mission, Fallen Diplomat

Barlow probably need not have gone to Wilna that fall. He had already mailed off copies of his treaty and claims convention before the invitation arrived announcing Napoleon's readiness to sign them. And although Bassano appeared to make Napoleon's signature contingent on his appearing at the emperor's winter headquarters, Barlow might have awaited the latter's return to Paris had he been less compulsive. Being Joel Barlow, however, meant finishing what he had begun, missing no opportunity to bring his mission to a swift and successful conclusion. Bassano's promising this result must have convinced him. He had been assured that, together, they would work out the final details under the emperor's eye, quickly overcome "all difficulties," and "conclude an arrangement without delay." For his part Bassano was so confident Barlow would accept the invitation that he promised to find him comfortable and "convenient" lodgings—and, as if the matter were settled, asked how many staff he planned to bring with him.[1]

Barlow in reply expressed regret at Bassano's not having received the draft documents he and Dalberg had posted to Wilna a week earlier. He might have saved himself the trip, he wrote, because by the time he got there he was sure the emperor would already have approved them. Be that as it may, he would leave Paris tomorrow, bringing his secretary and one servant. Although he did not name his traveling companions, they would be his nephew Thomas, who had served as legation secretary ever since Lee's return to Bordeaux, and a French coachman whom Barlow later referred to wryly as Lazy Louis. With winter fast approaching, Barlow was not unmindful of the hardships he would face along the way, but as he told Monroe, he "could not refuse without giving offence," and he believed the trip worthwhile if it brought a speedy end to his months of frustration. And lest the administration worry about his tendency to improvise, he assured the secretary of state that if Napoleon sought to sign more than a commercial treaty and a claims convention—a treaty of alliance, for example—"I shall not be at a loss how to answer."[2]

As he set off for Wilna, everything hinged on Napoleon's supposed willingness to indemnify for past shipping losses. That the emperor would sign the commercial treaty was a given, but Barlow seemed not to realize that the claims convention he and Dalberg had been discussing remained a work in progress. Unlike the draft commercial treaty, the formula for compensating American claimants was still evolving. Before the end of October, Petry, Dalberg, and Sussy all took a crack at modifying the original plan to the point where, despite assurances from Wilna, much clearly remained to be decided.

Petry took the opportunity to put forward what he called he called a more "dignified" solution than Barlow's original. Rather than allowing "speculation" to run rampant, as he was sure it would if Barlow were permitted to sell import licenses, he proposed an alternative. If claims totaled 30 million francs, as the American minister insisted, he believed this amount might be raised by setting aside one-fifth of the tariff revenues imposed on cargoes brought in by some eighty American licensees. Under this regimen France would do the licensing, not Barlow, whose motives he had no reason to trust. He even went so far as to calculate how much would be derived from the tariff set-asides on cargoes of cotton, coffee, sugar, etc.[3] Barlow himself must have seen some merit in this proposal, because Dalberg mentioned it as constituting the American minister's own fallback alternative.

Writing to Bassano on October 20, however, he expressed reservations about what might be called the Petry-Barlow plan. Such set-asides would not come out of the French treasury, to be sure, but they spelled lost revenue. Voicing this and other objections, Dalberg said he had tried to steer Barlow away from talk of licenses and tariff set-asides and had once again suggested that Americans might consider themselves indemnified if France were to arrange for the cession of East Florida or an expansion of the boundaries of Louisiana. Having heard this before, Barlow would have none of it. The future of East Florida, he rejoined, lay between Spain and the United States, and was unlikely to be determined as long as Europe was at war. As for Louisiana's boundaries, they were already fixed, comprising all that France had owned and already sold to the United States. Dalberg, forced to backtrack, told Barlow he doubted the emperor would agree to this latest plan. Calculating one-fifth of tariff receipts was too complicated, and estimating American claims at roughly 30 million francs was too imprecise. Barlow replied mildly that the total was not too high, and in fact his plan would probably recover only 20 to 25 million; even so, it was better to reach a broad settlement than resort to a "fastidious liquidation" of each individual claim.[4] There the matter rested.

Believing he had held Barlow at bay, Dalberg nonetheless wrote Bassano that some sort of licensing arrangement seemed unavoidable if France were to meet American claims for indemnification, without which, he reminded, Barlow had threatened a "rupture" and would not sign a commercial treaty. From a bargaining standpoint, however, he sensed some leeway. Although the American minister had put France's liability at 30 million francs, he would probably be satisfied with 20 million. And instead of eighty licensees, he would likely settle for sixty if France would agree to the 20 percent set-asides. Mustering this semblance of a recommendation, he wrapped up the records of his final dealings with Barlow and sent them off to Wilna.[5]

Sussy's input fell somewhat behind the curve. The minister of commerce, who saw only Barlow's original plan—the one calling for a 40-40 division of licensed importers—focused largely on revenue considerations. Tariff reductions for the first group—those licensed to import U.S. commodities—would cost the French treasury too much. He opposed it. On the other hand, he liked the idea of licensing Americans to bring in sugar and coffee. France was short of these "colonial" commodities, and if they were brought in at the current tariff levels, the treasury would suffer no loss. Moreover, Americans were good at finding such cargoes.[6]

Predictably Bassano found flaws in all the incoming proposals. His hostility toward any settlement surfaced starkly in a letter he wrote Serurier six days after Barlow arrived in Wilna. For one thing, he would have to ask Sussy for more factual data because he didn't trust Barlow's total claims figure of 30 million francs. He also looked askance at Barlow's proposal to license eighty American importers and seemed perplexed as to the difference between favoring them with a 20 percent tariff set-aside and a 20 percent tariff reduction, except that in both cases the French treasury stood to lose revenue. But above all, he questioned Barlow's authority to come forward with any licensing plan whatever, in light of Washington's longtime opposition to all forms of licensed commerce.[7] His reservations on this score may well have been a deciding factor. As Petry later explained to Barlow's successor, France had rejected Barlow's plan largely because it doubted Washington would accept its licensing feature.

This explanation, while eminently self-serving, was not far off the mark. Monroe did, in fact, roundly condemn the plan when he learned of it.[8] Still, to blame Barlow for failing to win the case for American claimants also skirted the reality that Napoleon up to that time had given no sign that he ever intended to indemnify them. Meanwhile, to Serurier, Bassano ventured to guess that if the emperor did accord licenses to Americans (with or without tariff concessions), he would also make them available to French and other importers. He was right on this score. Shortly after he returned from his Russian fiasco, Napoleon offered to sell two hundred additional licenses to all comers, a move that tacitly acknowledged Barlow's estimate of their revenue potential. As Bassano wound down his letter to Serurier, he mused wistfully on how simple it would have been if Americans had agreed to be indemnified by a French-orchestrated acquisition of East Florida. Unfortunately, their government preferred to deal directly with Spain.

Leaving the claims issue in limbo, Bassano highlighted to Serurier the special favors Americans would win from the proposed commercial treaty. Shipmasters bringing cargoes to France could now lade whatever return cargoes they wished (as long they equaled in value the cargoes they had brought in). France would also permit American importers to defer paying duties for six months and allow them to store cargoes until they could be, if not sold, re-exported. Moreover, although the treaty made these "facilities" reciprocal, Serurier should point out that Americans would benefit disproportionately because their commerce with Europe far outstripped that of France with the United States. They should also be gratified to know that the treaty renewed the former Convention's commitments to "free ships, free goods," a list of narrowly specified contraband, a tight definition of blockades, and the offer of wartime port privileges to each other's privateers. As for the last, even now France was permitting American prizemasters to sell captured vessels, along with captured cargoes not otherwise forbidden entry. With the American minister now in Wilna, he told Serurier, negotiations would continue. As yet, of course, nothing had been concluded; final decisions would await the emperors's pleasure.[9]

Once en route, Barlow enjoyed clocking the rate at which his carriage ate up the fourteen hundred miles between Paris and Wilna. Drawn by six horses, he and Tom made the trip in twenty-two days (and six hours) even with Lazy Louis at the reins, arriving on November 18, a day earlier than he had calculated. Counting off miles and hours each day came to him as obsessively as when he had paced off the rooms in the Tower of London more than twenty years before. And as the days passed, he and his nephew fell into a routine of sorts. Whenever they stopped to change horses, they posted the letters they had written during the day's ride—his to Ruth, Tom's to Clara—invariably assuring them that were both in good health. Until they reached the killing fields of Poland, their letters tended to dwell on the daily trivia that travelers feel compelled to describe. Crossing the Rhine on a pontoon bridge, for example, caught Tom's fancy, while Barlow, for his part, enjoyed the passing scene but began to have mixed feeling about his decision to keep rolling after dark. The nights, he told Ruth, "are long & dark, so we can't go fast," but at least, we "go steady and safe."[10]

Writing from their first layover, in Frankfurt, he reckoned they had covered 360 miles in eighty-three hours, stopping only for morning coffee. They could have made better time if Louis were not so "indolent." He missed Ruth badly, he told her; he worried about her health and even wept a little at the thought of her being unwell in his absence. On a lighter note, he promised that if Clara took good care of her and spared no expense, he would put her in his will and find her a husband.[11]

Berlin, their second night off the road, gave Barlow time to call on the French minister and accompany him to the theater and for Tom to take a side trip to Wittenberg to visit Martin Luther's tomb. They would leave for Königsburg tomorrow, he wrote, although after eight days of rain the mud would slow their progress. The earth, he wrote, "is full of water as a sponge," mud everywhere. "The carriage wheels whirl it over your head in a black rainbow that moves as you move." He supposed that "40 more days of these rains will be sufficient to puzzle the pigeon or the raven to find a resting place for the sole of its foot." They were crossing many rivers now: the Oder, the Elbe, the Spree, and soon the Vistula and the Neman. Wilna, he noted, lay on a tributary of the Neman. The journey was nearly over.[12]

A day spent in Königsburg, their last major stopover, afforded Barlow an opportunity to visit his banker and load a case of wine. Setting out once more, they ran into an abrupt change in the weather. With disconcerting swiftness, a bitter cold swept in across the Polish countryside, freezing the mud and making the roadway lumpy enough to slow their carriage. Even under cover, the cold was so intense it froze their water bottles overnight. Now, too, they began to pass wounded soldiers, their numbers swelling as they drove east. And along with the frost and the casualties came chilling news from the front. The letter he dropped off to Ruth on November 14 reported rumors that Napoleon was in retreat and "it is believed the tide will roll farther back."[13]

At the time, Barlow was not particularly alarmed. He was sure Napoleon's military genius would prevail and the Grande Armée would not be routed. If the emperor were forced to retire to his winter quarters, all the better, because Barlow would have a chance to deal with him face to face. Their pace quickened, and a few days later he was pleased to learn that Bassano, aware of his approach, had reached out to accommodate him. A day's ride from Wilna, the French commandant at Kowno told him he had received the foreign minister's orders to show him "every attention." He declined the offer of lodging but given the desperate scenes he and Tom had witnessed along the way, he welcomed the offer of an armed escort.[14]

As their carriage rattled through the streets of Wilna the next day, Barlow began to grasp the magnitude of Napoleon's losses. Though the city, with its thick medieval walls, was well stocked and capable of resisting a siege, he realized that instead it had become a choke point for the French retreat, with "at least a thousand waggons & carts crowding to get through the town all loaded with sick and dying soldiers." He was not surprised. On their approach, they had seen carnage on all sides, houses burned, thatch roofs stripped to feed horses or to make bedding for the wounded who lay in open carts. Others, he noted grimly, slept in the fields, living on horse meat—the remains of an estimated 25,000 horses that lay dead between there and Moscow. He himself had counted more than a hundred the day they arrived in the city. The human toll was also high but hard to reckon, he wrote, because soldiers were often buried where they fell.[15]

The postscripts Barlow added to his first letter from Wilna spoke to an eagerness to get on with treaty making. He called at Bassano's quarters twice the day he arrived but didn't find him in. When they did meet the following evening, he got the impression that in light of the deteriorating military situation, the emperor was expected to turn up fairly soon. According to fragmentary reports, French forces had been outflanked near Minsk and were fighting their way toward Wilna. As he explained to Ruth, "the enemies flying troops (Kosacks) are in swarms on both his wings." But if she put on her fur slippers and went upstairs to look at his maps, she would see that Napoleon's "situation tho' difficult will not embarrass him long. He will always beat his enemy."[16]

Had there been reliable news from the front, however, he would have known the Grande Armée was now in full and chaotic retreat. Falling back from Moscow, Napoleon had hoped to make a stand at Smolensk but had to abandon the city when the Russians threatened to encircle it. Worse, a day later, the city of Minsk, another potential rallying point, fell to the Russians. Had he held Minsk, the Grande Armée might have had enough food and supplies to last through the winter. By the time the remnant of that army reached Wilna, however, it had lost all hope of making a stand, and the emperor himself had barely escaped capture. Driven by hunger and bitter cold, the vanguard of this undisciplined mass led by Marshal Joachim Murat began flooding into Wilna on December 8.[17]

Until this happened and still hoping the emperor would soon be within diplomatic reach, Barlow regaled Ruth with his forays into the city's still lively social life. On one occasion, along with a dinner invitation came Bassano's warning that the Polish ladies present might try to seduce him. "Lord have mercy," he protested, "what a useless caution. What a blessed thing is age in these cases, it prevents the attack being made & preserves us against its success if it is made, so I say with Voltaire, ah Saint Pere, envoyez moi la tentation." Teasingly, he admitted he had been somewhat taken by a Polish princess, a dinner companion whose name he couldn't remember except that it ended "in the sky." But the age factor, he assured her, should "banish all ideas of danger in my going astray."[18]

On November 24 he sent Monroe a lengthy status report. Unable to shake off the horrors he had seen en route, he described "roads extremely cut up . . . a mass of mud lined alternately with rocks, deep sands & wooden causeways, & bordered with dead horses, sick & dying soldiers, broken waggon wheels & burnt villages, the fruits of glorious war." Turning to affairs of state, he reported that Bassano had sent the emperor a detailed account of what he and Dalberg had negotiated and that the foreign minister fully expected to get orders "to conclude the business in both its parts." Sizing up what he was hearing from other sources, however, Barlow was not sanguine. He put the situation obliquely: "The emperor's present embarrassment in his retrograde movement may however occasion a further delay." He expected Napoleon to win a few more skirmishes before he retired to Wilna but gradually convinced himself that a general retreat was about to descend on the city. He also began to think about getting out of its way. He told Monroe that if the emperor had not already signed the treaty and claims convention, he would leave the city to avoid "the immense crowd & confusion that must attend his approach."[19] He wrote the same to Ruth: no one knew where the emperor was, nor had he been heard from for the past twelve days. Fringe battles were rumored; soldiers were streaming in. He planned to leave the city before it was inundated.[20]

Two days later, however, he seemed ready to return to business as usual, his hopes once more buoyed. He would dine with Bassano that day and "apply for Haley's sailors." And because Napoleon was expected in Wilna within six days, he hoped his "affair will march much faster after that." Whether genuinely optimistic at this point or momentarily diverted, he kept a light touch in his letters to Ruth who, he knew, always appreciated his teasing hints of infidelity. Once more he recurred to the fleshly endowments of the Polish beauties he met at ducal dinners, his appreciation of their charms not to be confused, of course, with his undying love for his wife. He wrote, too, of renewing acquaintance with the Danish minister they had known in Paris, now his next-door neighbor. "He is the same General Walterdorff, who used to come see us," he reminded Ruth, and until the general's provisions arrived from Copenhagen, he and his son had a standing invitation to dine with them. He suggested she write to thank him for "looking after your husband and warning him to be watchful over his morals, especially his conjugal morals."[21]

Barlow did not describe his and Tom's last days in Wilna. When he wrote again to Ruth on December 13, they were in Warsaw, ending seven days on the road, three overnights in the carriage, and enduring subzero temperatures. Every so often, they would call out to Louis "to know whether he is still alive or still dead," their coachman so layered with furs and great coats that only his nose came "within some inches of the external air." His own heavy clothing and footwear, he told Ruth, had made him "as comfortable as it is possible to be." And lest she worry, he made no mention of the diarrhea that had sapped his energies for more than a week. Rather, he dwelt on the bravery of Napoleon's soldiers whose suffering led him to wonder how many had died in just the past ten days. "And still they keep fighting (I don't mean the dead ones) day & night & marching & freezing, starving." The wounded, he wrote, crawled only as far as the nearest dead horse. Worst of all was the sight of a soldier who had been eating his dead horse for a month, both of his legs shot off.[22]

Barlow had no reason to regret leaving Wilna. Napoleon had never been within reach, having bypassed the city, not wanting it known that he had deserted his army. He had stopped in a suburb only long enough to confer with Bassano before dashing on to Warsaw. The imperial sleigh had passed them on the road four days out of Wilna, Barlow noted, while they were asleep at a "post house" and had left Warsaw twenty-four hours before they arrived. "Perhaps all these movements will do no harm to our affair," he reflected, "tho' it is pretty clear that the trip to Wilna has done no good." He was eager to return to Paris as quickly as possible, he told Ruth, to pick up the threads of his negotiations, although he flinched at retracing the route they had come with the temperatures in northern Europe now hovering well below freezing. After talking over alternative routes, he and Tom, in concert with Petry, who had ridden with them from Wilna, agreed they might find warmer weather and better roads if they returned by way of Vienna and Munich, even though the more southerly route would add 150 miles.[23]

His last letter to Ruth, dated December 17, confirmed their decision to return by way of Vienna. They planned to leave Warsaw at four o'clock the next morning "by moon light and snowlight," but because the snow was thin and well packed, they would keep their wheels instead of mounting runners. Looking back but also forward in what must pass for a tender valedictory, he told Ruth that having enjoyed the company of the "most beautiful women" in Europe, he would now "fly back to the one that is more lovely & more divine, more every way endearing."[24] Nine days later he was dead.

Barlow's companions each left an account of his last days. Thomas Barlow later wrote Monroe that while still in Wilna, his uncle had begun to suffer headaches, fever, and an attack of diarrhea from which he had not fully recovered but insisted that he felt strong enough to travel. In Warsaw he seemed to recover from his headaches and fever, and it was not until they were once more on the road that he developed "a violent cold" and asked to stop in the town of Zarnovic (today Žarnovica, Slovakia), believing he simply needed to rest in bed for day or two. Despite what they described as "comfortable lodging" at the house of an "excellent family" and the attendance of two doctors, Barlow's pulmonary condition continued to worsen. The second doctor, whom Petry described as a man of "great reputation," arrived in the evening of the 25th, found Barlow in a coma, and announced solemnly that he had "no hope of saving him." Barlow died the next morning as Tom and Petry stood vigil. He was fifty-eight years old. The next day they buried him in Zarnovic where a monument to his memory now stands. The survivors consoled each other. "Mr. Petry," Tom wrote, "has been with me the whole time & and has shown every care & attention." Even Louis the coachman had "rendered all the services in his power." Petry, for his part, told Bassano he was devastated by the loss; they would return to Paris as quickly as possible.[25]

Joel Barlow left a lot of unfinished business. His death not only buried whatever hopes there were for a commercial treaty or a claims convention; it also left the legation without a clear-cut line of succession. Customarily the secretary of legation assumes the minister's duties as chargé d'affaires, but in this instance William Lee, the original appointee, had long since returned to Bordeaux, leaving the position open. Barlow had belatedly realized his oversight, and when he reached Wilna notified Monroe that he had just filled out a blank commission naming his nephew to the post. Praising Tom as "a young man of solid judgment" who had already been serving in a secretarial capacity, he asked that the president secure Senate approval so that he could be put on the public payroll. He had been paying his nephew's salary, he wrote, but the mission had cost him so much that he could not afford "to be deprived of this trivial advantage."[26]

Unfortunately this interim appointment by no means settled the question. Well before Thomas Barlow reached Paris, David Bailie Warden petitioned Bassano to recognize him as chargé d'affaires. Moved by ambition and doubtless by his dislike of the legation staff, the Paris consul wasted no time pressing his case. The day after he learned of Barlow's death, he wrote Bassano, arguing that as "consul general"—a title often appropriated by the holder of the Paris consulate—he was now the U.S. government's only duly accredited official in the French capital, adding that he was familiar with the business of the legation and well known to the foreign office. Bassano, unaware of the storm that was about to break, welcomed Warden's willingness to assume responsibility and invited him to call at the foreign office at four o'clock that afternoon.[27]

On the rue de Vaugirard, meanwhile, Barlow's private secretary, a young man named Marcadier, recounted the legation's dismay at the news of the minister's death. "Mrs. Barlow's position is dreadful," he wrote Monroe; he wasn't sure she would "survive the unexpected shock." And because the minister had not named a chargé, question had arisen as to who would transact the legation's official business. Looking for help and not yet informed of Tom's interim appointment, Marcadier said he had written William Lee urging him to come to Paris. He knew that Lee had once held the post of legation secretary and hoped he might be able "to put things in order." The situation was becoming critical, he warned. Shortly after news of the minister's death, Warden had turned up demanding the legation's "papers, seals & cypher," which Mrs. Barlow had refused to give him on grounds that her husband had confided some of those papers to Isaac Barnet.[28] Four decades later, Clara Baldwin described the encounter. Warden, she wrote, "was mortally wounded & all the jealousies of his narrow mind were roused; he complained bitterly to my sister that Mr. B. had not officially informed him of his intended journey and [had not] appointed him chargé d'affaires."[29]

With Ruth's blessing, Lee and Barnet teamed up to try to deflect Warden's power play. Whether William Lee really wanted the post for himself, he reminded Bassano from Bordeaux that he had served as legation secretary for eight months, knew the duties, and outranked all other consuls in length of service. If Bassano thought it proper, he would come to Paris and "take charge of our affairs." Three days later, now in Paris ostensibly to console Ruth, he asked for but was denied an audience.[30] By this time the foreign minister had decided to deal only with Warden, and later, when Thomas Barlow appeared on the scene, a foreign office adviser named Roux built a strong case for his having made the right choice. As Roux pointed out, Warden's consular appointment at least had his government's official approval; young Barlow's claim did not, and if France were to negotiate with him, Washington might repudiate any official actions he took. Moreover, Barlow's nephew had proved himself unfit for serious business when, having earlier announced that he would carry the news of his uncle's death back to Washington, he had changed his mind. Roux suspected Lee of having persuaded him to stay and contest Warden for control of the legation. In any event, the nephew's indecisiveness had "disposed of the difficulties he created"[31] and affirmed the foreign minister's good judgment. In retrospect Roux's judgment of Thomas Barlow's unfitness seems warranted. Even Ruth Barlow later described her nephew as "intelligent & good, but very timid & unconscious of his own worth," a judgment in which Clara Baldwin concurred.[32]

Lee, whose family was well settled in Bordeaux, apparently had no heart for doing battle in Paris and left no evidence that he followed up with the foreign office. Barnet, however, not to be outdone by his arch-rival, lost no time staking his claim. The same day Warden petitioned to be recognized as chargé, Barnet made his own case, enclosing a letter from Barlow authorizing him, he claimed, to take charge of "all legation affairs and functions."[33] This was not quite accurate. The letter authorized Barnet to handle such routine matters as issuing and recording passports, and arranging for the repatriation or re-employment of American seamen released from custody, but it did not foresee his acting in a diplomatic capacity or as the legation's official channel to the foreign office. An unsigned "note" to Bassano, probably from Roux, dismissed this basis for Barnet's claim, characterizing the letter as merely a show of confidence in the consul's ability to handle specific legation-related matters, whereas the authority to conduct negotiations Barlow had taken with him to Wilna. Warden, on the other hand, "enjoys a good reputation and has always conducted himself honorably."[34] Bassano was satisfied, but lest Washington question his choice, he explained to Serurier that Warden would serve only as a channel of communication. France would not negotiate with him or even recognize him as chargé.[35]

As to Warden's suitability, Barlow's successor soon found reason to disagree. When William H. Crawford arrived in Paris in July, he found Warden bitterly contesting Lee and Barnet for consular fees made increasingly profitable by an uptick in the sales of prize vessels. In one such prize case, Crawford managed to alienate Warden by ruling in Lee's favor. In the acrimonious exchanges that followed, the new minister roundly denounced Warden for having wrongfully solicited the office of chargé, then fought him for custody of the correspondence he had generated with the foreign office, and finally fired him, replacing him in the Paris consulate with Barnet.[36] Meanwhile, the slow collapse of the Napoleonic era defeated Crawford's sporadic efforts to obtain indemnification. The issue that had cost Barlow his life would remain on the books until 1831 when, under Andrew Jackson's threat of reprisal, the government of Louis Philippe agreed to settle. And in 1836 France finally came through with 25 million francs, an amount deemed adequate at that time to recompense Americans for their losses during the Napoleonic era.

As for the Barlow household, Ruth returned home in the late summer of 1813, believing she had honored Joel's wishes by keeping legation documents intact. In December she wrote Dolley Madison, with whom she had carried on a largely one-sided correspondence, telling her that she planned to spend the winter with the Fultons in New York City. She had no plans to return to Washington; "the sight of Kalorama would recall too painful ideas." Her sister Clara, she noted, had gone to New Haven to be with her mother, and her nephew Thomas would soon be in Washington bringing a large packet of correspondence for the secretary of state.[37] Ultimately Ruth did return to Kalorama, where she was joined by Clara, who subsequently added to the household by marrying Col. George Bomford, the U.S. Army's chief of ordnance. On the hilltop overlooking the capital, Ruth died five years later. When Clara died in 1845, Thomas, having inherited the estate, sold it and moved to western Pennsylvania.[38]

18 Having Served His Country, Not Always Well but Faithfully

To his contemporaries, Joel Barlow was a powerful presence, a man who spoke out passionately on issues he believed stood to exalt the new nation's place in a rapidly changing world. Indeed, few others of his generation so eloquently projected the exceptionalist view that Americans were singularly destined to light the world by their example and that no matter how often they might fail of imitation, their ideals would ultimately set the standard for political and economic freedoms, the likes of which the world could not help but admire and would surely emulate. Whether as prophet or publicist for America's singular destiny, he not only envisioned a transformative role for his country; he also meant to have a hand in shaping it. Barely out of Yale, he composed an epic poem he hoped would convince his countrymen of their unique role in history, while putting Europe on notice that it would soon have to reckon with a formidable catalyst for change rising in the west. Later in life, aspiring to become his country's educator-in-chief, he came forward with a plan to bring together America's most renowned teachers and scholars, its scientists and philosophers, to create something more than a traditional university—an academic entity that would produce and disseminate learning in ways that Europeans had never dreamed of. And finally, as diplomat, he fastened on the ideal of freeing American commerce—indeed commerce everywhere—from the interruptions of war and prohibitive tariffs. Nor were his efforts in vain. Though his poetry remains unread, the think tanks and free-trade agreements he envisioned have become fixtures in the today's world.

Barlow, of course, was not alone in striving to create a distinctive national identity. Like others of his day, he winnowed the best from the worst of his country's colonial heritage, cherishing the British legacies of law and governance, grateful for the writ of habeas corpus, the right of trial by jury, and the right of freeholders to be represented in the body politic, while joining like-minded reformers to root out the medieval remnants of monarchy and privilege. As a Jeffersonian activist, he carried the cause of political and social reform to England itself, siding with British "radicals" in their efforts to bring the old order to an end. And although he was not the only American who saw the French Revolution as a hopeful vehicle for human progress, he was among the few who came forward to take a personal hand in its battles to slough off the tyrannies of the past. And when it failed, he shared the disappointment of other Jeffersonians who watched as bloodshed and Bonapartism destroyed the republican ideals they had hoped to see take root.

For Barlow, defining the new nation also meant coming to grips with the economic distress Britain had long visited on its American colonies, effectively forcing them to exchange low-value raw materials for high-value manufactures, thereby stunting economic growth by creating chronic shortages of hard cash. Any long-term relief from this imbalance would, of course, have to await Americans developing their own manufacturing base. Still, in the short term he entertained the possibility that France, if she were shown the way, might belie the dictum that only Britain could provide Americans with the goods they could not yet make for themselves. France, he believed, given the opportunity, could replace Britain as Americans' principal trade partner, a switch that might not change the dynamics of dependency, although he believed it would. Accordingly he devoted much of his mission to France trying to negotiate a commercial treaty that he believed would dramatically expand Franco-American commerce by lowering tariffs and removing other obstacles to the free flow of trade. He held out the lure that if they succeeded, France would seize Britain's overseas markets for manufactured goods and Americans, for their part, would be free of their economic dependence on a common enemy.

Unfortunately, in this undertaking he found himself not so much ahead of his time as bound by its circumstances. To his disappointment, neither James Madison nor Napoleon Bonaparte warmed to his formula for expanding Franco-American commerce. His call for lower tariffs met with the administration's objection that in preparing for war, it needed more revenue from that source, not less. Nor could he persuade the administration that putting more ships and cargoes in the Atlantic outweighed the importance of securing indemnity for the seaborne property Napoleon had already seized and confiscated. And on his side, the emperor saw no reason to forgo valuable tariff revenue and contended with reason that if he made American vessels more welcome in French ports, British cruisers would simply step up their interceptions. At bottom, however, Barlow's argument failed largely because it ran athwart the economic reality that French industry was no match for Britain's in supplying manufactured goods to overseas markets. Nor would she come close to matching it for years to come, although, perhaps for reasons of national pride, no French official in Barlow's day would care to admit it.

Characteristically, whether engaged in diplomacy, business, or everyday life, Barlow was often well served by his talent for making friends. An obituary appearing in the May 4, 1813, issue of the *National Intelligencer* touched on this aspect of his life when it described him as a hard-driving, witty, sensitive man "sincerely beloved by all those whom he admitted to his company." Nor were many excluded from that company. Morever, those he befriended often played key roles in advancing whatever project he had before him. They ranged from the army officers who furnished him with letters of introduction when he set off to Philadelphia to sell subscriptions to his epic poem, to President Jefferson who thirty years later urged Congress to act on his proposal to establish a "national academy." Those friends—and sometime benefactors—were spread across a broad spectrum of time and circumstance, numbering scientists, revolutionaries, political leaders, businessmen, and fellow diplomats. And on occasion, his charm was determinative. When, for example, he finally managed to win over the temperamental dey of Algiers, he told Ruth he was sure that Ali Hassan "would give me his beard, hair by hair, if I were to ask for it." Nor would he have succeeded in North Africa had he not cultivated the goodwill of the Jewish banker, Macaiah Bacri, whose financial support was critical to the outcome.

The personal charm that lent force to his powers to persuade clearly counted for less, however, during his mission to France. Napoleon's top advisers, though they appreciated his engaging personality, gave him little reason to believe he could persuade them to sign a commercial treaty or even accord better treatment to American ships and cargoes. They refused even to discuss what his instructions firmly demanded: indemnification for the American property

France already confiscated. But if his suggestions for mending Franco-American relations met with rejection at the top, he often won over lesser officials, pursuing them relentlessly to consider ways to improve those relations. These men in turn passed his recommendations "up the line," where, once Congress had declared war on Britain, they received a warmer welcome. Consequently, by the time he left for Wilna, he had succeeded in firming up wartime port privileges for American privateers and had secured the release of scores of American seamen whom the French had detained because they had been found on board captured British prizes. In retrospect it seems unlikely that anyone else could have done more, or even as well, to extract minor favors from Napoleon.

But on the big issues, Barlow was often his worst enemy. As an exemplar of goodwill, he had few equals, but as an advocate of various causes he too often revealed a self-defeating tendency to overreach, to ask too much, and thereby weaken the fabric of his argument. During the Quasi-War, for example, he urged his fellow Americans to consider how sorely they had offended France in the recent past, but then he went on to warn the John Adams administration that if it continued its obtuseness, France would declare war on the United States and wreak terrible vengeance. The warning was not only overblown—it was also ill-timed. Adams was outraged when he heard of it, because he was already preparing another peace mission to France in the face of scalding Federalist opposition. Not one to forgive easily, Adams bore a grudge for twenty years before finally deciding that Barlow had meant well at the time. Meanwhile in France, as the prospects for peace began to brighten, Barlow lost whatever credibility he might have had with the Directory by topping off some conciliatory proposals with the suggestion that France also give up privateering, both in principle and practice. In this instance, he seemed to ignore the reality that without much of a navy, the Directory was not about to relinquish its only means of harassing British convoys. And finally, during his own mission to France, he overreached again when he decked out his draft commercial treaty with articles the French termed "innovations" and found patently unacceptable. Here, besides listing the customary courtesies afforded by commercial treaties, he tried to put France on record in favor of restricting maritime warfare, to put an end to privateering and paper blockades. Instead, his "innovations" gave his French opposites reason to delay the negotiations, extending a hiatus that coincided all too well with Napoleon's aim to keep Americans at arm's length until they had had enough of England to declare war. Axiomatically, diplomacy succeeds when both parties see advantage to themselves in what they agree to. Unfortunately Barlow too often held out mutual "advantages" whose time had not yet come. Not until 1856, at the end of the Crimean War, did the powers of Europe agree to ban privateering and set rigorous standards for naval blockades.

Among Barlow's more endearing qualities was the boyish enthusiasm he exhibited for whatever was new, untried, or challenging. Even while thrashing out treaties in North Africa, he relished the prospect of traveling on, junketing through Italy and on to Constantinople. Accompanied by his loving wife, he proposed to make treaties along the way, mixing travel with national interest and obviously intending to take pleasure in both. America's poet and nation builder never lost his zest for life's adventures and did his best to serve his country along the way. As member of an American generation who foresaw a better future for humanity, Barlow was a buoyant and sometimes prophetic player.

NOTES

CHAPTER 1. SEEKING FAME BUT WITHOUT FORTUNE

1 To Oliver Wolcott, Hartford, CT, 8 February 1779, from Theodore A. Zunder, ed., "Six Letters of Joel Barlow to Oliver Wolcott," *New England Quarterly* 2 (July 1929): 477.

2 To Noah Webster, New Haven, CT, 30 January 1779, item 518 in Joel Barlow Papers (MS Am 1448), Houghton Library, Harvard University, hereinafter cited as BP-HL.

3 To Wolcott, Hartford, 4 November 1779, Zunder, "Six Letters," 487.

4 To Samuel Hopkins, Paris, 14 March 1798, BP-HL, Letter Book, vol. 3.

5 See "The Prospect of Peace, a Poetical Composition delivered at Yale College . . . July 23, 1778," *The Works of Joel Barlow*, eds. William K. Bottorff and Arthur L. Ford (Gainesville, FL: Scholars' Facsimiles and Reprints, 1970), hereinafter cited as *Works*, vol. 2, (poetry), 1–12.

6 For Barlow's early years, see James L. Woodress, *A Yankee's Odyssey: The Life of Joel Barlow* (Philadelphia: Lippincott, 1958); Charles Burr Todd, *Life and Letters of Joel Barlow, L.L.D., Poet, Statesman, Philosopher, with Extracts from His Works, and Hitherto Unpublished Poems* (New York and London: G. P. Putnam's Sons, 1888), Samuel Bernstein, *Joel Barlow: A Connecticut Yankee in an Age of Revolution* (Cliff Island, ME: Ultima Thule Press, 1985), and most fully, Theodore Alfred Zunder, *The Early Days of Joel Barlow, a Connecticut Wit, Yale Graduate, Editor, Lawyer and Poet; Chaplain during the Revolutionary War: His Life and Works from 1754 to 1787* (New Haven, CT: Yale University Press, 1934).

7 To Esther Hull Barlow, New Haven, 6 July 1775, BP-HL, item 105.

8 From a handwritten biographical sketch, BP-HL, item 720.

9 Zunder, *Early Days of Joel Barlow*, 32.

10 To his tutor, Joseph Buckminister, Hartford, 19 March 1779, Henley-Smith Papers (hereinafter H-SP), Library of Congress (hereinafter LC).

11 Works, vol. 2, 123–358. A list of subscribers is attached to the text.

12 March 1788, BP-HL, item 531.

13 Zunder, *Early Days of Joel Barlow*, 104.

14 Barlow fell ill after the retreat from Long Island and returned to Yale that fall to complete both his undergraduate and master's degrees; Woodress, *Yankee's Odyssey*, 43.

15 "Near Paramus" and "Camp near Hackensack," 11 and 18 September 1780, BP-HL, items 126 and 127.

16 "Orange Town" and "Totaway," 2 and 18 October 1780, BP-HL, items 129 and 131.

17 Woodress, *Yankee's Odyssey*, 59.

18 For Barlow's whereabouts in the summer and fall of 1781, see BP-HL, items 141–48.

19 Redding, 2 March 1782, BP-HL, item 154.

20 Todd, *Life and Letters*, 31. On 9 March 1782, Barlow wrote Ruth that her brother Dudley "has told the old gentleman we are married & he is much displeased." He suggested that Dudley and her other brother, Abraham, tell him "your reasons for not speaking to him about it," BP-HL, item 156. For Barlow's semiapologetic letter to his father-in-law, see Redding, 20 March 1782, BP-HL, item 160.

21 Letters from Philadelphia, 2 and 12 November 1782, BP-HL, items 169 and 170.

22 BP-HL, item 170.

23 Zunder, *Early Days of Joel Barlow*, 207; and Woodress, *Yankee's Odyssey*, 85.

24 Todd, *Life and Letters*, 54.

25 Robert F. Durden, "Joel Barlow and the French Revolution," *William and Mary Quarterly*, 3rd Series, 8, no. 3 (July 1961): 328.

26 Woodress, *Yankee's Odyssey*, 86.

27 See his letter to Mrs. John Penn in John C. Fitzpatrick, *Writings of George Washington*, vol. 29 (Washington: Government Printing Office, 1939), 276.

28 Zunder, *Early Days of Joel Barlow*, 218.

29 For Barlow's role in founding the *American Mercury*, see Woodress, *Yankee's Odyssey*, 78–80; Zunder, *Early Days of Joel Barlow*, 171–76; and Arthur L. Ford, *Joel Barlow* (New York: Twane Publishers, 1971), 21.

30 Todd, *Life and Letters*, 48–49.

31 Quoted from Cantor's "Joel Barlow: Lawyer and Legal Philosopher," *American Quarterly* 10, part 4 (summer 1958): 170.

32 Ibid., 166.

33 See handwritten biographical sketch, BP-HL, item 720.

34 Ford, *Joel Barlow*, 24.

35 New Haven, 30 January 1779, BP-HL, item 518.

CHAPTER 2. SELLING WESTERN LANDS TO FRENCH ÉMIGRÉS

1 Theodore T. Belote, *The Scioto Speculation and the French Settlement at Gallipolis* (Cincinnati: University of Cincinnati Press, 1907), 10–14; Woodress, *Yankee's Odyssey*, 91–93.

2 Woodress, *Yankee's Odyssey*, 93.

3 Belote, *Scioto Speculation*, 22.

4 Woodress, *Yankee's Odyssey*, 91–93.

5 Belote, *Scioto Speculation*, 21.

6 Durden, "Joel Barlow and the French Revolution," 329.

7 New York, 24 May 1788, BP-HL, item 177.

8 See Zunder, "Joel Barlow and Seasickness" *Yale Journal of Biology and Medicine* 1 (1929): 385–92.

9 30 June 1788, Joel Barlow Diaries, Houghton Library call number "bMS Am 1448 (series 1), containing item 9 (25 March–12 September 1788), and item 10 (23 September–11 October 1788), hereinafter cited as Barlow Diaries with item number and date of entry.

10 Barlow Diaries, item 9, n.d.

11 Ibid.

12 Ibid.

13 Ibid., Calais, 7 September 1788.

14 Ibid., en route to Paris, n.d.

15 Woodress, *Yankee's Odyssey*, 98.

16 Barlow Diaries, item 9, 11 September 1788.

17 Ibid., London, 30 August 1788.

18 Ibid., London, 5 August 1788.

19 Ibid.

20 Ibid., London, 19 August 1788.

21 Ibid., London, 3 August 1788.

22 Ibid., London, 16 August 1788.

23 Ibid., Brussels, 12 and 23 September 1788.

24 Paris entries of 27 and 29 September 1788; Antwerp, 6 and 8 October 1788; Barlow Diaries, item 10.

25 Ibid., Paris, 3 October 1788.

26 Todd, *Life and Letters*, 87.

27 6 November 1794, BP-HL, item 529. Barlow did, however, write an outline for such a history, which appears in his Notebook, dated 1802. See item 18 in Joel Barlow Notebooks, BP-HL.

28 Belote, *Scioto Speculation*, 25.

29 To RB, Paris, 1 January 1790, BP-HL, item 178. For details of the endgame, see Belote, *Scioto Speculation,* 28–49.

30 Belote, *Scioto Speculation,* 47–49.

31 Todd, *Life and Letters*, 68–69; Woodress, *Yankee's Odyssey*, 111; Belote, *Scioto Speculation,* 34–35.

32 BP-HL, item 720; Woodress, *Yankee's Odyssey*, 111–12; Todd, *Life and Letters*, 72; Durden, "Joel Barlow and the French Revolution," 330.

33 Beatrice Davenport, ed., *A Diary of the French Revolution by Gouverneur Morris*, vol. 2 (Boston: Houghton Mifflin, 1939), 95.

34 Belote finds his failure to prosecute his partners "the sole reason we have to doubt [his] honesty," *Scioto Speculation,* 39n.

35 Paris, BP-HL, item 178.

36 To RB, Paris, 11 July 1790, BP-HL, item 185; see also Durden, "Joel Barlow and the French Revolution," 332.

37 To Robert Morris, Paris, 16 November 1790, Davenport, *Diary*, vol. 2, 50. Both Robert Durden and Melanie Miller make the point that Morris himself was involved in land sales to Europeans and disliked Barlow for having given such enterprises a bad name. See Durden, "Joel Barlow and the French Revolution," 331; Melanie Miller, *Envoy to the Terror: Gouverneur Morris and the French Revolution* (Dulles, VA: Potomac Books, 2005), 78.

38 Jean-Baptiste Petry to the duc de Bassano, Paris, letters of 10 and 18 September 1812, France, Archives Nationales, Ministère des Affaires Étrangères, Correspondance politique-Etats-unis (hereinafter AECP-EU), vol. 68, ff. 321–22v, 329–32.

CHAPTER 3. JOINING THE FRENCH REVOLUTION

1 *Works*, vol. 1, 91–210; Todd, *Life and Letters*, 90; Durden, "Joel Barlow and the French Revolution," 335–36.

2 BP-HL, item 66.

3 Woodress, *Yankee's Odyssey*, 119–23.

4 *Works*, vol. 1, 21–90. Durden gives the most detailed account of Barlow's dealings with British reformers in his "Joel Barlow and the French Revolution," 338–39.

5 Barlow was already campaigning in Chambéry when he was notified. Durden, "Joel Barlow and the French Revolution," 339.

6 Chambéry, 4 December 1792, BP-HL, item 196.

7 "A Letter Addressed to the People of Piedmont, on the Advantages of the French Revolution and the Necessity of Adopting Its Principles in Italy," *Works*, vol. 1, 313–58.

8 Chambéry, 25 December 1792, BP-HL, item 198.

9 Woodress, *Yankee's Odyssey*, 135.

10 Ford, *Joel Barlow*, 32.

11 23 May 1802, BP-HL, item 374.

12 Letters of 1 and 9 January 1793, London, BP-HL, items 538 and 539.

13 Letters of 28 January and 1 February 1793, Paris, BP-HL, items 540 and 541.

14 Six letters in March alone, BP-HL, items 202–8.

15 Paris, BP-HL, item 210.

16 Barlow had met Leavenworth in London. See Durden, "Joel Barlow and the French Revolution," 351.

17 Ibid.

18 Middletown, CT, 10 June 1794, BP-HL, item 645.

19 Paris, 8 November 1794, in George Gibbs, ed., *Memoirs of the Administrations of Washington and John Adams, Edited from Papers of Oliver Wolcott, Secretary of the Treasury*, vol. 1 (New York, 1846), 161.

20 Woodress, *Yankee's Odyssey*, 139–40.

21 Paris, 7 May 1793, BP-HL, item 212.

22 Howard C. Rice, "James Swan, Agent of the French Republic," *New England Quarterly* 10 (Sept. 1937): 464–86.

23 Paris, 19 April 1793, BP-HL, item 210.

24 Woodress, *Yankee's Odyssey*, 145.

25 Paris, 2 May 1793, BP-HL, item 211.

26 Woodress, *Yankee's Odyssey*, 146.

27 Altona, 12 November 1794, BP-HL, item 510.

28 H. G. Barnby, although he cites no sources, finds this to be the likeliest pattern of Barlow's operations. See his *The Prisoners of Algiers: An Account of the Forgotten American-Algerian War, 1785–1897* (New York: Oxford University Press, 1966), 130–31.

29 See Pierre Caron, ed., *La Commission des Subsistances de l'an II: Procès verbale et actes* (Paris: E. Leroux, 1925), two volumes. Volume 1 contains only three references to dealings with Barlow. The first, dated 4 December 1793, complained that Barlow was asking too much for his cargo of potash but permitted him to sell it at the established

price (p. 88). Four days later, the commission itself agreed to buy the potash (at its price) and to allow the re-export of goods he was unable to dispose of (p. 102). Third, an elaborate chart of Commission purchases, dated 28 January 1794, shows that Barlow landed a cargo of potash and pearl ash at Le Havre (p. 662).

CHAPTER 4. WAITING FOR A DIPLOMATIC OPENING TO ALGERIA

1 Before Barlow arrived on the scene, Humphreys had sounded out Benjamin Hichborn and had even drawn up a commission naming him U.S. consul to Algiers, only to have Hichborn beg off on grounds of ill health. See Barnby, *Prisoners of Algiers*, 130; Woodress, *Yankee's Odyssey*, 154.

2 Barnby, *Prisoners of Algiers*, 202.

3 Marseille, 10 August 1797, Joel Barlow's Letter Book, vol. 2, 223–35, Barlow Papers, Houghton Library, hereinafter cited as Barlow LB.

4 To secretary of state, Algiers, 18 March, 1796, Barlow LB, vol. 1, 59.

5 See his memoir, *The Captives: Eleven Years a Prisoner in Algiers* (La Porte, IN: J. B. Newkirk, 1899), compiled by his daughter, Jane Bancker Cathcart Newkirk. Also reproduced in Paul Baepler, ed., *White Slaves, African Masters: An Anthology of American Barbary Captivity Narratives* (Chicago: University of Chicago Press, 1999).

6 Barnby, *Prisoners of Algiers*, 82.

7 Jefferson recapped his earlier efforts in a report Washington conveyed to Congress on December 30, 1790. For the text of his report, see *Naval Documents Related to the United States Wars with the Barbary Powers, Naval Operations including Diplomatic Background from 1785 through 1891*, vol. 1 (Washington, DC: Government Printing Office, 1938), 18–22, hereinafter cited as *NavDocs.*

8 Barnby, *Prisoners of Algiers*, 73.

9 Ibid.

10 See Cathcart's account of Lamb's mission in *The Captives*, 35–40.

11 See Jefferson's instructions to Adm. John Paul Jones, Philadelphia, 1 June 1792, in United States Ministers, Instructions of the Department of State, vol. 5, 158–59, hereinafter cited as DI (diplomatic instructions).

12 To Jefferson, Algiers, 8 June 1786, *NavDocs*, vol. 1, 1–5.

13 Cathcart, *The Captives*, 40, 31.

14 Philadelphia, 13 July 1791, DI, vol. 5, 67–68.

15 See Jefferson's report to Congress, *NavDocs*, vol. 1, 24–25.

16 Ibid., 34–35.

17 Instructions of 1 June 1792, ibid., 156–68.

18 See Jefferson to David Humphreys, Philadelphia, 21 March 1793, DI, vol. 5, 256–57.

19 Ibid.

20 For Humphreys's "Circular concerning the Truce between Portugal and Algiers," Gibraltar, 8 October 1793, see *NavDocs*, 45–47. For George Logie's role in arranging the truce and the Portuguese foreign minister's disclaimer and promise of convoy, see Edward Church, U.S. consul, to secretary of state, Lisbon, dispatches of 12 and 22 October 1793, ibid., 48–49 and 52–53.

21 Alicante, 29 November 1793, Diplomatic Dispatches (Portugal), vol. 4, Records of the Department of State (hereinafter cited as DD), copy enclosed in Humphreys to secretary of state, no. 104, Madrid, 25 December 1793, DD (Spain), vol. 1.

22 Nathaniel Cutting to secretary of state, Lisbon, 10 February 1794, *NavDocs*, 63–68. As Humphreys's clerk, Cutting traveled with him to Alicante. Both were back in Lisbon by January 25. Cutting noted that George Logie, also in Lisbon, was at that moment "walking the Garden beneath my window." Logie, he wrote, had denied complicity in the Algerian truce, but not even the Portuguese government believed him.

23 This letter is reproduced in Frank Humphreys's *The Life and Times of David Humphreys*, vol. 2 (New York and London: G. P. Putnam's Sons, 1917), 188. See also Humphreys to secretary of state, Alicante, no. 102, 23 November 1793, DD (Portugal), vol. 4.

24 Skjoldebrand to Humphreys, Algiers, 13 November 1793, ibid. As his mission to Algiers drew to a close, Barlow wrote Humphreys that Skjoldebrand deserved high praise for having looked after the needs of the American captives before he arrived and for "giving me the most friendly assistance at every critical period of our affairs." He later told of Skjoldebrand's refusal to accept gifts valued at $2,500, which he was prepared to pay out of his own pocket if Washington declined to reimburse him. To Humphreys, Algiers, 4 March 1797, Barlow LB, 38–43.

25 Sjoldebrand made this suggestion in his letter of 13 November 1793, DD (Portugal), vol. 4. O'Brien endorsed it in a letter to Humphreys dated 12 November 1793, ibid.

26 Abigail Adams's description appears on a scrap of paper in Barlow's "Miscellaneous Papers" in the Houghton Library collection, item 720. It reads: "Col. H is from Ct., a dark complexioned, stout, well-made warlike looking gentleman of about 30."

27 Humphreys enclosed copies of his letters to Skjoldebrand and O'Brien, both dated 29 November 1793, in his dispatch no. 103, Alicante, 7 December 1793, DD (Portugal), vol. 4.

28 For his bootless talks with Short and Carmichael in Madrid, see his dispatch no. 107, Lisbon, 30 January 1794, ibid.

29 Dispatch no. 120, Lisbon, 18 April 1794, ibid.

30 Humphreys enclosed copies of these letters from Skjoldebrand and O'Brien in his dispatches nos. 121 and 122 of 26 April and 13 May 1794, respectively, ibid.

31 See dispatches nos. 122 and 123, of 13 and 18 May 1794, respectively, ibid.

32 Copy enclosed in his dispatch no. 124, 23 May 1794, ibid.

33 He also told O'Brien he wanted to hear no more about the overtures of unauthorized agents. Letter of 18 May 1794, ibid.

34 Letter of 11 August 1794, ibid.

35 Earlier that year, when Cutting left on a junket to Ireland, Humphreys repeated to Randolph what he had told Jefferson, that he felt "an insuperable reluctance to have any thing to do with public monies," adding that he would rather resign than have his accounts questioned. Dispatch no. 113, 6 March 1794, ibid. Six months later, he insisted that without a clerk or secretary, he was not prepared to disburse public funds. That had been Cutting's role, he explained, primarily in funneling funds to Alicante where Montgomery, in turn, had used them to reimburse Skjoldebrand for expenses associated with provisioning the captives. But now, Humphreys told Randolph, "it would be impossible for me to go through the druggery [sic] of counting with my own hand in dollars, as Mr. Cutting did 40,000." Dispatch no. 141 of 18 September 1794, ibid.

36 Lisbon, 11 August 1794, enclosed in dispatch no. 134 of the same date, ibid.

37 See Randolph to Humphreys, Philadelphia, 19 July 1794, *NavDocs*, 77–78, and Humphreys's dispatch no. 136, 20 August 1794, DD (Portugal), vol. 4, reporting his inability to identify the French agent.

38 Lisbon, dispatch no. 149, 10 November 1794, DD (Portugal), vol. 4.

39 Lisbon, dispatch no. 148, 30 October 1794, ibid.

40 For Humphreys's interpretation of Skjoldebrand's warning, see his dispatch no. 151, 29 November 1794, ibid.

41 Ibid.

CHAPTER 5. SETTING OUT TO COMPLETE DONALDSON'S TREATY

1 Humphreys was about to sail for Philadelphia when he learned that consular appointee Gabriels, a resident of Portsmouth, Virginia, had been told to consult with him en route to Algiers. Humphreys wrote Gabriels to wait at Gibraltar for his return. By that time, however, Humphreys had new instructions in which Gabriels did not figure. See his letter to Gabriels, Lisbon, 29 November 1794, enclosed in his dispatch no. 151 of the same date, DD (Portugal), vol. 4. For Heysell's ill-fated mission, see U.S. Consul Robert Montgomery to secretary of state, Alicante, 2 May 1795, in Dispatches from U.S. Consuls (Alicante), vol. 1, hereinafter cited as CD with name of consular post.

2 Barnby, *Prisoners of Algiers*, 118–19.

3 Randolph to Humphreys, Philadelphia, 4 April 1795, *NavDocs*, 96–97.

4 O'Brien to Montgomery, Algiers, 27 December 1794, and Montgomery to Humphreys, Alicante, 16 January 1795, CD (Alicante), vol. 1.

5 Randolph to Humphreys, Philadelphia, 28 March 1795, *NavDocs*, 94–96; same to same, 4 April 1795, ibid., 96–97.

6 "On Board the Brig *Sophia*, Delaware Bay, 8 April 1795," Humphreys, *Life of Humphreys*, vol. 2, 231–32.

7 Lisbon, 18 May 1795, *NavDocs*, 98–99.

8 Barnby, *Prisoners of Algiers*, 126–27.

9 Cathcart, *The Captives*, 158–61.

10 Ibid., 137–46, 150.

11 Punishment administered by being beaten on the soles of one's feet.

12 Cathcart, *The Captives*, 169–70.

13 Ibid., 174–75. The dey, Barlow later concluded, had signed the treaty because he disliked foreign consuls undercutting one another and in this instance was angry at Vallière for having lied about Donaldson's having carte blanche. He made no mention of Cathcart's role in exposing the French consul. To Monroe, Algiers, 24 May 1795, Barlow LB, vol. 1, 116–22.

14 Cathcart, *The Captives*, 177–80.

15 Ibid., 180.

16 Ibid., 180–85. Barlow's May 24 letter to Monroe (Barlow LB, vol. 1, 116–22) offers a somewhat more detailed account of these last-minute offers and counteroffers, but generally substantiates Cathcart's.

17 Cathcart declined to translate this response because he "thought it very uncharitable and improper." Cathcart, *The Captives*, 187.

18 Barnby, *Prisoners of Algiers*, 190.

19 Cathcart, *The Captives*, 241. Shortly thereafter, Donaldson went to live with the Skjoldebrand brothers.

20 Ibid., 188, 201.

21 Ibid., 188–89. Cathcart saw O'Brien off on 11 September and later remarked peevishly that Donaldson had paid four times more than was necessary for the ship to carry O'Brien at Alicante (pp. 192, 194).

22 Monroe voiced his discomfiture in this instance when he later critiqued how badly the administration had treated him during his mission to France. See his *A View of the Conduct of the Executive of the United States in the Foreign Affairs* (Philadelphia, 1797).

23 To Barlow, Lisbon, 7 September 1795, *NavDocs*, 118.

24 See his letters of 27 September and 2 October 1795, while Humphreys was still at Le Havre, Barlow LB, vol. 1, 1–3.

25 Department of State, 13 April 1796, quoted in Humphreys, *Life of Humphreys*, vol. 2, 240.

26 See his letter to Humphreys of 2 October 1796, Barlow LB, vol. 1, 1–3.

27 Cathcart, *The Captives*, 217.

28 To Humphreys, Paris, 28 December 1797, Barlow LB, vol. 2, 66–69, recounting his end-of-mission activities and recommendations.

29 Paris, 23 December 1795, Barlow LB, vol. 1, 5.

30 Marseille, 17 January 1796, BP-HL, item 237.

31 Marseille, 10 January 1796, ibid., item 230.

32 For Barlow's encounters with the Algerian contingent in Marseille, see his letters to Ruth of 6, 7, 11, and 17 January 1796, ibid., items 226, 227, 231, and 237, respectively.

33 Marseille, 10 January 1796, ibid., 230.

34 Letters to Ruth from Figueres, 26 January, and from Alicante, 6 February 1796, ibid., items 243 and 246.

35 He wrote Ruth on 9 February that if a boat were available, he would sail for Algiers at once (ibid., item 247), but three days later wrote Humphreys that he would wait in Alicante until Montgomery returned from Lisbon, presumably with further instructions, Barlow LB, vol. 1, 5–6.

36 Alicante, 22 February 1796, BP-HL, item 252.

37 Lisbon, 7 February 1796, in "The Diplomatic Journal and Letter Book of James Leander Cathcart, 1788–1796" in *Proceedings of the American Antiquarian Society for October 1954)*: 379–85; hereinafter cited as Journal.

38 Commenting on this letter, Cathcart noted acidly that Donaldson had refused to charter a boat to Lisbon, which meant that O'Brien had wasted time traveling overland from Alicante, ibid., 385.

39 Algiers, 6 February 1796, *NavDocs*, 132–33.

40 To the dey and regency of Algiers, Lisbon, 10 Feb , and to Barlow, 16 February 1796, ibid., 133–34, and 135–36.

41 Alicante, 26 and 29 February 1796, Barlow LB, vol. 1, 13–14 and 15–16.

42 Alicante, 27 February 1796, BP-HL, item 255. Barlow later explained to Pickering how desperate he believed the situation had become in late February, dispatch no. 2, Algiers, 8 April 1796, CD (Algiers), vol. 1, 125–26.

CHAPTER 6. SAVING THE TREATY, FREEING THE CAPTIVES

1 Algiers, 8 March 1796, BP-HL, item 257.

2 Cathcart glumly recorded Barlow's reliance on Bacri in his early attempts to get an audience with the dey, *The Captives*, 250–51. Although Barlow often spelled Bacri's first name "Micayo," Daniel Schwartz, professor of Judaic Studies at the George Washington University, writes that Micaiah is the most familiar Anglicization of the Biblical name Micah.

3 Ibid., 251.

4 Ibid., 245–51.

5 Ibid., 218.

6 Ibid., 247.

7 Algiers, 14 March 1796, BP-HL, item 258.

8 Looking back in this long letter of 3 April 1796, Barlow praised Donaldson's "firmness & prudence" in not involving Vallière in the treaty-making process. Fortunately, too, Donaldson had been able to capitalize on the dey's dislike of the British who were seizing Algerian vessels at the time and were known to be hostile to American interests. See Barlow LB, vol 1, 40–49.

9 BP-HL, items 259 and 260.

10 Barlow and Donaldson related this sequence in a letter they sent Humphreys on 5 April 1796, *NavDocs*, 143–44, copy in Barlow LB, I, 50–53. Barlow mentioned the gift of the horse in a letter to Ruth, 26 April 1796, BP-HL, item 262.

11 Cathcart to Humphreys, 6 April 1796, *Journal*, 391. Knowing Barlow was Humphreys's friend, Cathcart was careful to characterize him as an "accomplished gentleman," whose only defect was not knowing the language. Unable to resist a little troublemaking, he also described Donaldson as "amazingly piqued" that Humphreys had sent Barlow "to keep him honest," adding, however, that "no private pique" would keep him from doing his best to raise the treaty money. Ibid., 392.

12 See letter of 5 April 1796, *NavDocs*, 144. He asked Montgomery to coach Humphreys on how to transfer the funds and asked that the $18,000 "douceur" needed to grease the transaction not be made known to Bacri's associates because he planned to keep some of it for his son. To Montgomery, 6 April 1796, Barlow LB, vol. 1, 53–54.

13 Letter of 5 April 1796, *NavDocs*, 144.

14 8 April 1796, Barlow LB, vol. 1, 63–64.

15 12 April 1796, ibid., 65.

16 26 April 1796, BP-HL, item 262.

17 5 April 1796, *NavDocs*, 144. He elaborated on this advice to Humphreys in a letter dated 26 April, Barlow LB, vol., 82–84.

18 To secretary of state, 17 April 1796, ibid., 71–72.

19 Algiers, 8 May 1796, BP-HL, item 265.

20 To Monroe, Algiers, 19 April 1796, Barlow LB, vol. 1, 77–82.

21 This observation appears in a fifty-four-page report to Pickering, Algiers, 18 October 1796, Barlow LB, vol. 2, 72–126.

22 To Monroe, Algiers, 19 April 1796, vol. 1, 77-82

23 Algiers, 26 April 1796, BP-HL, item 262.

24 Writing to Oliver Wolcott on 27 April, he repeated what he had told Monroe: that the United States could benefit from making commercial treaties with Turkey and the Italian states, but that he could not afford the expense of undertaking this mission. See Barlow LB, vol. 1, 89–90. By late fall of 1796, he had given up the idea of a Turkish mission but informed Humphreys that at his request, the dey had written a letter of introduction that an American emissary could pick up on his way to Constantinople. To Humphreys, Algiers, 16 November 1796, Barlow LB, vol. 2, 156–57.

25 Barlow LB, vol. 1, 82–90.

26 Ibid., 68–69.

27 To Monroe, Algiers, 24 May 1796, ibid., 116–22. Here, at some length, Barlow recapitulated Donaldson's difficulty in securing the treaty and underscored French obstructionism during and since that time. Nonetheless, he hoped Monroe could persuade Paris to let Herculais continue to help him negotiate a treaty with Tripoli.

28 *Journal*, 337. For Cathcart's account of negotiating the truce with Tunis the previous November, see Cathcart, *The Captives*, 210.

29 22 May 1796, Barlow LB, vol. 1, 108–16.

30 19 May 1796, ibid., 104–5.

31 To Monroe, 31 May, and to Humphreys, 12 June 1796, ibid., 122–23 and 123–31.

32 Letters of 3 and 8 July 1796, BP-HL, items 270, 271.

33 To Humphreys, 24 June 1796, Barlow LB, vol. 1, 132.

34 For his letters to Monroe of 16 and 28 June 1796, see ibid., 131, 136–38.

35 He wrote Humphreys on July 3 that he was still "to windward of the old Boy, and I have very little doubt at this moment but that things might be kept snug for some months longer, if necessary," ibid., 142.

36 To Donaldson, 12 July 1796, *NavDocs*, 161–62.

37 For Barlow's explanation, see his letter to Donaldson a year later, 4 July 1797, Barlow LB, vol. 2, 172–75.

38 To Humphreys, 6 July 1796, Barlow LB, vol. 1, 143–45. See also his dispatch no. 7, to the secretary of state, 12 July 1796, *NavDocs*, 163–65.

39 Ibid.

40 Ibid.

41 Barlow put in this good word for himself near the end of a long letter to Humphreys dated 6 September. Now that the captives had been ransomed, he noted, the dey suspected the United States would default on the treaty money. Unless the money came quickly, he warned, Algerian corsairs might once more begin preying on American shipping. Barlow LB, vol. 2, 1–9.

42 To Donaldson, 12 July 1796, *NavDocs*, 161–62.

43 Barlow gave the Bacris a bill of sale for the *Fortune* but told Captain Calder to burn it because he had no intention of buying the vessel. The British later captured the *Fortune* while it was transporting a cargo of Bacri-owned wheat from Bône to Genoa. And because Donaldson's name appeared on the ship's papers—much to Barlow's puzzlement—the Bacris held the United States responsible for the lost cargo. In the end, the U.S. government paid for it. See his explanation to Stephen Cathalan, Marseille, 17 July 1797, Barlow LB, vol. 2, 175–76, enclosing a "certificate" relating to the *Fortune*, dated 19 July.

44 Letter of 12 July 1796, *NavDocs*, 161–62.

45 From his long report to secretary of state, 18 October 1796, Barlow LB, vol. 2, 72–126.

CHAPTER 7. WAITING OUT TREATIES WITH TUNIS AND TRIPOLI

1 See Barlow's letters to Famin and Donaldson of 2 August 1796, Barlow LB, vol. 1, 162–65 and 166–68, and to Monroe, Aug. 7, ibid., 173–75. A copy of the truce described Barlow as an "agent of the United States residing in Algiers," Famin as his employee, and granted a truce of six months during which American vessels will be "treated with respect," ibid., 182 –83. Although the deys of Algiers appointed the beys of Tunis and Tripoli, the latter often resisted ouster by military force.

2 Explained to Humphreys in his long letter of 6 September 1796, Barlow LB, vol. 2, 1–9.

3 To Monroe, 31 August 1796, Barlow LB, vol. 1, 185–86.

4 To Donaldson, 2 August, ibid., 166–68.

5 Letters of 7 August (sent on 25 August) and 31 August, ibid., 173–75, 185–86.

6 7 August 1796, ibid., 170–73.

7 8 September 1796, Barlow LB, vol. 2, 16–17.

8 7 September 1796, ibid., 12–13.

9 1 September 1796, BP-HL, item 274.

10 To Humphreys, 24 September 1796, Barlow LB, vol. 2, 20–30; Humphreys to secretary of state, Lisbon, 6 October 1796, *NavDocs*, 175–76.

11 To Humphreys, 24 September 1796, Barlow LB, vol. 2, 20–30 .

12 To secretary of state, 18 October 1796, ibid., 72–126.

13 24 September 1796, ibid.

14 To secretary of state, 18 October, 1796, ibid. See also to Humphreys, 9 October, LB, vol. 2, 62–64, and to Ruth Barlow, 9 October, BP-HL, item 278.

15 See Barlow's notation to the "Substance of the Dey's letter to the Bey of Tripoli," undated, addressee not specified, Barlow LB, vol. 2, 68–72.

16 To secretary of state, 18 October 1796, ibid.

17 Ibid.

18 His calculations appear in two letters to Donaldson dated 31 August 1796, ibid., 184–85, and 12 October, ibid., 65–67.

19 To Donaldson, 19 October 1796, ibid., 129–31.

20 To Humphreys, 4 August 1797, Barlow LB, vol. 1, 202–18.

21 8 October 1796, Barlow LB, vol. 2, 58–61.

22 Ibid., 33–49.

23 Ibid., 54–57.

24 To Famin and to Graves, 8 October 1796, ibid., 50–53 and 57, respectively.

25 Barlow's dismay at this turn of events was shared by Edward Rand, owner of the *Eliza* and a passenger on board. After the vessel put in at Palermo, Graves announced that he planned to take the stolen cargo to Bristol and then sail to the United States. When Rand reminded him of Barlow's instructions, Graves claimed they were "discretionary." The fallout from this sequence of events appears in a document referred to as the Graves Deposition, dated 18 April 1797, in Barlow LB, vol. 2, 81–103.

26 30 April 30, 1797, ibid., 109–10.

27 Algiers, 12 January 1797, *NavDocs*, 191–92.

28 For an overview of this controversy, see Rob Boston, "Joel Barlow and the Treaty with Tripoli: A Tangled Tale of Pirates, a Poet, and the True Meaning of the First Amendment," *Church and State* 50, no. 6 (June 1997), 11–14. The bey signed the treaty on 4 November 1796, Barlow signed it on 3 January 1797, and the Senate ratified it on 10 June 1797. See text in David Hunter Miller, ed., *Treaties and Other International Acts of the United States of America, 1776–1863*, vol. 2 (Washington: Government Printing Office, 1931), 363–85.

29 Letter of 12 January 1797, *NavDocs*, 191. Ray Irwin suggests that a contributing factor may have been the dey's anger at Tunisians having earlier plundered a shipwrecked Algerian vessel. See his *The Diplomatic Relations of the United States with the Barbary Powers, 1776–1816* (Chapel Hill: University of North Carolina Press, 1951), 87.

30 See "Observations of Richard O'Brien on negotiations for peace with Tunis," City of Tunis, 9 December 1796, *NavDocs*, 184–86. Famin was piqued at not being invited to join in these negotiations. Letter of 17 October 1796, Barlow LB, vol. 2, 127.

31 See Barlow's long dispatch to secretary of state, 18 October 1796, ibid.

32 Dealing with the dey was a "strange comedy," he told Ruth, in which he had acted out a "most painful and despairing role." Although the latter seemed skeptical of "the sincerity of our government, he saw in my tranquillity and constancy something that won him over." Still, knowing how "capricious" the dey could be, he hoped he could retain the regent's goodwill until the end of his mission. Algiers, 20 November 1796, BP-HL, item 284.

33 To Donaldson, 1 February 1797, Barlow LB, vol. 3, 18–19.

34 6 February 1797, BP-HL, item 289.

35 To William Little, 20 December 1796, Barlow LB, vol. 2, 172–75; to Aloïs Herculais (in Tunis), 21 December 1796, ibid., 180–84; and to Capt. Joseph Ingraham (U.S. Consul, Tripoli), 1 February 1797, Barlow LB, vol. 3, 10–15. Barlow instructed Little to invest any profits in U.S. government bonds, split evenly between accounts for Ruth and Herculais, the latter as half-owner of the *Friendship*. To Ruth, 30 December 1796, BP-HL, item 288.

36 To R. and J. Montgomery, 1 February 1797, Barlow LB, vol. 3, 20–23. Same to same, 24 May 1797, ibid., 117–18, noting that half the profits should be credited to the "house of J. C. Bacry & Co," the other half to him.

37 From Barlow's long dispatch to secretary of state, 18 October 1796, Barlow LB, vol. 2.

38 Algiers, 24 March 1797, Barlow LB, vol. 3, 73–75.

39 To the U.S. minister in Paris, 14 March 1797, *NavDocs*, 199–201.

40 Ibid.

41 Barlow was right. Much later, he reported that the dey had recalled his troops at the end of January when the bey sent an apology and a gift. At that time he realized the dey would play no further role in his negotiations with Tunis and that he would be left to his own devices. To secretary of state, Marseille, 17 August, 1797, Barlow LB, vol. 3, 237–44.

42 To Famin, 20 March 1797 and to Cathalan, 28 April, Barlow LB, vol. 3, 66–70 and 108–9, respectively.

43 To Famin, 9 June 1797, ibid., 144–56.

44 Ibid.

45 Marseille, 19 July 1797, ibid., 183–86. Famin signed the Tunisian treaty on 28 August 1797; Humphreys forwarded it to Philadelphia on 14 November. After the Senate amended Articles 11, 12, and 14, Cathcart (U.S. consul, Tripoli) and Gen. William Eaton signed it again on 28 March 1798. The Senate ratified the amended treaty on 24 December 1799. See annotated text in *NavDocs*, 210–15.

46 Marseille, 1 August 1797, BP-HL, item 308.

47 Marseille, 4 August 1797, Barlow LB, vol. 3, 192–94. George Clark was the nephew of the Montgomery brothers, sent to Algiers at Barlow's request.

48 Marseille, 4 August 1797, ibid., 202–18. Barlow's itemized expenses appear in dated entries but on unnumbered pages in his Letter Book, vol. 4. By September 1797 he calculated that the government had spent a total of $706,986.86 on his mission, of which it owed him $6,089.10.

49 Marseille, 4 August 1797, Barlow LB, vol. 3, 200.

50 Ibid., 201.

51 BP-HL, item 320.

52 Marseille, 4 August 1797, Barlow LB, vol. 3, 194–96.

CHAPTER 8. CRITIQUING U.S. POLICY TOWARD FRANCE

1 To William Vans Murray, Paris, 8 October 1797, in Misc. Letters, William Vans Murray Papers, Library of Congress.

2 E. Wilson Lyon's phrase in his "The Directory and the United States," *American Historical Review* 43 (April 1938): 524.

3 James D. Richardson, *A Compilation of the Messages and Papers of the Presidents, 1789–1897*, vol. 1 (Washington: Bureau of National Literature, 1896), 266.

4 For the abuse leveled at Murray during the Senate's confirmation of his appointment, see the author's *William Vans Murray, Federalist Diplomat: The Shaping of Peace with France, 1797–1801* (Syracuse, NY: Syracuse University Press, 1971), 137.

5 Barlow LB, vol. 3, 80–109. Barlow enclosed a note asking that the letter be circulated quietly but not published unless the diplomatic crisis worsened. At the same time, however, he left the question of its publication entirely up to Baldwin. See BP-HL, item 70.

6 See, for example, Adams's references to France in his messages to Congress of 16 May and 22 November 1797, Richardson, *Messages,* vol. 1, 233–39 and 250–54, respectively.

7 Paris, 26 July 1798, BP-HL, item 529; also reproduced in Gibbs, *Memoirs*, vol. 2, 111. Barlow revealed his familiarity with Gerry's diplomacy in a letter to his New York broker, James Watson, Paris, 26 July 1798, LB, vol. 3, 132–34.

8 Paris, 2 October 1798, BP-HL, item 516.

9 For Adams's somewhat bloodthirsty letter to Washington, see Charles Francis Adams, ed., *The Works of John Adams, Second President of the United States*, vol. 8 (Boston: Little, Brown, 1854), 624–25. And for his second thoughts on Barlow's motives, vol. 9, 241.

10 Woodress writes that Federalist newspapers "worked themselves into a fine frenzy" over the letter to Baldwin but did not alter it appreciably. For Barlow's rebuttal, titled "On the System of Policy Hitherto Pursued by Our Government, Paris, 4 March 1799," see Bottorff, *Works*, vol. 1, 365–93.

11 Ibid., 369.

12 Ibid., 372–73.

13 Ibid., 375–76.

14 For the text of Jay's Treaty, see Miller, *Treaties*, vol. 2, 245–67.

15 "Memoir on Certain Principles of Public Maritime Law, Written for the French Government," 5 December 1799, in Bottorff, *Works*, vol. 1, 449.

16 Ibid., 475–76.

17 Ibid., 460–64.

18 To M. Dobrée (U.S. consul at Nantes), Paris, 12 Ventose, an 8 [3 March 1800], Barlow LB, vol. 3, 266–68.

19 Stephen Kurtz suggests that Adams himself contributed to the delay, believing that the Ellsworth Commission's bargaining position would be improved when three new American frigates nearing completion put to sea. See his "The French Mission of 1799–1800: Concluding Chapter in the Statecraft of John Adams," *Political Science Quarterly* 80 (December 1965): 555–56.

20 This letter, dated 12 February 1799, was sent to all five members of the Executive Directory. See Barlow LB, vol. 3, 194–204.

21 Paris, 26 Prairial, an 8 [16 June 1799], ibid., 236–38.

22 For details of Adams's last-minute struggle to overcome his cabinet's opposition to sending the mission, see Alexander DeConde's *The Quasi-War: The Politics and Diplomacy of the Undeclared War with France, 1797–1801* (New York: Scribner's, 1966), 217–22.

23 For his letters to Lyle of 28 July and 23 September 1799, see Barlow LB, vol. 3, 243–44 and 252–53.

24 Weston, CT, 24 September 1799, BP-HL, item 536.

25 Ibid.

26 Paris, 17 April 1800, ibid., item 101.

27 To Aaron Barlow, Paris, 1 October 1800, ibid., item 103.

28 Paris, 27 August 1800, ibid., item 341.

29 Barlow wrote either to Ruth or Fulton nearly every day between 16 August and 13 September. See BP-HL, items 331–58.

30 Cynthia Owen Philip, in her *Robert Fulton: A Biography* (New York: F. Watts, 1985), puts all three on the psychiatrist's couch: Ruth's letters to Fulton are "erotic"; Barlow's "egocentricity possibly masked a deep-seated fear of Ruth"; Barlow and Fulton may have been "lovers." But then she concludes that Fulton was more talk than action. "His tone is that of an impotent man. He seems incapable of loving anyone but himself" (105–7).

31 Barlow wrote to Fulton on 13 August 1802, when the latter was staying with William and Susan Lee in Bordeaux. On the reverse side of this letter, Fulton replied: "Tell Mrs. B if I had not fell in love with her first I certainly should have with Mrs. L[ee]. But in such platonic love as mine I believe the best way is to love both." BP-HL, item 410.

32 See his letters to Ruth of 2 September 1800 and to Fulton of 6 September, ibid., items 347 and 351.

33 To William Lee, Paris, 12 April 1799, Barlow LB, vol. 3, 224–25.

34 Le Havre, 6 October 1800, BP-HL, item 526.

35 Le Havre, 6 October 1800, among five letters to Meigs, ibid., item 506.

36 Paris, 17 April 1800, Barlow LB, vol. 3, 270–71.

37 Paris, 25 April, 1800, ibid., 226–31.

38 New Haven, 13 October 1808, BP-HL, item 641. For more on Barlow's religious beliefs, see Merton Christensen, "Deism in Joel Barlow's Early Work: Heterodox Passages in the Vision of Columbus," *American Literature* 27, no. 4 (January 1956): 509–20. Barlow's cosmology was vaguely materialistic. In his "Note Book," dated 1802, he defined "Nature, or the Universe, or God" as being "merely physical & cannot be either intellectual or moral." Morality was a human concept derived from "social organization and mutual dependence." BP-HL, item 12.

39 Washington, 9 June 1822, in Mary Lee Mann, *A Yankee Jeffersonian: Selections from the Diary and Letters of William Lee of Massachusetts, Written from 1796 to 1840* (Cambridge, MA: Harvard University Press, 1958), 191.

40 Paris, 10 March 1801, BP-HL, item 657.

41 Paris, 20 January 1796, ibid., item 546.

42 Letters of 6 July and 8 December 1796, ibid., items 558 and 565.

43 Letters of 9 August and 16 December, 1796, ibid., items 562 and 566.

44 Paris, 12 November 1796, ibid., item 564.

45 Letters of 20 February, 12 March, and 5 April 1796, ibid., items 573, 574, and 576.

46 See his letters of 20 October and 12 December 1810, and 6 March 1811, in Mann, *Yankee Jeffersonian,* 130, 132, and 134, respectively.

47 Paris, 22 May 1796, BP-HL, item 557.

48 Paris, 29 April 1797, ibid., item 578.

49 Algiers, 8 July 1796, ibid., item 271.

CHAPTER 9. KEEPING BUSY IN PARIS, RIDING OUT THE POLITICAL STORM AT HOME

1 Letters of 20, 28, and 30 July 1802, BP-HL, items 398, 402, and 403, respectively.

2 London, 28 July 1803, ibid., item 527.

3 To Lady Hamilton, Paris, 21 September 1801, LB, vol. 3, 281–84.

4 Paris, 5 January 1802, ibid., 289–93.

5 To William Herries, Paris, 29 September 1802, ibid., 310–11.

6 Whether Barlow rented the Vaugirard property or sold it and rented it back when he returned remains uncertain. From London in November 1804, he wrote Abraham Baldwin that he had sold all his property in France (BP-HL, item 78). But from Paris in November 1811, he wrote his nephew Stephen that he and Ruth were again living in their former house on Vaugirard (ibid., item 478).

7 See eight letters to RB, Paris, between 5 and 17 May 1802, BP-HL, items 361–68.

8 To RB, Paris, 9 May 1802, ibid., item 363.

9 To RB, Paris, 17 May 1802, ibid., item 368.

10 To RB, Paris, [8 June 1802], ibid., item 382. (Here and hereinafter, brackets indicate where I've substituted modern dating for Barlow's use of the French revolutionary calendar.)

11 To RB, Paris, [24 July 1802], ibid., item 400.

12 To RB, Paris, [18 June 1802], ibid, item 387.

13 To RB, Paris, [14 June 1802], ibid., item 385.

14 To RB, Paris, [12 July 1802], ibid., item 394. This and other letters addressed to Ruth that summer contained advice to Fulton.

15 To RB, Dover, [1 July 1802], ibid., item 389.

16 To RB, Paris, [26 July 1802], ibid., item 401.

17 Barlow told Ruth that Livingston and others regarded undersea warfare as not playing by the rules and that it "was better for the morals & general happiness of all people, that the fighting should be done on the ocean." Paris, 4 June 1802, ibid., item 380.

18 To RB, Paris, [30 July 1802], ibid., item 403.

19 To RB, Paris, [13 August 1802], ibid., item 410.

20 See letters to Monroe and Dearborn, Paris, 17 and 20 March 1802, LB, vol. 3, 293–97 and 298.

21 To U.S. consul, Bordeaux, Paris, 14 July 1801, ibid., 277–78; and to Thomas Dabney, Paris, 17 February 1803, ibid., 312–13.

22 To RB, Paris, August 19, 1802, ibid., item 413.

23 To RB, Paris, [15 and 19 August 1802], BP-HL, items 411 and 413.

24 To RB, Paris, [July 20, 1802], ibid., item 398.

25 London, 28 July 1803, ibid., item 527.

26 To Fulton, Paris, [20 May 1802], ibid., item 372.

27 To Fulton, Paris, [25 May 1802], ibid., item 375.

28 Kalorama, 15 December 1807, ibid., item 455.

29 "Agreements for sale and eventual manumitting of two negro slaves, Washington, 23 July 1811," in BP-HL (Misc. Papers), item 707.

CHAPTER 10. HOME AT LAST: TOUTING A NATIONAL INSTITUTION OF LEARNING

1 Still useful overviews of this era are Irwin's *Diplomatic Relations* and James A. Field, Jr., *America and the Mediterranean World, 1776–1882* (Princeton, NJ: Princeton University Press, 1969).

2 Bottorff, *Works*, vol. 1, 371–780.

3 See Josiah Meigs to Barlow, Athens, GA, 20 October 1809, BP-HL, item 625.

4 Clemenceau's proposal appears as a marginal note in a copy of *The Columbiad* owned by the family of Richard B. Parker, author of "The Story of Joel Barlow and His Kalorama," in *Neighbors of the Cosmos Club* (Washington: Cosmos Club, 2001). The note writer cites the *Hartford Courant* as the source.

5 See Howard Rice, "James Swan, Agent of the French Republic, 1794–1796," *New England Quarterly* 10 (September 1937): 485. The quoted passage is from a descendant's account of Swan's prison accommodations published in *Proceedings, Massachusetts Historical Society* 4: 47.

6 To RB, Paris, [7 May and 24 July 1802], BP-HL, items 362 and 400. Barlow chuckled at Skipwith's having listed his age as thirty-two on the wedding register,

having given his age as fifty on the passport Barlow had borrowed when he went to England that summer. In fact, he was thirty-seven.

7 Philip, *Fulton*, 185.

8 Ibid., 203.

9 To Fulton, Washington, 30 March 1806, BP-HL, item 494.

10 Philip, *Fulton*, 235.

11 Mann, *A Yankee Jeffersonian*, 19.

12 Ibid., 146

13 Washington, 30 March, 1806, BP-HL, item 494.

14 Cf. TJ to JB, 3 May 1802, ibid., item 615, and JB to Noah Webster, 30 January 1779, item 518.

15 Letters of 3 May 1802 and 9 January 1804, ibid., items 615 and 616.

16 To Oliver Wolcott, Hamburg, 6 November 1794, ibid., item 529.

17 Hamburg, 8 November 1794, Gibbs, *Memoirs*, vol. 1, 161.

18 To Abraham Baldwin, Paris, 3 January 1801, BP-HL, item 74.

19 Paris, 28 December 1798, in Barlow Notebooks, 1798–1801, ibid., item 12.

20 New York, 28 August 1805, ibid., item 506.

21 Although this tour of Federalist New England was far from triumphal, Barlow was pleased when a New Haven audience of 150 turned out for a reception held in his honor by Republican members of the Connecticut legislature and "other respectable Republicans." Reported by the *American Mercury* (Hartford), 7 November 1805.

22 Cf., "Prospectus of a National Institution to be Established in the United States," in Bottorff's *Works*, vol. 2, 479–522, and a printed copy of the Logan bill at the end of the Houghton Library's microfilm reel labeled "bMS Am, Series III."

23 Bottorff, *Works*, vol. 2, 486.

24 Ibid., 499–505.

25 Ibid., 508–14.

26 Ibid., appendix, 517–20.

27 See Houghton Library microfilm referenced above.

28 Richardson, *Messages*, vol. 1, 410.

29 Algiers, 13 January 1797, BP-HL, Barlow LB, vol. 3, 5–6; more accurately called the Philadelphia Society for Promoting Agriculture, founded in 1785.

30 Paris, 26 September 1811, BP-HL, item 528.

31 Paris, 21 August 1801, ibid., item 506.

32 Paris, 2 September 1802, Barlow LB, vol. 3, 307–8.

33 Steven Brown, head of the University of Georgia archives, confirms that Barlow's presentation copy of *The Columbiad* did survive a devastating library fire in 1830. Its title page is inscribed "Presented by the author to the University of Georgia in 1808." Mr. Brown adds: "Readable or not, I'm glad it survived as a tangible relict of the friendship between Barlow and Meigs."

CHAPTER 11. NURTURING NEPHEWS, DEFENDING A PRESIDENT

1 To Stephen Barlow, Paris, 6 September 1802, BP-HL, item 437. Among Barlow's miscellaneous papers at the Houghton Library is a genealogy of Aaron's sons who, at the time of his death, included Elnathan, twenty-five; Samuel, twenty-three; Stephen, twenty-one; Daniel, nineteen; Aaron, Jr., eighteen; and Thomas, seven. A letter from Aaron written in the fall of 1799 describes Elnathan and Daniel as living at home, Samuel having gone to Ohio, Stephen studying law, and Aaron, Jr., teaching school and preparing for college. Ibid., item 536.

2 To the directors of the Ohio Company, Paris, 6 September 1802, Barlow LB, vol. 3, 303–4.

3 6 September 1802, BP-HL item 437.

4 Ibid.

5 To Stephen Barlow, Philadelphia, 1 February 1807, ibid., item 446.

6 See, for example, his letter to Stephen, New York, 19 August 1806, ibid., item 443.

7 Kalorama, 24 March 1808, ibid., item 459.

8 Kalorama, 12 October 1808, ibid., item 461.

9 See letters of 28 and 24 January 1808, ibid., items 456 and 457.

10 Ibid.

11 Kalorama, 11 December 1808, ibid., item 462.

12 Kalorama, 28 May 1810, ibid., item 466.

13 Paris, 21 November 1811, ibid., item 478.

14 Kalorama, 15 December 1807, ibid., item 455.

15 Kalorama, 20 February 1808, ibid., item 458.

16 Kalorama, 12 October 1808, ibid., item 461.

17 Kalorama, 23 September 1810, ibid., item 468.

18 Kalorama, 26 September 1810, ibid., item 469.

19 Kalorama, 17 October 1810, ibid., item 470.

20 Kalorama, 31 October 1810, ibid., item 472.

21 Kalorama, 18 February 1811, ibid., item 476.

22 Hampton Roads, VA, 5 August 1811, ibid., item 477.

23 See letters of 21 November 1811, and 22 April 1812, ibid., items 478 and 479.

24 The Barlows took up residence in Washington sometime in the fall of 1807. A letter to Stephen from Philadelphia is dated 5 October, but a second on November 6 is datelined "Belair," and a third on 15 December explains the name change. Barlow wrote: "I find the name of Belair has already been given to many places in Maryland and Virginia, so by the advice of friends we have changed it to one that is quite new, Calorama, from the Greek, signifies fine view, and this place presents one of the finest views in America." BP-HL, items 453–55.

Besides the original property, Shannon Lee, reference librarian of the Historical Society of Washington, DC, has identified deeds for at least four more parcels of land Barlow purchased in 1809.

25 To RB, Georgetown, letters of 10 and 17 March 1807, ibid., items 435–36.

26 Philip, *Fulton,* 191.

27 Webster to JB, New Haven, 12 November 1807, BP-HL, item 637.

28 New Haven, 5 April 1810, ibid., item 638.

29 Ford, *Joel Barlow*, 43.

30 See "Oration Delivered at Washington, July Fourth, 1809," Bottorff, *Works*, vol. 1, 525–36.

31 *The Federalist Papers* (Garden City, NY: Anchor Books, 1966), 24.

32 Bottorff, *Works*, vol. 1, 529.

33 Ibid., 534.

34 Ibid., 525.

35 Ibid., 532–33.

36 Ibid., 535.

37 Ibid., 535–36.

38 Smith's screed appeared in the *National Intelligencer*, 2 July 1811. For Barlow's *Review of Robert Smith's Address*, see Bottorff's *Works,* vol. 1, 551–86.

39 For excerpts from the British and French decrees mentioned in this chapter, as well as citations to their original sources, a handy reference work is Ruhl J. Bartlett's *The Record of American Diplomacy: Documents and Readings in the History of American Foreign Relations* (New York: Knopf, 1964).

40 Bartlett, *Record of American Diplomacy*, 124–25.

41 This was one of several orders-in-council in November 1807. Texts are reproduced in *Debates and Proceedings of the Congress of the United States*, 10th Cong., 2th Sess. (Washington: Gales and Seaton, 1834–56), 1698–1701.

42 Bartlett, *Record of American Diplomacy*, 125–26.

43 Ibid., 127–28.

44 Ibid., 128–29.

45 Ibid., 134; Madison to William Pinkney, Washington, 23 May 1810, Madison Papers, LC, reel 26.

46 See Bartlett, *Record of American Diplomacy*, 135, for the Cadore Letter.

47 Madison himself admitted that when he responded to the Cadore Letter, he had neglected to insist on the restoration of these vessels. He may have assumed they would be freed as part of a general accommodation with France. His embarrassment showed in a letter he wrote to Armstrong on 19 October 1810. See Madison Papers, LC, reel 12.

48 Bottorff, *Works*, vol. 1, 564.

49 Ibid., 563–64.

50 Ibid., 564, 568.

51 Ibid., 566.

CHAPTER 12. WATCHING THE WORSENING RELATIONS WITH BRITAIN AND FRANCE

1 See Bradford Perkins, *The First Rapprochement: England and the United States, 1795–1805* (Philadelphia: University of Pennsylvania Press, 1955).

2 Perkins, "Sir William Scott and the *Essex*," *William and Mary Quarterly*, 3rd Series, 22 (1956), 169–83.

3 For an extended account of the origins of the Non-Intercourse Act, see Burton Spivak, *Jefferson's English Crisis: Commerce, Embargo, and the Republican Revolution* (Charlottesville: University of Virginia Press, 1979), 31–47; also Herbert Heaton, "Non-Importation, 1806–1812," *Journal of Economic History* 1 (November 1941): 178–98.

4 See Donald R. Hickey, "The Monroe-Pinkney Treaty: A Reappraisal," *William and Mary Quarterly*, 3rd Series, 44, no. 1 (January 1987): 66–88.

5 For this sequence of events, see J. Leitch Wright, Jr., *Britain and the American Frontier, 1783–1815* (Athens: University of Georgia Press, 1975), 152–54.

6 For more on the context and ramifications of the Rambouillet and Trianon decrees of 23 March and 5 August 1810, see Peter P. Hill, *Napoleon's Troublesome Americans: Franco-American Relations, 1804–1815* (Washington: Potomac Books, 205), chaps. 9 and 10, passim.

7 This rebuff is contained in a note addressed to the duc de Cadore, dated 7 February 1811, expressing Napoleon's wishes. See Archives Etrangères de France, Correspondance Politique, États-Unis, vol. 67, 15, hereinafter cited as AECP-EU. The signature on the note is illegible.

8 Russell to secretary of state, Paris, 2 May 1811, Archives of the U.S. Department of State, Diplomatic Dispatches, France (hereinafter cited as DD-F), vol. 12. The duc de Bassano replaced Cadore as minister of exterior relations in April 1811.

9 See Smith's explanation to Russell, Washington, 6 March 1811, DI, vol. 7, 148–49.

10 For this dustup between Russell and Pinkney over the *New Orleans Packet*, see Hill, *Napoleon's Troublesome Americans*, 102–4.

11 Reported by David Bailie Warden (U.S. consul, Paris) to John Graham, 4 January 1813. See Department of State, Dispatches from U.S. Consuls (Paris), vol. 4.

12 Conclusion reached by Frank Edgar Melvin, *Napoleon's Navigation System: A Study of Trade Control during the Continental Blockade* (New York: AMS Press reprint, 1970), 88; John Holland Rose, *The Life of Napoleon I* (New York: MacMillan Company, 1907), 203–6; and Audrey Cunningham, *British Credit in the Last Napoleonic War* (Cambridge: Cambridge University Press, 1910), 60.

13 Emmanuel de Las Casas, *Memorial de Sainte Hélène (par Las Casas)*, vol. 4 (Paris: Edition Garnier Frères, 1961), 200.

14 Melvin, *Napoleon's Navigation System*, 207–8.

15 See Armstrong to the comte de Champagny (later the duc de Cadore), Paris, 13 February 1809, AECP-EU, vol. 62, 42.

16 For exchanges on this issue, see Monroe to Serurier, 29 June 1811, and Serurier to Monroe, 30 June, ibid., 65, 323–23v, and 324–25; and Serurier's dispatches to Bassano of 25 and 30 June, ibid., 252–54, and 265–69v.

17 See Russell to Cadore, 1 October 1810, and Cadore's reply of 8 October, DD-F, vol. 12; and Cadore's "Copie des instructions de M. Serurier," October 1810, Archives Nationales de France, Série AFIV, côte 1681A, dossier 4.

18 Note to Cadore, 17 December 1810, DD-F, vol. 12.

19 To secretary of state, 4 December 1810, ibid.

20 See Russell to Cadore, 12 January 1811; Cadore to Russell, 18 January, DD-F, vol. 12; and Russell to Smith, 21 January, *American State Papers, Foreign Relations* (hereinafter cited as *ASP-FR*), vol. 3 (Washington: Gales and Seaton, 1832–59), 501; and Cadore to Serurier, no. 5, Paris, 9 February 1811, AECP-EU, vol. 65, 43–44.

CHAPTER 13. BEGINNING THE FRENCH MISSION— WITH LIVELY EXCHANGES

1 *National Intelligencer*, 8 August 1811.

2 For these astonished reactions, see Madison to John Quincy Adams, Washington, 15 November 1811, Madison Papers, LC, reel 13; Monroe to Foster, 1 October, *ASP FR*, vol. 3, 445–46; and Serurier to Ministre des Relations Extérieures, Washington, 8 August, AECP-EU, vol. 66, 19.

3 Richardson, *Messages,* 1, 491–96.

4 Ibid.

5 For these two letters to Fulton, the first, Hampton Roads, 11 August 1811, and the second "off the capes of Virginia," 5 August, datelined Hampton Roads, see BP-HL, items 499 and 500.

6 To Stephen, 5 August, 1811, BP-HL, item 479; to Monroe, 5 August, DD-F, 13.

7 To Stephen, 21 November 1811, BP-HL, item 478.

8 Paris, 26 November 1811, Mann, *Yankee Jeffersonian*, 144.

9 Paris, [September 1811], ibid., 117.

10 Bassano to Barlow, Paris, 21 September 1811, AECP-EU, vol. 64, 334. Barlow had planned to hold the *Constitution* long enough to send back a progress report, but uncertain of Napoleon's return to Paris and doubtful that he could track him down in Holland, he decided to use the frigate to ferry Jonathan Russell across the channel to his post as chargé in London. To Monroe, Paris, 29 October 1811, DD-F, 13.

11 To Monroe, Paris, 29 September 1811, DD-F, 13.

12 Paris, 26 September 1811, BP-HL, item 528.

13 Bassano's note to Serurier, no. 13, 24 October 1811, AECP-EU, vol. 64, 335–37.

14 For Petry's long report to Bassano, 15 November 1811, see AECP-EU, vol. 66, 285–95.

15 Ibid. 286–86v.

16 Ibid.

17 Ibid., 286v–87.

18 Ibid., 289.

19 Ibid., 291.

20 Ibid., 293v–295.

21 Dispatch no. 3, Paris, 21 November 1811, DD-F, 13, enclosing both his account of his audience with Napoleon on 17 November and his note to Bassano of 10 November.

22 Ibid.

23 Ibid. Richard Glover makes the case that Napoleon might have achieved naval superiority had he not embarked on his Russian campaign in his "The French Fleet, 1807–1814: Britain's Problem and Madison's Opportunity," *Journal of Modern History* 39 (September 1957): 233–52.

24 Dispatch no. 3.

25 Ibid.

26 Barlow to Monroe, dispatch no. 4, Paris, 12 December 1811, DD-F, 13.

27 Two notes to Bassano, both dated 30 November 1811, copies enclosed in Barlow's dispatch no. 5, Paris, 31 December 1811, ibid.

28 It was Bassano who told of having pleaded "no reproach," lest Barlow's hurtful account of this exchange offend the administration. See his dispatch no. 16, Paris, to Serurier, 30 December 1811, AECP-EU, vol. 64, 413.

29 AECP-EU, vol. 64, 378–85v.

30 Ibid., 380.

31 Ibid., 381.

32 Ibid., 382v–85.

33 For Bassano's "Rapport à Sa Majesté" of 5 December 1811, see AECP-EU, vol. 64, 386–94.

34 Ibid., 387v–88v., 389.

35 Ibid., 389v.

36 Ibid., 390.

37 In his dispatch no. 5 of 31 December 1811 (DD-F, vol. 13), Barlow noted having mentioned this possibility to Petry.

38 Bassano's "Rapport à Sa Majesté" of 5 December 1811, 391v.

39 Ibid., 394.

40 Ibid., 392.

CHAPTER 14. OUTLINING A TREATY, WAITING FOR A RESPONSE

1 Bassano to Barlow, Paris, 27 December 1811 (excerpts enclosed in Barlow's dispatches nos. 5 and 5-A, sent under one cover to Monroe, Paris, 31 December, DD-F, vol. 13).

2 Dispatch no. 5-A, 31 December, DD-F, vol. 13.

3 Dispatch no. 5, 31 December, DD-F, vol. 13.

4 Paris, 1 January 1812, Madison Papers, LC, reel 13.

5 Dispatch no. 16, Paris, 30 December 1811, AECP-EU, vol. 64, 407–14.

6 Ibid., 410–10v.

7 Ibid., 410v–11.

8 See Bassano to Serurier, dispatch no. 17, Paris, 30 December 1811, same date as no. 16 but entered in vol. 66, AECP-EU, 442–45v. Bassano apparently realized that Serurier needed a more detailed account of French goodwill. His dispatch no. 16, twice as long, is obviously the sequel to no. 17.

9 Dispatch no. 5. This mailing of 31 December 1811 also enclosed copies of Bassano to Barlow, 21 December (his response to Barlow's note of 10 November): same to same, 21 December (announcing the release of three U.S. vessels and twenty-three American seamen); and Barlow to Bassano, two notes of 30 November (one questioning the success of the Continental System, the other defending the administration's conduct vis-à-vis Britain).

10 For the "project of a Treaty" Barlow sent to Bassano on 17 January 1812, see dispatch no. 6, Paris, 28 January 1812, DD-F, vol. 13.

11 Ibid.

12 Ibid.

13 "Rapport à Sa Majesté," 27 February 1812, AECP-EU, vol. 69, 18–19.

14 See dispatches nos. 7 and 8, Paris, 8 February and 3 March 1812, DD-F, 13.

15 Washington, 23 April 1812, DI, vol. 7, 191–94.

16 Ibid., 200–205. For Monroe's critical marginalia, see Madison Papers, reel 13.

17 Dispatch no. 9, Paris, 16 March 1812, DD-F, 13.

18 Bassano admitted the oversight and assured Serurier that it was unintentional, that "the navigation and commerce of the United States are every day more favored by the French government." Paris, 27 April 1812, AECP-EU, vol. 69, 36–37v.

19 Ibid.

20 To Bassano, Paris, 1 May 1812, DD-F, 13.

21 Dispatch no. 12, Paris, 12 May 1812, enclosing Bassano's note of May 10, ibid.

22 See Serurier's dispatches of 21 June and 21 July 1812, AECP-EU, vol. 70, 275v–76 and 310–11. For Bassano's insistence, even to Serurier, that the decree was genuine, see his letter of 26 May, ibid., vol. 69, 56–58v.

23 Barlow to Russell, Paris, 11 May 1812, DD-F, 13.

24 Dispatch no. 14, Paris, 14 May 1812, ibid.

25 Bradford Perkins, in his *Prologue to War: England and the United States, 1805–1812* (Berkeley: University of California Press, 1969), chapter 9, recounts in detail the politics attending the ministry's decision to suspend the orders.

CHAPTER 15. SORTING OUT THE ISSUES IN FRANCO-AMERICAN COBELLIGERENCY

1 Dispatch no. 10, Paris, 22 April 1812, DD-F, 13.

2 Dispatch no. 11, Paris, 22 April 1812, ibid.

3 "Rapport à Sa Majesté," 17 April 1812, AECP-EU, vol. 69, 22–25.

4 Ibid., 24.

5 Ibid., 24v–25.

6 Bassano to Barlow, Paris, 20 April 1812, AECP-EU, vol. 69, 26. Dalberg, a native of Mainz, first came to Napoleon's attention when he represented the Margrave of Baden during the negotiation of the Treaty of Lunéville in 1801. The emperor, who often chose his councillors of state from French-occupied areas, named him a "duc of the empire" in 1810. Louis Gabriel Michaud, *Biographie universelle ancienne et modern* (Paris: Plons, 1843), vol. 10, 32–39.

7 AECP-EU, vol. 69, 28–29v.

8 Ibid.

9 Ibid.

10 See his dispatches nos. 12 and 13, Paris, of 12 and 22 May 1812, DD-F, 13.

11 See Barlow to Dalberg, 5 June 1812, copy enclosed in his dispatch no. 14 of 13 July, ibid. Barlow spent several weeks composing this note, which explains the time lapse between the date he began to write it and the date he sent a copy to Monroe.

12 Ibid.

13 Ibid.

14 Ibid.

15 Paris, 17 July 1812, copy enclosed in dispatch no. 15, 11 August, DD-F, 13.

16 Bassano to Dalberg, Paris. 10 May 1812, AECP-EU, vol. 69, 60–76.

17 Ibid.

18 Ibid.

19 Ibid.

20 Accompanying this short note of 28 May was a much longer but undated analysis Dalberg entitled "Examen des rapports entre la France et les États-unis en 1812," vol. 69, 78–80.

21 See Decrès to Bassano, Paris, 6 June 1812, AECP-EU, vol. 68, 200–02; and Bassano to Dalberg, Thom, 9 June, ibid., vol. 69, 133–35v.

22 Ibid.

23 See Dalberg's "Examen."

24 Paris, 17 June, AECP-EU, vol. 68, 243–44v.

25 See pp. 444–45 in Irving Brant, "Joel Barlow, Madison's Stubborn Minister," *William & Mary Quarterly*, 3rd Series, 15, no. 4 (October 1958).

26 Dalberg to Bassano, Paris, 18 June, and Petry to Bassano, 13 June 1812, AECP-EU, vol. 69, 138–38v and 139–141.

27 Paris, 18 June 1812, H-SP.

28 Paris, 15 July 1812, AECP-EU, vol. 68, 249–51v. Given Parliament's hostility, Petry doubted the British ministry would revive the orders. Therefore, unless France took counteraction, it must anticipate a return to full-bodied Anglo-American commerce.

29 Paris, 17 July 1812, copies enclosed in Barlow's dispatch no. 15, 11 August, DD-F, 13.

30 Ibid.

31 Paris, 29 July 1812, AECP-EU, vol. 69, 172–73.

32 For the eighteen-page position paper Petry sent Bassano on 31 July 1812, see AECP-EU, vol. 68, 262–71.

33 Ibid., 262–62v.

34 Ibid., 268.

35 To Bassano, Paris, 8 August 1812, enclosed in his dispatch no. 15 of 11 August, DD-F, 13.

36 Paris, 28 July 1812, AECP-EU, vol. 68, 259–60v.

CHAPTER 16. BRAINSTORMING A SOLUTION TO THE INDEMNITIES ISSUE

1 Wilna, 10 August 1812, AECP-EU, vol. 69, 198–200v.

2 Ibid.

3 Paris, 11 August 1812, ibid., 201–4.

4 For Dalberg's undated counterproposal, ibid., 205–12.

5 For Barlow's response of 13 August, detailing seven items he would add to Dalberg's counterproposal, and the latter's qualified acceptance of these additions on 17 August, see AECP-EU, vol. 69, 213–17v, and 218. Dalberg wrote Bassano on 21 August that he doubted Barlow would accept much of his counterproposal but that Sussy had approved it as a basis for negotiation, ibid., 220–21.

6 Wilna, 21 August 1812, ibid., 227–27v.

7 Paris, 9 September 1812, AECP-EU, vol. 68, 318–20v.

8 Paris, copy enclosed in his dispatch no. 15, 11 August 1812, DD-F, 13.

9 See Bassano's correspondence with the naval ministry's prize division in October 1812 (AECP-EU, vol. 68, 356–57), and Decrès's "Rapport à Sa Majesté," 14 October 1812, ibid., 366.

10 See David Bailie Warden to Monroe, Paris, 26 April 1813 (CD, Paris), 4.

11 To Bassano, Paris, 26 August 1812, AECP-EU, vol. 68, 295–96v.

12 Paris, ibid., 308–9.

13 To Bassano, Paris, 27 and 30 August 1812, AECP-EU, vol. 69, 231–31v, and 233–33v.

14 Ibid.

15 Ibid.

16 Paris, 8 September 1812, ibid., 236–236v.

17 Dalberg enclosed an undated copy of Barlow's initial indemnity plan in his letter to Bassano of 8 September 1812, ibid., 238–39.

18 Ibid.

19 To Bassano, Paris, 10 September 1812, AECP-EU, vol. 68, 321–32v.

20 Ibid.

21 Ibid.

22 Wilna, 18 September 1812, AECP-EU, vol. 69, 242–45.

23 Ibid.

24 Paris, 5 October 1812, ibid., 248–49.

25 See *The Papers of James Madison (Presidential Edition)*, vol. 5 (Charlottesville: University of Virginia Press, 2004), 144–45.

26 See intercepted letter, Barlow to Madison, 26 September 1812, in AECP-EU, vol. 68, 345–50v; also Petry to Bassano, Paris, 26 September 1812, ibid., 341–42v.

27 To Bassano, Paris, 5 October 1812, ibid., vol. 69, 248–49.

28 Petry to Bassano, letter of 26 September 1812, ibid., vol. 68, 342.

29 See Bassano's invitation, 11 October 1812, ibid., vol. 69, 253–53v; and Barlow to Monroe, 25 October, DD-F, 13.

30 Paris, 26 October 1812, AECP-EU, vol. 69, 276–78v.

31 See Bassano to Feltre, Wilna, 30 November 1812, vol. 68, 462–63v, enclosing his letter from Barlow of 28 November 1812, ibid., 465–67.

32 Ibid.

33 Feltre to Bassano, Paris, 3 December 1812, ibid., 471–72.

34 See Barnet to Bassano, Paris, 19 December 1812, ibid., 495–97, requesting the foreign minister to assure the duc de Feltre that the credentials of the persons whose names he was submitting had received "the most scrupulous attention."

35 Letter of 28 November 1812, Wilna, ibid., 465v.

36 For more on Haley's voyages, see Edgar Stanton Maclay, *A History of American Privateers* (New York: D. Appleton, 1899), 275–77. Haley was not new to the Franco-American scene. Not only a former officer in the French navy, he had also served as a courier for the State Department in 1808, at which time he had thrust himself uninvited into John Armstrong's negotiations with various French officials. For details of his quasi-diplomatic activities, see the author's *Napoleon's Troublesome Americans*, 49–51.

37 Ibid., 44.

38 Wilna, 23 November 1812, DD-F, 13.

39 See Bassano to Feltre, 20 July 1812, and the latter's reply of 31 August, AECP-EU, vol. 68, 256, and 301.

40 See Bassano to Barlow, 10 November 1812, ibid., 430, repeating Feltre's misgivings.

41 Letter of 28 November 1812, Wilna, ibid., 464–64v.

42 Paris, 19 November 1812, ibid., 454–54v.

43 See Warden to Barlow, Paris, 11 December 1811, DD-F, 13, and Barlow's letters to Bassano of 17 December 1811 and 23 January and 14 March 1812, ibid.

44 Paris, 26 June 1812, ibid.

45 Paris, 29 June 1812, ibid.

46 See postscript in Barlow's letter conveying his correspondence with Warden to the State Department, ibid.

CHAPTER 17. FAILED MISSION, FALLEN DIPLOMAT

1 Wilna, 11 October,1812, DD-F, 13.

2 See Barlow's letters to Bassano and Monroe of 25 October 1812, ibid.; and Barlow to Bassano, 24 October, AECP-EU, vol. 69, 350–51.

3 Petry to Bassano, 24 October 1812, ibid., vol. 68, 372–72v.

4 Paris, ibid., vol. 69, 313–24.

5 Ibid.

6 To Bassano, Paris, 22 October 1812, ibid., 342–47.

7 Wilna, 25 November 1812, ibid., 374–85.

8 Petry reported having given William H. Crawford this reason for rejecting Barlow's plan (to Bassano, 7 September 1813, AECP-EU, vol. 71, 355–56). For Monroe's shocked reaction when he first learned of the plan, see Serurier's dispatch no. 68, 10 September 1812, (ibid., 67, 283–87v). Crawford would later tell the French foreign office that the administration was "most decidedly opposed to the license system in every form." To Monroe, dispatch no. 12 (private), 1 December 1813, DD-F, vol. 14.

9 See letter of 25 November 1812, AECP-EU, vol. 69, 374-89.

10 Courcelles, 29 October 1812, H-SP.

11 Frankfurt, 30 October 1812, ibid.

12 Königsburg, 11 and 12 November 1812, ibid.

13 Stalloponin [Stalluponen], 14 November 1812, ibid.

14 Kowno [present day Kaunas], 17 November 1812, ibid.

15 Wilna, 18 November 1812, ibid.

16 Postscript dated 20 November 1812.

17 See, for example, Alan Palmer, *Napoleon in Russia* (New York: Simon and Schuster, 1967), 227–52, for an account of the French army's retreat.

18 Wilna, 22 November 1812, H-SP.

19 Wilna, 23 November 1812, DD-F, vol. 13.

20 Wilna, 26 November 1812, H-SP.

21 Wilna, 28 and 30 November 1812, ibid.

22 Ibid.

23 Ibid.

24 Ibid.

25 See Thomas Barlow to Ruth Barlow, 27 December 1812, BP-HL, item 667; and Petry to Bassano, 27 December, enclosed in Bassano to Daniel Parker, Paris, 13 January 1813, DD-F, vol. 13; also Thomas Barlow to Monroe, Paris, 27 January, ibid. Thomas sent his letter of 27 December via Parker who broke the news to Ruth. Bassano, too, recognized Parker's role in consoling Barlow's widow, which explains how Petry's account ended up in Diplomatic Dispatches. For letters of thanks to Bassano for extending his condolences, see Parker's of 14 January and that of Marcadier (Barlow's private secretary) the next day, AECP-EU, vol. 67, 380 and 381–82.

26 Dispatch no. 22, 23 November 1812, DD-F, 13.

27 For this exchange between Warden and Bassano, see AECP-EU, vol. 67, 383 and 384.

28 Paris, 13 January 1813, DD-F, 13.

29 See BP-HL, item 674.

30 See Lee's letters of 21 and 24 January 1813, AECP-EU, vol. 67, 392–92v and 397–97v.

31 See Roux's "Note à Son Excellence," 2 February 1813, ibid., 402–5v, in response to Thomas Barlow to Bassano, 2 February, ibid., DD-F, 13.

32 Ruth Barlow to Dolley Madison, New York, 16 December 1813, BP-HL, item 655; and Clara Baldwin Bomford to Dolley Madison (n.d.), ibid., item 674.

33 To Bassano, Paris, 15 and 18 January 1813, AECP-EU, vol. 67, 385–85v and 386–86v.

34 Ibid., 389–90v.

35 Paris, 6 March 1813, ibid., 420, at the conclusion of a lengthy explanation of all that had transpired since Barlow's death, ff. 413–20.

36 For details of Crawford's problems with Warden, see *Napoleon's Troublesome Americans*, 219–20.

37 New York, 16 December 1813, BP-HL, item 655.

38 For the later lives of Barlow's family members, see Woodress, *Yankee's Odyssey*, 308–9, and Bernstein, 209.

BIBLIOGRAPHY

NATIONAL ARCHIVES OF THE UNITED STATES

Diplomatic and Consular Instructions of the Department of State (microfilm)
Reel 1 (January 1791 to August 1793)
Reel 2 (February 1793 to November 1796)
Reel 3 (June 1795 to January 1797)

Dispatches from U.S. Consuls (microfilm)
Algiers, vol. 1, part I (April 1785 to November 1795)
Algiers, vol. 1, part 2 (February to November 1796)
Algiers, vol. 2 (1796 to 1798)
Alicante, vol. 1 (1788 to 1834)
Gibraltar, vol. 1 (1791 to 1795)
Tunis, vol. 1 (1797 to 1800)

Dispatches from U.S. Ministers to France
Vol. 12 (26 September 1810 to 29 October 1811)
Vol. 13 (29 September 1811 to 26 March 1813)

Dispatches from U.S. Ministers to Portugal
Vol. 4 (January to November 1794)

Dispatches from U.S. Ministers to Spain
Vol. 1 (1792 to 1795)
Vol. 2 (1795 to 1796)
Vol. 3 (1796 to 1797)

Records of the Department of State, United States Ministers, Instructions
Vol. 5 (1797 to 1801)
Vol. 6 (1801 to 1808)
Vol. 7 (1808 to 1815)

ARCHIVES NATIONALES DE FRANCE

Correspondance Politique, États-Unis

BARLOW PAPERS

Connecticut Historical Society Museum
Houghton Library, Harvard University
Huntington Library
Library of Congress
  Henley-Smith Papers
  Madison Papers (microfilm)
Massachusetts Historical Society
New York Public Library
University of Georgia

NEWSPAPERS

American Mercury (Hartford)
Columbian Centinel (Hartford)
Federal Republican (Baltimore)
Gazette of the United States (Philadelphia)
Gazette Nationale ou le Moniteur Universel (Paris)
Independent Chronicle (Boston)
National Intelligencer (Washington)

WORKS BY BARLOW

The Works of Joel Barlow. 2 vols. William K. Bottorff and Arthur L. Ford, eds. Gainesville, FL: Scholars' Facsimiles & Reprints, 1970.

Vol. 1 (Prose)

"A Letter to the National Convention of France, on the Defects of the Constitution of 1791 and the Extent of the Amendments Which Ought to Be Applied." London: J. Johnson, Saint Paul's Churchyard, 1792, 21–90.

"Advice to the Privileged Orders in the Several States of Europe. Resulting from the Necessity and Propriety of a General Revolution in the Principles of Government." Part I. London: Childes and Swayne, 1792, 91–210. Part II. Paris, 1793, 213–312.

"A Letter Addressed to the People of Piedmont, on the Advantages of the French Revolution and the Necessity of Adopting Its Principles in Italy." New York: Columbia Press, 1795, 313–58.

"Two Letters to the Citizens of the United States and One to General Washington, Written from Paris in the Year 1799 on Our Political and Commercial Relations." New Haven, CT: Sidney Press, 1806, 359–479.

"Prospectus of a National Institution, To Be Established in the United States." Washington: Samuel H. Smith, 1806, 479–522.

"Oration Delivered at Washington, July Fourth, 1809 at the Request of the Democratic Citizens of the District of Columbia." Washington: R. E. Weightman, 1809, 523–52.

"A Review of Robert Smith's Address to the People of the United States, Originally Published in the *National Intelligencer.*" Philadelphia: John Binns, 1811, 553–86.

Vol. II (Poetry)

"The Prospect of Peace, a Poetical Composition delivered at Yale-College . . . July 23 [1778]," 1–12.

"The Conspiracy of Kings" (1792), 67–84.

"Hasty Pudding: A Poem" (1793), 87–98.

The Vision of Columbus (1787), 123–358.

The Columbiad (1807), 371–780.

PRIMARY SOURCES

Adams, Charles Francis, ed. 10 vols. *The Works of John Adams, Second President of the United States.* Boston: Little, Brown, 1854.

American State Papers: Foreign Relations. 6 vols. Washington: Gales and Seaton, 1832–59.

Bartlett, Ruhl J. *The Record of American Diplomacy: Documents and Readings in the History of American Foreign Relations.* New York: Knopf, 1964.

Boyd, Julian, P., ed. *The Papers of Thomas Jefferson.* Princeton, NJ: Princeton University Press, 1950.

Caron, Pierre. 2 vols. *La Commission des Subsistances de l'an II: Procès verbale et actes.* Paris: E. Leroux, 1925.

Cathcart, James Leander. *The Diplomatic Journal and Letter Book of James Leander Cathcart, 1788–96.* Philadelphia: American Antiquarian Society, 1955.

———. *The Captives: Eleven Years a Prisoner in Algiers.* La Porte, IN: The Herald Print, 1899.

Correspondance de Napoléon 1er. 34 vols. Paris: Plon, 1858–70.

Davenport, Beatrice Cary, ed. 2 vols. *A Diary of the French Revolution by Gouverneur Morris, 1752–1818.* Cambridge, MA: Harvard University Press, 1939.

Debates and Proceedings of the Congress of the United States. 42 vols. Washington: Gales and Seaton, 1834–56.

Fitzpatrick, John C. 39 vols. *Writings of George Washington.* Washington: Government Printing Office, 1933–44.

Ford, Paul Leicester, ed. 12 vols. *The Works of Thomas Jefferson.* New York: G. P. Putnam's Sons, 1904–05.

Gibbs George, ed. 2 vols. *Memoirs of the Administrations of Washington and John Adams, Edited from the Papers of Oliver Wolcott, Secretary of the Treasury.* New York: Printed for the Subscribers, 1846.

Hamilton, Stanislaus Murray, ed. 7 vols. *The Writings of James Monroe.* New York: Putnam's, 1898–1903.

Hunt, Gaillard, ed. 9 vols. *The Writings of James Madison.* New York: Putnam's, 1900–10.

King, Charles R., ed. 6 vols. *The Life and Correspondence of Rufus King.* New York: G. P. Putnam's Sons, 1894–1900.

Mann, Mary Lee, ed. *A Yankee Jeffersonian: Selections from the Diary and Letters of William Lee of Massachusetts, Written from 1796 to 1840.* Cambridge, MA: Harvard University Press, 1958.

Miller, David Hunter, ed. 8 vols. *Treaties and Other International Acts of the United States of America, 1776–1863.* Washington: Government Printing Office, 1931–48.

Monroe, James. *A View of the Conduct of the Executive of the United States in Foreign Affairs.* Philadelphia: Benjamin Franklin Bache, 1797.

Naval Documents Related to the United States Wars with the Barbary Powers, Vol. I: Naval Operations including Diplomatic Background from 1785 through 1801. Washington: Government Printing Office, 1938.

Richardson, James D. 11 vols. *A Compilation of the Messages and Papers of the Presidents, 1789–1897.* New York: Bureau of National Literature, 1896–1910.

Rutland, Robert A., et al., eds. 4 vols. *The Papers of James Madison, Presidential Series.* Charlottesville: University of Virginia Press, 1984.

SECONDARY WORKS

Ammon, Harry. *James Monroe and the Quest for National Identity.* New York: McGraw-Hill, 1971.

Bacon-Foster, Carra. "The Story of Kalorama," *Records of the Columbia History Society,* vol. 13 (Washington): 98–118.

Barnby, H. G. *The Prisoners of Algiers: An Account of the Forgotten American-Algerian War.* New York: Oxford University Press, 1966.

Belote, Theodore Thomas. *The Scioto Speculation and the French Settlement at Gallipolis: A Study in Ohio Valley History.* Cincinnati, OH: University of Cincinnati, 1907.

Bernstein, Samuel. *Joel Barlow: A Connecticut Yankee in an Age of Revolution.* Cliff Island, ME: Ultima Thule Press, 1985.

Boston, Rob. "Joel Barlow and the Treaty with Tripoli: A Tangled Tale of Pirates, a Poet and the True Meaning of the First Amendment. *Church and State* 50, no. 6 (June 1997): 11–14.

Brant, Irving. *James Madison, Secretary of State, 1800–1809.* Indianapolis, IN: Bobbs-Merrill, 1952.

———. *James Madison, the President, 1809–1812.* Indianapolis, IN: Bobbs-Merrill, 1954.

———. "Joel Barlow, Madison's Stubborn Minister." *William and Mary Quarterly,* 3rd series, 15, no. 4 (October 1958): 438–51.

Brissot de Warville, Jacques-Pierre. *New Travels in the United States of America, Performed in 1788.* New York: Berry and Rogers, 1792.

Cantor, Milton. "Joel Barlow: Lawyer and Legal Philosopher." *American Quarterly* 10, no. 2 (1958): 165–74.

Christensen, Merton A. "Deism in Joel Barlow's Early Works: Heterodox Passages in *The Vision of Columbus.*" *American Literature* 27 (January 1956): 509–20.

Clauder, Anna C. *American Commerce as Affected by the Wars of the French Revolution and Napoleon, 1793–1812.* Philadelphia: University of Pennsylvania Press, 1932.

Coulter, E. Merton. *Abraham Baldwin: Patriot, Educator, and Founding Father.* Arlington, VA: Vandemere Press, 1987.

Cunningham, Audrey. *British Credit in the Last Napoleonic War.* Cambridge, UK: Cambridge University Press, 1910.

Davenport, Beatrice. 2 vols. *A Diary of the French Revolution by Gouverneur Morris.* Boston: Houghton Mifflin, 1939.

DeConde, Alexander. *The Quasi-War: The Politics and Diplomacy of the Undeclared War with France, 1797–1801.* New York: Scribner's, 1966.

Dell Isola, Maria. "Joel Barlow: Précurseur de la Société des Nations." *Revue de Litterature Comparée* (April–June 1934).

Dorfman, Joseph. "Joel Barlow, Trafficker in Trade and Letters." *Political Science Quarterly* 59 (March 1944): 83–100.

Du Pont de Nemours, P. S. *Notice sur la vie de M. Barlow, ministre plénipotentiaire des États-Unis d'Amérique auprès de S. M. l'Empereur et Roi. Mercure de France,* April 10, 1813.

Durden, Robert F. "Joel Barlow in the French Revolution." *William and Mary Quarterly,* 3rd series, 8, no. 3 (July 1961): 327–54.

Field, James A., Jr. *America and the Mediterranean World, 1776–1882.* Princeton, NJ: Princeton University Press, 1969.

Ford, Arthur L. *Joel Barlow.* New York: Twane Publishers, 1971.

Glover, Richard. "The French Fleet, 1807–1814: Britain's Problem and Madison's Opportunity." *Journal of Modern History* 34 (September 1957): 233–52.

Heaton, Herbert. "Non-Importation, 1806–12." *Journal of Economic History* 1 (November 1941): 178–98.

Hickey, Donald R. "The Monroe-Pinkney Treaty: A Reappraisal." *William and Mary Quarterly,* 3rd series, 44, no. 1 (January 1987): 66–88.

Hill, Peter P. *Napoleon's Troublesome Americans: Franco-American Relations, 1804–1815.* Washington: Potomac Books, 2005.

Hulbert, A. B. "The Methods and Operations of the Scioto Group of Speculators" *Mississippi Valley Historical Review* 1 (March 1915): 502–15.

Humphreys, Frank Landon. *The Life and Times of David Humphreys.* 2 vols. New York and London: G. P. Putnam's Sons, 1917.

Irwin, Ray W. *The Diplomatic Relations of the United States with the Barbary Powers, 1776–1816.* Chapel Hill: University of North Carolina Press, 1931.

Kurtz, Stephen J. "The French Mission of 1799–1800: Concluding Chapter in the Statecraft of John Adams." *Political Science Quarterly* 80 (December 1965): 543–72.

Las Casas, Emmanuel, comte de. *Memorial de Sainte Hélène (par Las Casas).* Paris: Edition Garnier Frères, 1961.

LeFebvre, Georges. "Le commerce extérieure, de l'an II." *La révolution francaise,* 78: 133–54.

Lyon, E. Wilson, "The Directory and the United States." *American Historical Review* 43 (April 1938): 514–32.

Maclay, Edgar Stanton. *A History of American Privateers.* New York: D. Appleton, 1899.

Melvin, Frank Edgar. *Napoleon's Navigation System: A Study of Trade Control during the Continental Blockade.* New York: AMS Press, 1970 (reprint).

Miller, Melanie. *Envoy to the Terror: Gouverneur Morris and the French Revolution.* Washington: Potomac Books, 2005.

Palmer, Alan. *Napoleon in Russia.* New York: Simon and Schuster, 1967.

Parker, Richard B. "The Story of Joel Barlow and His Kalorama." *Neighbors of the Cosmos Club.* Washington: Cosmos Club, 2001.

Paullin, Charles O. *Diplomatic Negotiations of the American Naval Officers, 1778–1883.* Baltimore: Johns Hopkins University Press, 1912 (reprint 1967).

Perkins, Bradford. *The First Rapprochement: England and the United States, 1795–1805.* Philadelphia: University of Pennsylvania Press, 1955.

———. *Prologue to War: England and the United States, 1805–1812.* Berkeley: University of California Press, 1961.

———. "Sir William Scott and the *Essex.*" *William and Mary Quarterly,* 3rd series, 22 (1956): 169–83.

Philip, Cynthia Owen. *Robert Fulton: A Biography.* New York: F. Watts, 1985.

Rice, Howard C. "James Swan, Agent of the French Republic." *New England Quarterly* 10 (September 1937): 464–86.

Rose, John Holland. *The Life of Napoleon I.* New York: The Macmillan Company, 1907.

Ross, Frank E. "James Leander Cathcart: Troublesome, Litigious Trifler." *Americana* 28, (1934), 477–85.

———. "The Mission of Joseph Donaldson, Jr., to Algiers, 1795–97." *Journal of Modern History* 7 (1935): 422–33.

Spivak, Burton. *Jefferson's English Crisis: Commerce, Embargo, and the Republican Revolution*. Charlottesville: University of Virginia Press, 1979.

Todd, Charles Burr. *Life and Letters of Joel Barlow, L.L.D., Poet, Statesman, Philosopher, with Extracts from His Works, and Hitherto Unpublished Poems*. New York and London: G. P. Putnam's Sons, 1886.

Virginskii, Victor Semenovich. *Robert Fulton, 1765–1815*. Washington: Smithsonian Institution and National Science Foundation, 1976.

White, Henry Clay. *Abraham Baldwin, One of the Founders of the Republic*. Athens, GA: McGregor, 1926.

Wright, J. Leitch, Jr. *Britain and the American Frontier, 1783–1815*. Athens: University of Georgia Press, 1975.

Woodress, James L. *A Yankee's Odyssey: The Life of Joel Barlow*. Philadelphia: Lippincott, 1958.

Zimmermann, James F. *Impressment of American Seamen*. New York: Columbia University Press, 1925.

Zunder, Theodore Alfred. *The Early Days of Joel Barlow, a Connecticut Wit: Yale Graduate, Editor, Lawyer and Poet; Chaplain during the Revolutionary War—His Life and Works from 1754 to 1787*. Hamden, CT: Archon Books, 1969 (reprint).

———. "Joel Barlow and George Washington." *Modern Language Notes* 1 (April 1929): 254–56.

———. "Joel Barlow and Seasickness." *Yale Journal of Biology and Medicine* 1 (1929): 385–90.

———. "Six Letters of Joel Barlow to Oliver Wolcott, Junior." *New England Quarterly* 2 (1929): 479–80.

INDEX

ABOUT THE AUTHOR

Professor of history emeritus Peter P. Hill has published extensively in the field of early Franco-American relations. His major publications include *Napoleon's Troublesome Americans: Franco-American Relations, 1804–1815*; *French Perceptions of the Early American Republic, 1783–1797*; and *William Vans Murray: Federalist Diplomat; The Shaping of Peace with France, 1797–1801*. Professor Hill taught U.S. diplomatic and U.S. early national history at the George Washington University for nearly forty years before he and his wife retired to Brunswick, Maine, where between visits to the Bowdoin College library, he now spends summers sailing on Casco Bay and winters cross-country skiing.